INSPIRE / PLAN / DISCOVER / EXPERIENCE

AUSTRIA

DK EYEWITNESS

AUSTRIA

CONTENTS

DISCOVER AUSTRIA 6

EXPERIENCE VIENNA 58

EXPERIENCE AUSTRIA 148

NEED TO KNOW 308

Left: Stylish building façade in Upper Austria
Previous page: Snowy mountain resort of Schladming
Front cover: Picture-postcard village of Hallstatt

DISCOVER

Red tiled roofs dotting Graz's cityscape

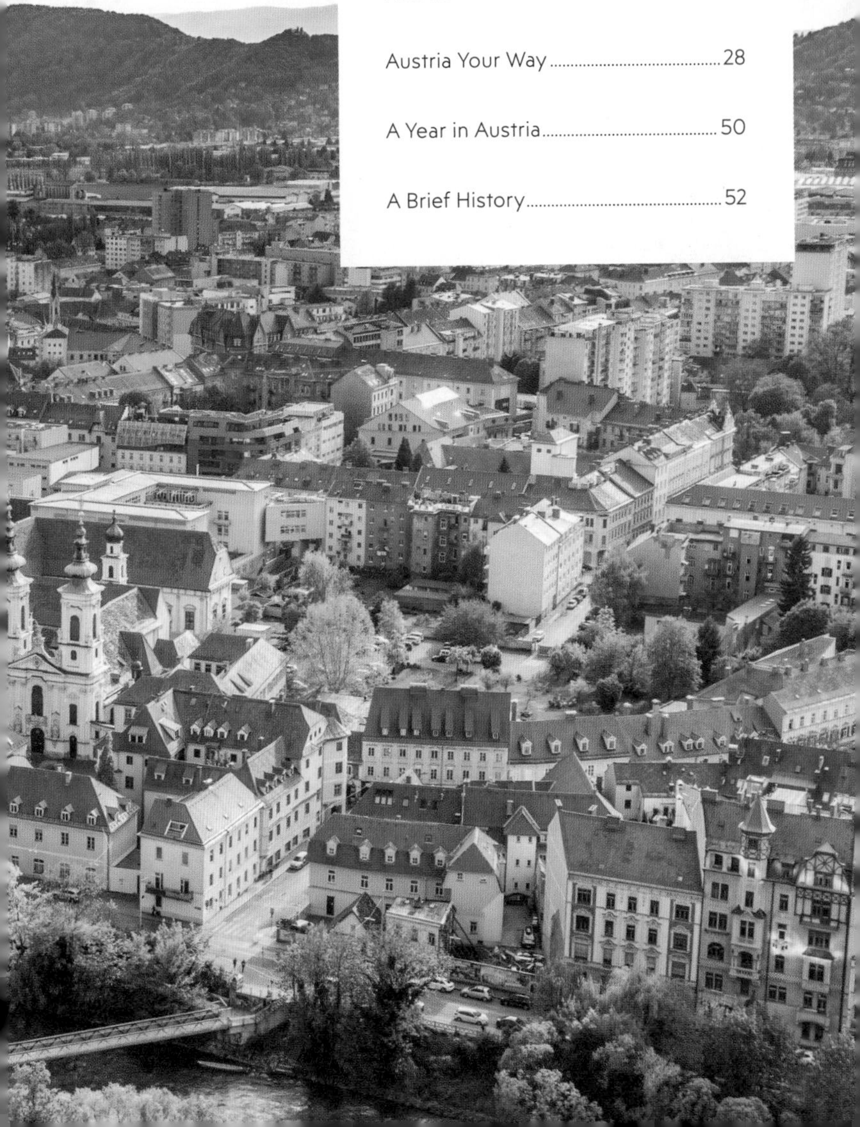

WELCOME TO
AUSTRIA

Situated at the very heart of Europe, Austria is a harmonious blend of high culture and pristine nature. You'll never be far from the swell of a Schubert symphony, the swoop of a ski run, rustic wine trails or fairytale palaces in this small but varied country. Whatever your dream trip to Austria includes, this DK Eyewitness travel guide is the perfect companion.

1 Taking in the gorgeous view of the Austrian Alps.

2 Idyllic vineyard in the Lower Austria region.

3 Treats at a Christmas market stall in Vienna.

4 The town of Hallstatt amid lush greenery.

For centuries, Austria was a formidable European power whose influence stretched far beyond today's modest borders. And that cosmopolitan empire still has a palpable presence: just wander the cobblestoned streets of the capital or gaze up at Melk Abbey on the Danube. The Habsburgs' penchant for palaces and fortresses, along with collections of old masters to fill them, has also left a swathe of grand buildings to explore, from Vienna's Schönbrunn to Innsbruck's Schloss Ambras. Beyond the historic landmarks, the Habsburgs' wide-roaming influence is evident in the rich, spiced cuisine here, from fragrant strudel to liquor-laced coffees enjoyed in a Viennese *Kaffeehaus*. Add to this the musical offerings of Mozart and *The Sound of Music* and you have a country that offers a cultural experience like no other.

Away from its buzzing cities, Austria is a land of the great outdoors. It's no wonder that the lyrical beauty of its Alpine peaks, sparkling lakes and lush pastures has enchanted artists and explorers. Every journey here can be a similarly inspiring adventure, from the daredevil verticals of the Zillertal's glacial highs to pram-friendly hiking trails in the Salzkammergut and warm water dips in the pretty Wörthersee.

With so many different things to experience, Austria can seem overwhelming. We've broken the country down into easily navigable chapters, with detailed itineraries, expert local knowledge and comprehensive maps to help you plan the perfect visit. Whether you're staying for the weekend or longer, this Eyewitness guide will ensure that you see the very best of the country. Enjoy the book, and enjoy Austria.

REASONS TO LOVE
AUSTRIA

A natural wonderland oozing effortless natural charm, the rich culture and history of its cities, and an abundance of intriguing traditions – there are endless reasons to love Austria. Here, we pick some of our favourites.

1 WORLD-CLASS WINTER SPORTS

Be it vertiginous black runs, blistering backcountry or family-friendly snow parks, Alpine Austria *(p42)* promises winter fun for all. For the downhill jaded, there's glacier climbs and snowshoe touring.

LAKE LIFE *2*

Though landlocked, Austria is chock-full of serene waters, from the forested clutch of beauties in the Salzkammergut *(p218)* to the deep dark blue of Carinthia's Wörthersee *(p304)*.

3 VIENNA'S CAFÉ CULTURE

The *Kaffeehaus (p68)* is a Viennese institution and ubiquitous across the capital. Savouring coffee and cake in a centuries-old café is a time-honoured tradition.

MUSICAL HERITAGE 4

Austria's classical lineage is second to none. Whether you're at the opera or enjoying a park performance, the sounds of Mozart, Haydn and Beethoven fill every corner of the country.

THE BELVEDERE 5

Stretching from the Jugendstil pavilions of Karlsplatz to the exquisite gardens of the palace itself, the Belvedere *(p124)* is imperial Vienna at its most awe-inspiring.

AN EVENING IN A HEURIGER 6

For an escape from gilded Vienna, head to a neighbourhood *Heuriger* (wine tavern). Pull up a bench, order a jug of Wiener Gemischter Satz and raise a glass with the locals.

MEDIEVAL TOWNS 7

The rural reaches of Carinthia and Styria are home to a trail of remarkably preserved medieval towns. Murau *(p201)* is the prettiest, and Friesach *(p301)* is circled by Austria's last moat.

JOURNEYING INTO ICE CAVES 8

A subterranean landscape of ice palaces, crystalline lakes and nature's own surreal sculptures await underground. To top it off, Eisriesenwelt *(p255)* is the world's largest.

9 STRUDEL

While Vienna might claim it as their own, the concoction of baked apples, rum-soaked raisins and buttery sheets of pastry beckons from every cake shop across the country.

10 FOLLOWING THE SECESSION

The avant-garde architecture of the Secession movement (p48) shocked fin-de-siècle Vienna to the core. See their Jugendstil curves at the Wiener Secession (p126).

HIKING THE ALPS 11

Austrians know how to slow down, and hiking is one of their favourite ways to do it. Pull on your boots: towering mountains and flower-strewn meadows await you.

CHRISTMAS MARKETS 12

From the end of November, wooden huts spring up in towns and cities throughout the country, selling traditional handicrafts, *Glühwein* (mulled wine) and roasted chestnuts.

EXPLORE
AUSTRIA

This guide divides Austria into seven colour-coded sightseeing areas, as shown on the map below. Find out more about each area on the following pages.

Regensburg

Deggendorf

Landshut

Augsburg

GERMANY

Braunau

Munich

Landsberg am Lech

Memmingen

Rosenheim

Salzburg

Hallein

Bodensee

Bregenz

Reutte

Wörgl

St Johann in Tirol

Dornbirn

Seefeld

Inn

Schwaz

SALZBURGER LAND
p234

Feldkirch

Landeck

Innsbruck

TYROL AND VORARLBERG
p258

Bludenz

SWITZERLAND

Brunico

Lienz

ITALY

Cortina d'Ampezzo

EUROPE

Udine

Pordenone

FINLAND

NORWAY

SWEDEN

ESTONIA

North Sea

RUSSIA

LATVIA

Baltic Sea

DENMARK

LITHUANIA

UNITED KINGDOM

NETHER-LANDS

BELARUS

IRELAND

GERMANY

POLAND

BELGIUM

CZECH REP.

UKRAINE

Venice

SLOVAKIA

FRANCE

SWITZ.

AUSTRIA

HUNGARY

Adriatic Sea

CROATIA

ROMANIA

SERBIA

ITALY

BULGARIA

SPAIN

GREECE

TURKEY

GETTING TO KNOW
AUSTRIA

Cradled by magnificent mountains that span two-thirds of the country, Austria is a hotspot of Alpine drama, with buzzing cities scattered throughout. From the imperial opulence of Vienna to the bucolic outpost of Styria, each region has its own distinct personality.

PAGE 58

VIENNA

Once the capital of a great empire, with Baroque pomp at every turn to prove it, modern Vienna remains a city at the very heart of Europe. A cornucopia of culture, Vienna's art and architecture scene packs a punch – this is where you'll find the country's grandest palaces and finest art scene. You'll also find a cosy *Kaffeehaus* on nearly every street, where lingering over a light lunch while tucking into a book is customary. And when the sun goes down, you can dress in your finest and indulge in some of the world's most celebrated music, courtesy of the Vienna Philharmonic.

Best for
Habsburg palaces, elegant cafés, museums and galleries

Home to
Stephansdom, The Hofburg Complex, Burgtheater, Schönbrunn Palace

Experience
Taking in the incredible 19th- and 20th-century art collections of the MuseumsQuartier

PAGE 150

LOWER AUSTRIA AND BURGENLAND

Vienna's sophistication spills out to the surrounding region of Lower Austria: the largest province in the country and where the mighty Danube leads to the pretty Wachau valley. To the south lies bucolic Burgenland and its graceful capital Eisenstadt, surrounded by green flatlands. Down by the Hungarian border is the watersports mecca of Neusiedler See, while the villages circling its banks are home to some of Austria's best wine producers and their cellar doors.

Best for
Day trips from Vienna, castle hopping and wine tasting

Home to
St Pölten, Eisenstadt, Neusiedler See, Melk Abbey

Experience
Riding the steep and picturesque Schneeberg Mountain Railway

PAGE 178

STYRIA

This southern province can often feel like Austria in microcosm. Pristine Alpine rivers and peaks mark the north and west, rolling vine-covered hills of "Styrian Tuscany" lie to the south, and forests, spa towns and hilltop castles dot the east. The region's riverside capital, Graz, is the main draw, home to a unique and flourishing culinary scene, convivial bars and pubs and a historic centre of terracotta rooftops. In the west, winter sport is unrivalled on the Dachstein, the highest peak in the region and home to the best cross-country skiing trails.

Best for
Medieval towns, Gothic churches and skiing

Home to
Graz, Österreichisches Freilichtmuseum, Schladminger Tauern, Mariazell Basilika

Experience
Wine tasting in a Buschenschank *(cellar door) along the South Styrian Wine Road*

$\rightarrow$

PAGE 210

UPPER AUSTRIA

Though perhaps a less well-known part of the country, Upper Austria is a prosperous, industrious region, with natural beauty that's all the more stunning for its lack of mass tourism. The province's capital, Linz, is known for its innovative museums and galleries, but also has an old town centre that's both beguiling and upbeat. Spas and abbeys line the Danube here as they do in Lower Austria, but there's also small pastel-toned towns, many limestone peaks, magnificent abbeys and pretty wheatfields along the riverbanks.

Best for
Natural wonders, rustic charm and a festive capital

Home to
Linz, Salzkammergut Lakes, The Danube Valley

Experience
A riverside bike ride from the village of Steyr to Sierning

PAGE 234

SALZBURGER LAND

A region of high mountains, Salzburger Land is a mecca for winter sports and summer mountain walks. The baroque beauty of its best-known city, Salzburg, never fails to enchant, its old town seemingly trapped in an 18th-century time warp and where a Mozart aria or concerto is waiting to be heard around every corner. Surrounding the city, its eponymous little region is a world of ice caves and limestone peaks, and turreted towns set by vividly hued lakes. Austria's most scenic mountain road, the Grossglockner Hochalpenstrasse, crosses the southern part of the province.

Best for
Classical music concerts, traditional spa towns and accessible nature trails

Home to
Salzburg, Gasteinertal

Experience
An outdoor concert in a Baroque square at the annual Salzburg Festival

TYROL AND VORARLBERG

Downhill thrills, après-ski clubbing and picturesque Alpine villages deliver the quintessential Austrian experience in this Alpine stretch of land, famous for spectacular scenery and world-renowned resorts. But there's so much more to these two regions, whether you're cycling in the Zillertal past fields of rare wildflowers in the summer, taking on a circuit dedicated to cheese in the Vorarlberg, or kicking back in Innsbruck's old town surrounded by *Schloss*-topped peaks.

Best for
Winter sports, hiking and Alpine culture

Home to
Innsbruck, Bregenz, Zillertal

Experience
Skiing and boarding 365 days a year on the Hintertux Glacier

CARINTHIA AND EAST TYROL

Down south, Austria's chocolate-box vistas turn rugged and wild, with dark forested slopes reflected in the mirror-like surface of lake after lake – thousands of them, in fact. The largest, and warmest, Wörthersee, is also its most urbane, its lush banks dotted with historic baths and tranquil resort hotels. Klagenfurt, a traditional stately market city, will surprise too with its vibrant, artsy atmosphere. Beyond the mountains you'll also find verdant rolling hills interspersed with medieval villages and astounding castles.

Best for
Austria's highest mountains, glacial lakes and historic villages

Home to
Klagenfurt, Hohe Tauern National Park

Experience
Taking a dip in one of the historic baths that line Wörthersee

←

1 Strolling through the grounds of Schloss Mirabell.

2 Traunsee lake surrounding the town of Traunkirchen.

3 The idyllic Wolfgangsee.

4 Trick fountains in the gardens at Schloss Hellbrunn.

Austria brims with travel opportunities, from cultural visits to the capital *(p66)* to grand tours of its diverse regions. These itineraries will help you make the most of your trip.

5 DAYS

in Salzburg and the Salzkammergut

Day 1

Spend the day exploring one of the most stunning Baroque towns in Europe, Salzburg *(p238)*. Wander through the old town and visit the Kollegienkirche for a taste of 18th-century architecture at its best. Spend some time at Mozarts Geburtshaus, the house where the composer and the city's famous son was born, before heading to Hohensalzburg *(p244)*, the hilltop fortress that overlooks the town centre. In the evening, stroll among the famous gardens at Schloss Mirabell before a traditional dinner of schnitzel at Bärenwirt *(p239)*.

Day 2

No visit to Salzburg is complete without a trip to Schloss Hellbrunn *(p250)*, 4 km (2 miles) south of the town. Spend the morning exploring the 17th-century retreat and its well-preserved interiors, surrounded by stunning gardens. Then make your way to Werfen *(p255)*, 40 km (25 miles) south, to see the Eisriesenwelt ice caves and their spectacular stalagmites, as well as the imposing Hohenwerfen fortress. The Berggasthof Zaismann *(www. zaismann.at)* is halfway between the caves and the fortress and perfect for an early dinner before heading back to Salzburg.

Day 3

Travel to one of the most picturesque lakes in the Salzkammergut region, the Wolfgangsee *(p219)*, fringed by the pretty villages of Strobl, St Gilgen and St Wolfgang. The last is famous for its pilgrimage church, home to a stunning Gothic altarpiece. Weisses Rössl *(www. weissesroessl.at)*, the resort hotel that inspired an operetta in the 1920s, is the perfect place to end your day, with glorious lake views.

Day 4

Reserve most of the day for Hallstatt *(p232)*, arguably the most breathtaking of the Salzkammergut settlements. With Bronze Age artifacts in the local museum, a historic graveyard and a salt mine high above town, there's a great deal to see. In the afternoon take a trip to Dachsteinhöhlen *(p227)*, a network of caves high above the southern end of the Hallstätter See. Back in Hallstatt for dinner, the menu at Seehotel Grüner Baum *(www.gruenerbaum.cc)* offers freshly caught fish from Lake Hallstatt.

Day 5

Spend a lazy morning at one of the many spas at Bad Ischl *(p230)*, situated between the Wolfgangsee and the Traunsee and oozing with Habsburg tradition. Take a tour of Emperor Franz Josef's summer retreat, the Kaiservilla, followed by a trip to one of the town's traditional patisseries, Café Ramsauer *(www.cafe-ramsauer.at)*. Head next for the craggy peaks of the Traunsee, the Salzkammergut at its most picturesque. Tour the delightful historic town of Traunkirchen *(p229)* before eating at the Bootshaus *(www.dastraunsee.at)* on the edge of the lake.

←

1 Exploring the miniature world of Minimundus.

2 Strolling through the Landhaus in Graz.

3 Klagenfurt city centre.

4 The beautiful towers of Millstatt Abbey.

5 DAYS

in Southern Austria

▌ Day 1

Dedicate the day to exploring Graz (p182), whose old town is one of the best preserved in the region. Check out the cathedral and the Landhaus, one of the most beautiful Renaissance buildings in Styria, while the gorgeous Renaissance façade of the Landeszeughaus is topped only by the amazing collection of medieval weapons inside. The thoroughly modern Kunsthaus – whose shape is thought to resemble an alien – will provide a contrasting end to the day before dinner at the Weitzer hotel *(www. hotelweitzer.com)*, overlooking the Mur.

▌ Day 2

Head north of Graz for the Styrian village of Stübing *(p190)*. Its unique collection of buildings, representing Austria's regional architecture through the ages, was transported here from almost every part of the country, and strolling through the village makes for a perfect morning. It's well worth packing a picnic and spending most of the day here, before driving on to Murau *(p201)* to visit its Gothic Matthäuskirche and enchanting castle. Try the region's specialities at the elegant Rosenhof *(www.rosenhof-murau.at)*, with a glass of Austrian wine to end the day.

▌ Day 3

Drive south through the lush green hills of northern Carinthia towards Klagenfurt *(p292)*, stopping at the perfectly preserved medieval town of Friesach for lunch at Speckladle Höferer *(p301)*. Drive on to the dramatic medieval castle of Hochosterwitz *(p298)* and spend some time touring the grounds and admiring the views. Arrive in Klagenfurt well in time for last orders at the Felsenkeller beerhall *(www.schleppe-felsenkeller.at)*.

▌ Day 4

Spend the morning wandering the streets of old Klagenfurt, making sure not to miss Dom St Peter und Paul. Stop for lunch and a coffee at Cafe am Platz *(www. cafeplatzl.com)* before heading out to the Wörthersee *(p304)*, Austria's warmest lake and perfect for swimming and water sports. The road to the lake runs through Europapark and the Minimundus *(p293)* exhibition, with over 170 miniature models of the world's most famous buildings. From the terrace of the Maria Loretto bar and restaurant *(www. restaurant-maria-loretto.at)* there are superb views to the far side of the lake.

▌ Day 5

Kick off your final day with a walk around the town of Villach *(p300)*, a popular health resort, with a detour to the village of Maria Gail to see the lovely 14th-century frescoes in the church. Then head north for Spittal an der Drau *(p301)*, dominated by the Goldeck peak – perfect for short hikes – and the Schloss Porcia, one of the most significant Renaissance buildings in Austria. Find time to see the Benedictine abbey at Millstatt *(p302)*, on the shore of Millstätter See, before dinner on the lake at the Hotel Forelle *(www.hotel-forelle.at)*.

7 DAYS
in Eastern Austria

▌*Day 1*

After spending two cultural days in Vienna *(p66)*, head out of the city to the beautiful Vienna Woods (Wienerwald) *(p176)*, which have long been a favourite weekend destination for the Viennese. Be sure to stop off for a stroll in the small, picturesque town of Mödling – once a retreat for artists – before driving south to Gumpoldskirchen, a small wine-making town that has become famous for its countless *Heurige* (wine bars). After a tipple or two, enjoy local food, such as potato soup and fresh lamb, at Weinbau Straitz & Straitz *(www.straitz.com)*.

▌*Day 2*

Drive southeast to the picturesque town of Eisenstadt *(p156)* and head straight to Schloss Esterházy, the Baroque chateau whose main attraction is the Haydnsaal, a concert hall named after Joseph Haydn. After admiring its beautiful frescoes, continue taking your fill of Haydn at Haydn-Haus, a museum with a fascinating collection of the composer's possessions. From here it is a short distance to the

Neusiedler See *(p158)*, ringed by fishing villages and grassy plains. The town of Rust, with its seasonally nesting storks, is the most scenic of the lakeside settlements, and Hofgassl *(www.hofgassl. at)* serves the best spare ribs in Austria.

▌*Day 3*

Travel west via Wiener Neustadt to the Schneeberg, popular for cosy breaks in winter and pleasant hikes in summer. Go back in time at Semmering, home to the world's first mountain railway, before heading north to Mariazell *(p194)*, central Europe's main pilgrimage centre for Roman Catholics. Visit the Gothic basilica before having a beverage at the Brauhaus Mariazell *(www.bierundbett.at)*, which has been brewing its own beer for centuries.

▌*Day 4*

Head to St Pölten *(p154)*, a lively market town with a well-preserved Baroque centre, for a breakfast treat at the historic Café im Palais Wellenstein *(www.cafe-im-palais.at)*. Reserve most of the day to

1 Hiking on the Schneeberg during the summer.

2 Pretty church towers dominating the Waidhofen old town skyline.

3 Sailboats docked beside a restaurant on Neusiedler See.

4 Brewing beer at Brauhaus Mariazell.

explore the stunning abbey at Melk (p160), located 30 km (19 miles) west. The abbey contains a host of artworks, a historic library and a Baroque church. End the day at the ruins of the medieval castle in Dürnstein (p164) before dining on the terrace of Hotel Schloss (www.schloss.at).

Day 5

Start the day at Krems (p171), once Vienna's rival city and home to splendid buildings, not least the Piaristenkirche which towers above the town. A short drive to the south, Stift Göttweig (p166) is a Benedictine abbey that crowns a hilltop on the south bank of the Danube. Grab a bite to eat at a table on the terrace of the abbey's restaurant just in time to watch the sun set over the surrounding hills.

Day 6

After breakfast, spend the day exploring the quaint towns and historic villages of the Waldviertel (p174). North of Krems is one of Austria's most famous castles, Schloss Rosenburg, while the ceiling

frescoes at the gorgeous Benedictine abbey at Altenberg are also worth stopping to admire. In the afternoon head west to Zwettl, which is home to several original Baroque houses and one of the region's gems, a magnificent Cistercian monastery. The Gasthaus zur Goldenen Rose (www.goldene-rose.at), set in a house built in 1599, is perfect for dinner.

Day 7

Devote the last day of your tour to two small towns on the Ybbs river, Neuhofen (p168) and Waidhofen (p170). The attractive onion domes of the churches above the river at Waidhofen are a brilliant photo opportunity, and don't miss the clock on the north tower of the Stadtturm, which has shown the hour as 11:45 since 1534, the time of a famous Habsburg victory over the Turks. Neuhofen is home to the Ostarrichi Kulturhof, a fascinating museum of Austrian history. The locally sourced steaks at the Gasthaus Palme (www.gasthaus-zur-palme.at) make for a perfect end to the tour before heading back to Vienna.

7 DAYS

in the Austrian Alps

Day 1

Begin your week in Tyrol's vibrant capital, Innsbruck *(p262)*. A stroll around the compact medieval centre makes for a pleasant morning, with its many attractive decorative façades, of which the Goldenes Dachl is the most highly celebrated. Get a taste of Innsbruck's imperial heritage with a visit to the Hofkirche before lunch (and Sachertorte) at its historic Café Sacher *(www.sacher.com)*. Browse local shops as you stroll along the elegant boulevard of Maria-Theresien-Strasse, with its famous views of the Alps. Come evening, try some traditional Austrian dishes at Zum Hirschenwirt *(p264)*.

Day 2

Spend a day in the pretty mountain village of Seefeld *(p279)*, northwest of Innsbruck. Don't miss the Archduke Leopold V chapel, which houses a crucifix dating from the early 16th century said to have miraculous powers. After lunch at the Südtiroler Stube *(p279)*, head up the Härmelekopf peak via one of many leisurely hiking routes. Return to

Innsbruck for dinner and drinks at Die Wilderin *(www.diewilderin.at)*, famous for its farm to table kitchen, in the old town.

Day 3

Head west from Innsbruck to Imst before turning south into the Ötztal *(p280)*, one of Austria's longest, deepest and most majestic Alpine valleys. The remote village of Obergurgl, surrounded by high peaks, is a fabulous ski resort in winter and offers great hikes during the summer. Check out the terrace at the Zirben Alm Obergurgl restaurant *(www.zirbenalm.at)* for amazing views of the valley before returning to Innsbruck via the lively resort of Sölden. Be sure to take the cable car up to the eternal snows of the Rettenbach glacier, where the café and restaurant *(www.oetztalergletscher.com)* is perfect for an early dinner.

Day 4

Continue west by road or rail over the Arlberg Pass, the stark mountain barrier that divides Tyrol from Austria's westernmost province, Vorarlberg.

1 Innsbruck's Renaissance-era Goldenes Dachl.

2 The pretty Archduke Leopold V chapel in Seefeld.

3 Obergurgl village shrouded in a blanket of snow.

4 Mountain biking in the verdant Arlberg mountains.

5 Kufstein fortress perched above the small town.

The world-famous mountain resort of St Anton *(p282)* is famed for its riotous après-ski in winter, but is more relaxed in summer. It's also a paradise for walkers: if you're visiting with family in tow, try the popular Mutspuren route, which takes in a number of small lakes. Meanwhile, the more adventurous can explore 350 km (217 miles) of mountain bike tracks. Nearby Lech *(p280)* is a serene spot for dinner, with the terrace at Hotel Arlberg *(www.arlberghotel.at)* overlooking the river.

Day 5

Kitzbühel *(p278)* is a pretty medieval town where, if you are visiting January, you can watch the legendary Hahnenkamm downhill ski race. From spring to autumn, take the Hornbahn cable car up onto the high Alpine meadows to see the gorgeous Alpine Flower Garden. Take a trip to the quaint town of Kufstein *(p278)* to see the Heldenorgel (Heroes' Organ), the world's largest free-standing organ, at its historic fortress, then head back to Kitzbühel in time for a dinner of Austrian goulash at Huberbräu-Stüberl *(p279)*.

Day 6

Begin the morning south of Kitzbühel in the green pastures of Pinzgau *(p256)*, ideal for gentle walks. Follow the rustic road west towards the spectacular foaming waters of the Krimmler Wasserfälle *(p257)*, stopping to take pictures, then head east towards the lakeside centre of Zell am See *(p256)*, the starting point for the breathtaking mountain road over the Grossglockner Pass. Take a swim in the crystal-clear waters of the Zellersee before a meal at the Seensucht restaurant *(www.restaurant-am-see.at)* on the edge of the lake.

Day 7

Rise early and make your way to Hintertux *(p272)* at the far end of the Zillertal, a picture-postcard valley of pretty villages squeezed between the lofty Alps. You can ski on the glacier here year round, but the slopes close at lunchtime in the summer, so get in early. Finish your week by heading back to Innsbruck for a final taste of local food and wine at Sitzwohl *(www.restaurantsitzwohl.at)*.

On the Water

Austria has so many glistening lakes, it can be hard to pick a favourite. The Salzkammergut *(p218)* offers the gentle Wolfgangsee, which is perfect for bathing, and Mondsee , a sailing paradise. If you're looking for wild, untamed beauty, the three lakes of the Gosauseen *(p230)* can't be rivalled, with one of the clearest lakes, Vorderer Gosausee, in the country. In the south, the shallow Neusiedler See *(p158)* is perfect for watersports, while swimmers will love the Strandbad Klagenfurt, a beach on warm-water Wörthersee *(p304)*.

→

Sailing on the crystal-clear waters at Mondsee, with Schafberg peak behind

AUSTRIA FOR
THE GREAT OUTDOORS

Austria's natural beauty is intoxicating and provides vistas every bit as lyrical as a Mozart opera. Superb skiing might be the country's most famed outdoor asset but there are plenty of other ways to immerse yourself in the natural world here, from hiking its forest trails to swimming in its many lakes.

ENVIRONMENTAL PROTECTION

Austria has some of Europe's most strict conservation laws, due to both a deeply embedded respect for nature and an aware-ness of the Alpine ecosystem's fragility. Almost 60 "biogenetic" reserves and three major wilderness areas ensure endangered species, habitats and flora are protected. Austrians love visitors to get intimate with their natural world, but don't pick flowers or rocks, and take rubbish with you.

The Mountains are Calling

It's no wonder that walking in Austria is a joyous pastime, with monumental peaks, dramatic scenery and a chance to breathe in the fresh mountain air. The Pinzgauer Spaziergang *(p256)* is one of the most beautiful trails in the Alps, running at an altitude of about 1,000 m (3,280 ft) above the valley floor. Have your camera at the ready, as you'll want to stop for breathtaking photographs. Tyrol buzzes in summer with impressive views from the Stubaital *(p279)*, while Schladming *(p192)* in Styria welcomes mountain bikers .

→

Looking out over the Tyrol from the Stubai glacier viewing platform

An Icy Underworld

Below the ground, Austria offers up ice-bound, other-worldly landscapes that evoke myth and legend. In Abtenau, the natural limestone Eisriesenwelt *(p255)* is the largest ice cave in the world, with 42 km (26 miles) of stalagmites and stunning ice galleries to explore – all in freezing temperatures. In upper Austria, the twinkling, vast Dachsteinhöhlen *(p227)* cave system is covered by 500-year-old permafrost. The ice mountains, glaciers and frozen water-falls here have existed since the last ice age.

← Marvelling at the treasures at Dachstein-höhlen

TOP **5**
AUSTRIA'S ALPINE FLOWERS

Edelweiss
From July to September, the national flower dots the high valleys.

Gentian
Purple gentian blooms in summer until October.

Arnica
The yellow-orange medicinal plant flowers in the summer.

Columbine
Dark columbine blooms from as early as April.

Golden Hawk
This flower graces the alpine meadows well into September.

The thundering three tiers of the Krimmler Wasserfälle ↑

Venture into Forests

Almost half of Austria is covered in lush forest, from urban boltholes like the Vienna Woods and its 240 km (150 miles) of marked hiking trails, to the deep green reaches of the Alpine Bregenzerwald. Nestled within verdant greenery are breath-taking waterfalls, too. The Krimmler Wasserfälle *(p257)* are the highest in Europe and the country's most dramatic. It is photo-genic from most angles, but the best shots are taken from the Wasserfallweg (where you'll also be bathed in the falls' spray).

Habsburg Fortresses

The Habsburgs were huge renovators, and many of the Baroque edifices you can visit are alterations of far earlier buildings. Take the funicular up to Festung Hohensalzburg *(p244)*, where the stronghold's 11th-century bones were given a 16th-century makeover, or amble through Burg Aggstein *(p170)* to trace its 12th-century origins.

←

Festung Hohensalzburg, one of the best-preserved fortresses in Europe

AUSTRIA FOR
CASTLES AND PALACES

Dotted with grandiose castles, lavish palaces and monumental fortresses, Austria's cities and countryside alike brim with stories of the past. Follow in the footsteps of royals, bring history alive with classical music concerts and traditional festivals and marvel at imposing architecture.

TOP 3 MOUNTAIN-TOP CASTLES

Hohensalzburg
Salzburg's fine medieval fortress is one of Europe's largest *(p244)*.

Hohenwerfen
A 900-year-old rock castle in Werfen with the Alps on the horizon *(p255)*.

Burgruine Aggstein
The fairytale 12th-cenutury ruin overlooks the Danube *(p170)*.

→

The sumptuous state rooms at the Residenz palace in Salzburg

The Royal Way of Life

Palace hopping is a fine pursuit in Austria, and with their lavish decorations and embellished gardens, many palaces are more or less as the royals left them. For those fascinated by Empress Elisabeth, or Sisi, her dressing rooms at Schönbrunn *(p138)* and Hofburg *(p78)* give a fascinating insight into her strict daily beauty rituals. The fine tapestries, frescoes and Flemish and Dutch masterpieces at Salzburg's Residenz *(p240)*, meanwhile, highlight the wealth of the city's prince-archbishops.

↑ A performance held at the open-air stage built for the Grafenegg Music Festival

Music with a View

For centuries, music has been a grand accompaniment to royal life in Austria's palaces, and this tradition is continued today with their romantic grounds serving as sumptuous venues. The most spectacular is held at Vienna's Schönbrunn *(p138)*, where Mozart's operas and Strauss' waltzes ring out over the Orangery in the summer or fill the gilded Grand Gallery year round. Near-perfect acoustics make Eisenstadt's Haydnsaal – Schloss Esterházy's *(p157)* Baroque concert hall where Haydn often performed – a sublime setting for a performance of the composer's seminal string quartet work. Meanwhile, Grafenegg Castle *(www.grafenegg.com)* hosts the popular Grafenegg Music Festival over August and September, where you can enjoy top wine while classical music fills the castle grounds.

Step Back in Time

Curious to know what life was like in medieval Austria? Get a taste of the Middle Ages with a meal by candlelight at Burgtaverne Kreuzenstein *(www.burgtaverne-kreuzen stein.at)*, furnished to mirror a typical tavern, or immerse yourself in falconry with flying demonstrations at Burg Landskron *(www.burg-landskron.at)*. Burg Aggstein *(p170)* hosts an atmospheric medieval craft market, where roasted oxen is a speciality.

↑ Fairytale turrets at Burg Kreuzenstein and falconry demonstrations at Burg Lanskron *(inset)*

Did You Know?

The word strudel means "vortex" or "whirlpool" in German.

Pick a Pastry

In the perfect global village, a place on the main street would always be reserved for an Austrian pastry and coffee shop. That the French name for pastry is *Viennoiserie* underlines the Viennese tradition of sweet baking, and café culture *(p68)* is huge here. Treats on offer generally include classic *Apfelstrudel*, *Cremeschnitte* (puff pastry filled with custard), and *Punschkrapferl* (pink-fondant-topped pastry laced with rum).

←

Apple strudel cake sprinkled with sugar powder and cinnamon

AUSTRIA FOR
FOODIES

Long associated with Vienna's signature schnitzel and Sachertorte, Austrian cuisine is far more varied and flavoursome than most people realize. Age-old traditions refuse to budge here, with enticing cafés, welcoming *Würstel* stalls and traditional taverns dotting every town and city.

Wine Not?

The wine regions of Austria are delightfully distinct, all offering regional varietals and their own atmosphere. The Wachau and Kamptal regions attract wide acclaim with their popular whites, Grüner Veltliner and Riesling, and have a large network of wine cellars and touring routes, while Neusiedler See is known for its robust reds, particularly Zweigelt. For something more rustic and laid-back, check out the small producer vineyards found in the south's Burgenland and Styria. Even Vienna produces significant amounts within its city limits, one of the only cities its size to do so. Head to a neighbourhood *Heuriger* – a rustic, often open-air wine "shack" – for these hyper-local wines.

A tempting display of cakes for sale at Demel in Vienna and Zauner Bakery in Bad Ischl, Upper Austria *(inset)*

Piece of Cake

You could map where you are in Austria by the sweet speciality that's served with your mid-morning coffee. If it's Sachertorte, you'll be in Vienna. A buttery *Gugelhupf* will mean it's Tyrol, and the nutty berry layers of the Linzer Torte will naturally mean you're in Linz. In Salzburg the cake of choice is a meringue confection, the Salzburger Nockerl.

Choose a Classic

Austrian cuisine is a direct legacy of the country's imperial past, when culinary traditions from Europe influenced Viennese cooks. No trip to Austria is complete without trying the national dish, Wiener Schnitzel. Fries might seem like a great match, but to be faithful to tradition, opt for potato salad. You'll also find paprika-spiced Austrian goulash in many forms throughout the country.

→

↑ Sampling lush red wines at a winery just outside Vienna

The classic Wiener Schnitzel - veal, breaded and fried

Austrianwear

Tracht - an assortment of folk costumes - is still worn for many formal occasions, including weddings and balls in Austria. An entire branch of the textile industry here is devoted to the design and manufacture of these outfits, and you can find at least one specialist retailer for them in every town. Men sport green loden jackets and Lederhosen, the familiar leather breeches; for women, it's all about the Dirndl, a tight-bodice dress with puffed sleeves, a full skirt and apron.

$\rightarrow$

Inspecting vibrant fabric at a handicraft workshop in Salzburg

AUSTRIA FOR
TRADITIONS

Austria may be one of the most modern countries in Europe, but its people are still fiercely protective of their local traditions. Many are an excuse for locals to don folk costumes and feast on seasonal comfort food; for visitors, they offer a fascinating glimpse into Austria's old-world heart.

The Christmas market in Maria-Theresien-Platz in Vienna ↑

Appreciate Advent

Christmas is a particularly special time of the year in Austria, and the first Sunday of Advent sees the opening of the *Christkindlmarkt*. These charming markets fill town and city squares with rustic huts offering traditional handicrafts and Christmas foods. *Glühwein* (mulled wine) will keep you warm as you browse, and roast chestnuts and gingerbread are always on hand. In Vienna, Rathausplatz hosts the largest market, but to get away from the tourist hordes, head to Art Advent on Karlsplatz. Innsbruck's Hungerburg, meanwhile, is the perfect place to meander through while marvelling at the Dolomite.

TOP 3 TRADITIONAL GIFTS

Snow Globe
An Austrian invention, these dreamy domes are beautifully crafted.

Mozartkugeln
These Mozart-wrapped pistachio and chocolate balls date back to 1890 and are still produced by the confectioner's descendants.

Gmundner Ceramics
Fine vintage pieces that can be found in Gmund's second-hand shops for next to nothing.

Artisan Life

Austria's traditional handmade goods are still in high demand, with specialist shops across the country. Get walking to Salzkammergut to pick up beautifully crafted Goiserer boots - perfect for hiking. A couple of families in Burgenland still produce the decorative indigo patterns that have been part of local dress since the 17th century. Check it out at Blaudruckerei Koó's workshop *(www.originalblaudruck.at)*.

← Goiserer boots, made in the Salzkammergut region since the days of the early Alpinists

Classic Celebrations

If you're looking for a taste of local life, you'll find it at Austria's festivals. *Perchtenlauf* processions across the country kick off Carnival season with parties and masquerade balls, while the Alpine regions mark autumn with *Almabtrieb*, when cattle are brought down from high summer pastures and adorned with bells. If you're in the country for New Year's Day, it's hard to miss *Neujahrsschiessen*, where local squads dressed in traditional costumes raise musket rifles.

↑ Cattle adorned with wildflowers and ribbons for *Almabtrieb*

Habsburg Collections

Avid collectors and patrons of the arts, the Habsburg emperors amassed thousands of rare treasures over their 650-year rule. Precious masterpieces of the imperial collection are housed in Vienna's Kunsthistorisches Museum *(p104)*, which holds the world's largest collection of Bruegel, as well as works by Rembrandt and Titian. The Albertina *(p80)* also houses over 140 works by Albrecht Dürer, alongside drawings by Raphael and Rubens.

→

Admiring the works of the old masters at the Kunsthistorisches Museum

AUSTRIA FOR
ART LOVERS

Austria's artistic heritage is world-class, with one of the finest collections of art in the world, renowned art fairs and a variety of edgy galleries. Much of it can be found in Vienna, but other cities across the country also have a booming contemporary art and design scene waiting to be discovered.

Take to the Streets

Street art has an increasing presence in the Austrian capital and can even be found in its stately centre with the aptly named Street Art Passage, a tunnel running from Breite Gasse to the hallowed MuseumsQuartier. For the densest, most vibrant walls, trace the banks of the Donaukanal. Perhaps surprisingly, some of the most artistic street art can be found in Austria's third-largest city, Linz. Mural Harbor, an open-air gallery, has around 300 (and counting) graffiti pieces decorating old industrial buildings. Opt for a guided tour and you may even get the chance to create a piece of graffiti art yourself.

Relaxing by colourful art on the banks of Vienna's Donaukanal ↑

Following the Secession

The Vienna Secession, led by Gustav Klimt, was an art movement formed in 1897 that rejected the artistic conventions of the day, seeking to release creativity from the confines of academic tradition. In Vienna, seek out Klimt's *The Kiss* at the Belvedere *(p124)* or *Beethoven Frieze* at the Wiener Secession *(p126)*. Outside the capital, get your fill of the art of Klimt and his contemporary Oscar Kokoschka at Linz's Lentos Kunstmuseum *(p215)*, or of the renowned Expressionist work of his contemporary Egon Schiele in his birthplace of Tulln *(p166)*.

←

Klimt's *Amalie Zuckerkandl* (1917), one of his many masterpieces

TOP 3 MODERN GALLERIES

Wiener Secession
The world's oldest artist-run independent institution specifically dedicated to contemporary art remains an important forum for experimental art in Vienna *(p126)*.

Künstlerhaus Graz
An impressive range of international installation and video art is held in an airy mid-century modern pavilion in Graz's Stadtpark *(www.km-k.at)*.

Salzburger Kunstverein
This gallery has been championing international and Austrian artists since 1844, and has been located in the red Künstlerhaus since 1885 *(www.salzburger-kunstverein.at)*.

INSIDER TIP
Design Month Graz

This UNESCO City of Design has a month-long programme of exhibitions, workshops and lectures from mid-May to mid-June. Head to www.designmonat.at for more details.

Shock of the New

Along with grand old masters, Austria's galleries brim with fine collections from the second half of the 20th century. Over in Graz, the edgy Kunsthaus *(p184)* leads the way in eclectic art from the last four decades, while in the capital, mumok's *(p103)* extensive collection focuses on art from the 1960s and 70s and combines Nouveau Réalisme, Pop Art and Viennese Actionism.

→

The futuristic exterior of Vienna's mumok in the MuseumsQuartier

Let off Steam

Steam trains are the perfect way to enchant the kids while you sit back and gaze at Austria's spectacular scenery. On the Schafberg Railway, the country's steepest cog railway, kids can visit the captain and even take the controls themselves. The Zillertal steam train treats small children to their own play carriage, and older kids can check out the Swarovski crystal carriage with tens of thousands of sparkling stones that almost eclipse the vertical views.

$\rightarrow$

Enjoying the views from the vintage Schafberg steam locomotive

AUSTRIA FOR
FAMILIES

With hands-on museums, fairytale fortresses and gentle cycle trails, Austria knows how to keep the kids entertained. The winter brings a wonderland of snow-dusted peaks and Christmas markets, while the summer is perfect for lakeside swimming and picnicking in edelweiss-strewn meadows.

Awesome Adventures

With an enviable collection of adventure parks, Austria is guaranteed to amuse the kids (as well as tire them out). Vienna's Prater *(p145)*, home to the Wurstelprater amusement park and its roller coasters, ghost trains and ferris wheel, is a joy for youngsters and parents alike. On Wörthersee's shores you'll find Europapark Klagenfurt *(www.klagenfurt.at/die-stadt/freizeit/ europapark)*, a green expanse with a "miniature world" – Minimundus – plus a skate park and even open-air chess to check out. If you're looking to make a splash, head to Pirate World Aquapulco *(www.piratenwelt.at)*, just outside of Linz. Part of Bad Schallerbach's sprawling thermal spa complex, it has aquatic activities suitable for parents with babes in arms, while a wave pool will keep older children entertained.

$\rightarrow$

The iconic Wiener Riesenrad Ferris wheel at Vienna's Wurstelprater

Hands-on Museums

Austria's museums will spark young minds with a range of activities and exhibits. At the MuseumsQuartier's ZOOM *(p102)*, there are hands-on craft workshops where kids can get creative. Children can climb the musical piano staircase at the Haus der Musik *(www. hdm.at)*, while the Technisches Museum *(p146)* has excellent interactive exhibits. Outside Vienna, at Stübing's Österreichische Freilichtmuseum (Austrian Open-Air Museum), little ones can listen to Austrian fairy tales while older children learn about traditional customs and try their hand at crafts. In Linz, the Biologiezentrum *(p215)* combines up-close encounters with creepy-crawlies and interactive activities.

←
An old air ambulance on display at the Technisches Museum

TOP 3 FAMILY-FRIENDLY HIKING TRAILS

Flori's Adventure Trail, Flachau
Keep the youngsters entertained with a cool fairy-tale world, a fun bird-nest swing, as well as a skywalk and many puzzle stations.

Bruno's Mountain World, Dachstein
A number of activity stations keep kids motivated when little legs get tired.

Eng, Karwendel Mountains, Tyrol
This gentle terrain trail, lined with centuries-old maple trees, is suitable for buggies and strollers.

The Great Outdoors

With its lush grasslands and snow-capped mountains, Austria is a huge playground. Family cycling is a pastime here, and there are plenty of beautiful kid-friendly trails along the Danube, where children's bikes and seats can be hired. It's also easier than you think to get the kids involved in skiing. Laid-back Heiligenblut is known for its ski kindergarten, while Galtür has a great beginners' area and family-oriented slopes.

↑ Decked out in ski gear at the kid-friendly ski resort of Galtür

Bear Witness at Mauthausen

During the Third Reich, more than 50 concentration camps were built on Austrian territory. Though most were destroyed after the war, some sites have been preserved, including those at Gusen and Ebensee. The most important memorial is the former camp at Mauthausen (p220) where, between 1938 and 1945, over 100,000 prisoners were executed or died working its infamous quarry. The sick bay, living quarters, gas chambers and "ash dump" make for an eye-opening and undeniably harrowing visit. You can also learn about the history of the Jews in the Austro-Hungarian Empire at Vienna's excellent Jewish Museum (p88).

AUSTRIA FOR
HISTORY BUFFS

Sprawling empires make for lively history trails and Austria is no exception. The Habsburgs' lengthy rule has done much to shape the character of Vienna, while the countryside offers stark reminders of rich and often turbulent history, with Iron-Age mines and remnants of war to explore.

On the Couch

Vienna and Freud go hand in hand - locals joke that Vienna's nickname the "City of Dreams" owes its genesis to Freud's writings on the subconscious. And indeed the city had a big influence on his work. He wrote many of his best works at his rooms on Berggasse 19, and both his lodgings and consulting rooms are open to visit at the Freud Museum (p110). Freud-aficionados should also visit Café Korb (www.cafekorb.at), where his Vienna Psychoanalytic Society regularly met.

←

Learning about Freud's work at the Sigmund Freud Museum

HIDDEN GEM

Danube 4 AD

On the banks of the Danube, between Vienna and Bratislava, lay the Roman city of Carnuntum *(p173)*, an important 1st-century frontier post. Inspect archaeological finds in the museum and wander around subtly atmospheric ruins in the surrounding fields. A vividly recreated Temple of Diana is a particular highlight.

←

Taking in the Holocaust memorial from World War II at Mauthausen

Hail the Habsburgs

The Habsburgs' rule reached its apotheosis in the Austro-Hungarian Empire, and by the time of its defeat in 1919, it had become a global cultural force. Nothing symbolizes the grandeur and hubris of its late 19th-century days more than Vienna's Ringstrasse *(p114)*, around which you can see the city's major sites. A tour of the Hofburg Complex *(p78)* is also a powerful reminder of the glory of the Habsburg Empire.

→

Austrian Parliament, one of the imposing sites on the Ringstrasse

Unearth the Past

Austria brims with historic sites that preserve a bygone era. The network of ancient salt mines at Salzwelten Hallstatt *(p232)* remains the oldest settlement in Europe, and Hallstatt Museum's collection of finds offer a rich insight into the value of mining here. For a touch of the macabre, head to Salzburg's Stift St Peter *(p242)*, where catacombs are carved into rock .

←

An exhibit showcasing explorers underground at the Hallstatt Museum

Waters for Wellness

Austria's history of healing waters dates back to the Middle Ages and today spa holidays on the slopes marry relaxation with wonderful landscapes. Bad Gastein offers a slew of spa hotels and varied slopes to enjoy between massages. Spa traditionalists should head to Bad Ischl to soak in the town's thermal baths after a day on the piste.

→

Relaxed guests at the family-friendly Haus Hirt spa hotel in Bad Gastein

AUSTRIA AT
HIGH ALTITUDE

Few nations are more serious about their snow sports than Austria, but its ice-clad landscape offers much more than a race downhill. Whether you hanker for traditional Alpine hospitality or immerse yourself in off-piste partying until dawn, Austria's Alps have a resort to suit every taste.

GLACIER SKIING

Austria leads the world in glacier resorts, but the global retreat of glaciers is felt nowhere more keenly than here. It's predicted that around 90 per cent of its glaciers will have melted long before the end of the century, causing risks of floods, avalanches and the degradation of natural habitats. Austria's Alpine organization has called for a stop to the expansion of ski areas and other mass tourism initiatives on and around the most pristine of its glaciers. Many resorts have also implemented eco-friendly policies, including ISO-certified cable cars at Kaprun.

White Nights

For those who take their après-ski as seriously as their downhill, Austria's resorts are the place to be. Ischgl mixes all-night clubbing with traditional sing-alongs, while Soll is a more laid-back, affordable choice. Kitzbühel is a favourite for celebrity spotting but doesn't shirk on the late night fun and vies with St Anton am Arlberg for the most raucous resort title. You can also party at one of the country's best Alpine festivals, the Electric Mountain, at Sölden.

Partying to electronic and dance music at the Electric Mountain festival at Sölden ↑

Top Thrills

If you're looking to take it to the extreme, you're in the right place. Austria's steepest run is known as Harakiri, and thrillseekers can head to Mayrhofen for this 78 per cent gradient that takes no prisoners. Almost up there with Harakiri is Ischgl's steep drops from Greitspitz and Palinkopf, but the Piz Val Gronda aerial tram has made this resort heaven for freeriders, too. Sölden has two glaciers and three peaks that tower over 3,000 m (9,042 ft), which can be experienced in a scenic 50 km (31 mile) route. Powerhounds have only one heli-option: Lech Zürs in the Arlberg.

$\longrightarrow$
Expert skier about to navigate a vertiginous Apline slope

Winter Walks

If you're seeking a day off, in need of forest therapy or are simply a slope beginner, Austria's hiking, snowshoeing and Nordic walking trails suit every need. The Hohe Tauern National Park offers more than 400 km (250 miles) of ploughed winter hiking trails, while Zell am See has 30 km (19 miles) of trails that range from gentle walks around the lake to snowshoe-only routes up Schmittenhöhe.

$\longleftarrow$
Walking through a sparkling blanket of snow in Zell am See

Cross-Country

A number of resorts offer a far cheaper and more tranquil alternative to downhill skiing. Seefeld's 279 km (173 miles) of tracks take in idyllic villages and there's even a floodlit area for night-time gliding. Hohentauern's gentle 13 km (8 miles) of well-maintained trails are perfect for all abilities.

$\longrightarrow$
Spectacular views on a cross-country trail in Hohentauern

On The Mozart Trail

The spirit of prodigy Wolfgang Amadeus Mozart is still felt around every corner in Salzburg. See where his passion for opera began at Mozarts Geburtshaus *(p241)*, where the master was born, before heading to the Mozart-Wohnhaus *(p242)* – his later family residence – to see unmissable relics such as his pianoforte.

←

Getting the perfect picture of the iconic yellow Geburtshaus

AUSTRIA FOR
CLASSICAL
MUSIC LOVERS

No other country in the world can equal Austria for its musical history, scores of illustrious classical composers and continued dedication to classical music. It's huge breadth of performances cater for everyone from the occasional opera whistler to professional musicians on sabbatical.

TOP 4 CLASSICAL MUSIC FESTIVALS

Wiener Festwochen
Symphonies across Vienna in May and June *(www.festwochen.at).*

Salzburger Festspiele
Great musicians play in July and August *(www.salzburgerfestspiele.at).*

Styriarte
A summer celebration of Baroque music in Graz *(www.styriarte.com).*

Schubertiade
A spring-to-summer festival of chamber music in Vorarlberg *(www.schubertiade.at).*

Tracing the Viennese Tradition

Western classical music is synonymous with the Viennese School, when Haydn, Mozart and Beethoven composed in the city in the late 18th and early 19th centuries. A century later, the second school was born, led by Arnold Schönberg and his pupils. Attend performances of both school's compositions in the city's concert halls, see original scores at their residences and pay your respects at the Zentralfriedhof *(p136)* cemetery.

The adorned graves of Mozart and Beethoven at the Zentralfriedhof ↑

↑ Applauding the fine orchestra and conductor at the Wiener Konzerthaus

Visit a Venue

With a packed musical calendar and atmospheric venues, performances are easily accessible in Austria. In Vienna, the Musikverein *(p128)* is one of the finest concert halls in the world with impeccable acoustics, while the Wiener Konzerthaus *(www.konzerthaus.at)* is the place to see intimate choral works. Salzburg also supports its musical roots with sumptuous venues. On a budget? The Mozarteum *(p241)* offers excellent student performances and a "pocket opera" programme.

💬 INSIDER TIP
Schönbrunn's Summer Eve

Each summer the Vienna Philharmonic Orchestra hosts the Sommernachtskonzert *(www.sommernachts konzert.at)*, a free open-air concert at Schloss Schönbrunn *(p138)*.

Musical Museums

Austria's cities are alive with fantastic museums dedicated to its rich musical legacy. Get up close to Haydn's original scores at Haydnhaus *(p144)*, or picture Mahler composing his masterpieces at one of the huts he retreated to on lakes Wörthersee and Attersee. If you're looking to turn up the tempo, head to Vienna's Haus der Musik *(www.hdm.at)*, where you can try your hand at conducting a virtual version of the Vienna Philharmonic.

Gustav Mahler's piano at ↑ his house at Steinbach, on Attersee, and conducting at Haus der Musik *(inset)*

Vibrant Venues

The capital may have the richest collection of venues, but charming intimate spaces abound throughout Austria. The Austrian Film Museum *(www.filmmuseum.at)* in Vienna has a lively schedule of classic and contemporary cinema, while Salzburg's Mozartkino *(www.mozart kino.at)* showcases local productions. In Innsbruck, Leokino *(www.leo kino.at)* is best for arthouse films.

→

A screening at Mozartkino, one of the oldest cinemas in the world

AUSTRIA FOR
FILM BUFFS

This photogenic country is a natural on the big screen. The setting for many legendary films, Austria has also inspired some of the best cinematic stories. Film lovers can track down iconic locations, enjoy the country on screen at thriving cinemas or revel in movie magic at festivals.

The Third Man

Post-World War II Vienna, caught between a troubled past and an uncertain future, is the perfect noir setting for *The Third Man* (1949), from the novel by Graham Greene. Devotees can revel in the hoard of treasures at the Third Man Museum *(www. 3mpc.net)* or re-enact the final scene in the grimy sewers of the city on the Third Man Tour *(www.drittemanntour.at/en)*. And if you're wondering what all the fuss is about, the Burg Kino *(www.burgkino.at)* screens the film every week.

←

Tracing the film's iconic locations on Vienna's Third Man Tour

TOP 5 AUSTRIA ON SCREEN

Sissi (1955)
Portrays the Habsburg royal, Elisabeth.

Where Eagles Dare (1968)
A WWII epic starring Clint Eastwood.

Amadeus (1984)
Mozart biopic that conjures the splendour of the Viennese School.

Before Sunrise (1995)
This cult hit focuses on two young lovers wandering in Vienna.

The Piano Teacher (2001)
Controversial thriller set at the Vienna Conservatory.

The Hills are Alive

Salzburg deserves a supporting-actor Oscar nod for its role in the evergreen 1965 family musical, *The Sound of Music*. If the film is indeed one of your favourite things, you can join countless daily tours of the locations, or even tick the sights off on your own. Sing your Do-Re-Mis from Werfen Picnic Meadow to the Winkler Terrace, channel your inner von Trapp through the lakeside at Schloss Leopoldskron, and end your tour where the film also dramatically climaxes – at the Felsenreitschule.

→

Schloss Leopoldskron, a beautiful location used in *The Sound of Music*

Film-ivals

With a vast calendar of festivals, Austria has plenty to keep film fanatics entertained. The Viennale *(www.viennale.at)* takes place each October at classic cinemas in Vienna. For more niche events, try Linz's Crossing Europe *(www.crossingeurope. at)*, which exhibits the work of young filmmakers, or check out documentaries on the natural world at the Innsbruck Nature Festival *(www.inff.eu/en)*.

→

Enjoying a movie at the Viennale, the largest film festival in the capital

Flourishing Jugendstil

In 1896, a generation of avant-garde artists, architects and designers started an architectural revolution: the Vienna Secession. The movement's roots in Jugendstil (Art Nouveau) are evident in the richly decorative motifs on the buildings of this era. Look out for Secession accents throughout the city: the Wagner Apartments *(p129)* feature gold detailing; the Karlsplatz Pavillons *(p128)* are a gold and green delight; and the Wiener Secession *(p126)* is renowned for its golden ligree dome.

←

Otto Wagner's east Karlsplatz Pavillon, detailed in gold ligree

AUSTRIA FOR
ARCHITECTURE ENTHUSIASTS

Beautiful Baroque churches, sumptuous Secessionist icons and innovative modern masterpieces: there's more to Austria than its Alpine vernacular and imperial palaces *(p30)*. Stroll the streets for a glimpse of the intriguing buildings that shape the country's beautiful landscape.

TOP 3 GEMS OF ARCHITECTURE

Swarovski Kristallwelten
Part outdoor gallery, part theme park near Innsbruck *(p275)*.

mumok
An imposing breeze-block art gallery in Vienna *(p103)*.

Kunsthotel Fuchspalast
Colourful and quirky hotel in St Veit an der Glan *(p300)*.

Red Vienna

"Red Vienna" was the city's nickname during the 1920s and 1930s, when the Social Democratic Party governed Vienna for the first time. The period saw a boom in the construction of utilitarian social housing, of which Karl Ehn's Karl-Marx-Hof *(p142)* is the most famous. Head out of the city centre by tram to see this example, the world's longest residential building.

→

The imposing exterior of the Karl-Marx-Hof in Heiligenstadt

↑ The monumental abstraction of Wotrubakirche

Modern Masterpieces

Austria's eclectic mix of modern buildings will entice architecture enthusiasts. On the outskirts of Vienna, maverick eco-designer Friedensreich Hundertwasser's *(p140)* fairy tale apartment block is the most visited site. Just outside the city in Mauer is the brutal Wotrubakirche *(p147)*, a church that defies tradition, built with 152 blocks of concrete, while the futuristic Kunsthaus *(p184)* has transformed the serene city of Graz.

💬 INSIDER TIP
Take a Tour

Guided walking tours by Space and Place offer an alternative perspective of Vienna. Join their Vienna Ugly Tour *(www.spaceandplace.at/vienna-ugly)* to discover 19 of the city's least attractive buildings.

Baroque Splendour

Particularly typical of the Austrian architectural landscape are the vast abbeys built in the Middle Ages and modernized during the late Baroque period. The Pfarrkirche in Schwaz *(p275)* typifies the lightness of Baroque, with its opulent star vaulting resting on slender columns and its interior lit up by vast windows, while Salzburg's Dom *(p242)* is one of the earliest twin-towered churches of the modern era found north of the Alps.

→ The light-filled interior *(inset)* of Salzburg Dom, one of the best examples of the Early Baroque style

A YEAR IN
AUSTRIA

JANUARY

New Year's Day Concert *(1 Jan)*. World-famous extravaganza of Austrian music, played by the Vienna Philharmonic Orchestra at the Musikverein in the capital.

△ **Hahnenkamm World Cup Ski Race** *(24–26 Jan)*. This notorious downhill race is honoured with plenty of après-ski revelry in Kitzbühel.

FEBRUARY

△ **Opernball** *(20 Feb)*. The grandest ball in Austria takes place at Vienna's State Opera to celebrate the nationwide pre-Lenten *Fasching* (Carnival) season.

MAY

△ **Gauderfest** *(1–2 May)*. Austria's huge spring festival is celebrated with strong beer, oompah bands, ornate horse-drawn carriages and costumed parades in Zell am Ziller.

Wiener Festwochen *(2nd week May–mid-Jun)*. The country's biggest arts festival of opera, theatre and performing arts in the capital.

JUNE

△ **Donauinselfest** *(late Jun)*. Europe's largest open-air music festival features three days of live rock and pop, sunbathing and barbecues beside the Danube in Vienna.

Midsummer Night Celebration *(20 Jun)*. Bonfires and folkloric festivities mark the summer solstice across the country, with big celebrations in Tyrol.

SEPTEMBER

△ **Herbstgold** *(early–mid-Sep)*. An international festival of music by Haydn across Eisenstadt.

International Bruckner Festival *(mid-Sep–early Oct)*. This prestigious event starts with a series of concerts accompanied by laser lighting on the banks of the Danube in Linz.

Wiener Wiesn-Fest *(mid-Sep–early Oct)*. Vienna's very own Oktoberfest-style beer festival.

OCTOBER

Almabtrieb *(early Oct)*. Villages welcome home their flower-bedecked cattle, as they return from the high Alps for winter, with music and feasting.

△ **Long Night of Museums** *(early Oct)*. Museums and galleries across the country extend their usual hours, opening from 6pm to 1am for just one night.

MARCH

△ **Spring Festival** *(first 3 weeks)*. Classical concerts from top ensembles, including the Vienna Symphony Orchestra, herald the arrival of spring in Bregenz.

APRIL

Easter Carols *(Mar/Apr)*. Ancient Passiontide songs are performed in the streets of various towns, including Grossarl and Traunkirchen, during Holy Week.

△ **Easter Markets** *(early Apr)*. Market stalls throughout the country are adorned with painted eggs, chocolate rabbits, floral decorations, Easter bread and other seasonal treats.

Donaufestival *(mid-Apr–mid-May)*. Festival of contemporary theatre and music in Krems.

JULY

Festival of Early Music *(mid-Jul–end Aug)*. World-renowned festival of early music and Baroque operas held in Innsbruck.

△ **Salzburger Festspiele** *(late Jul–late Aug)*. This world-class series of classical concerts and theatre in Salzburg celebrates its hundredth year in 2020 and is one of Europe's top cultural events.

AUGUST

△ **Marien Schiffsprozession** *(15 Aug)*. Colourful processions mark the Feast of the Assumption throughout Austria, most notably at Wörthersee.

Jazzfestival Saalfelden *(late Aug)*. Free jazz concerts performed by several hundred artists.

NOVEMBER

St Martin's Day *(11 Nov)*. Art exhibitions, wine tastings and feasting on *Martinigans* – roast St Martin's goose – across the country.

△ **Weihnachtsmärkte** *(late Nov–late Dec)*. Christmas starts early in Austria, with seasonal music, traditional decorations and roasted chestnuts in markets across the nation.

DECEMBER

△ **St Nikolaus** *(5–6 Dec)*. Krampus the "bad Santa" and his *Perchten* (elves) appear in evening parades; then children receive Christmas gifts from St Nikolaus.

Silvester *(31 Dec)*. Fireworks usher in the new year. Vienna celebrates with Strauss's *Die Fledermaus* opera, Beethoven's Ninth and the celebrated Emperor's Ball.

A BRIEF
HISTORY

This small, neutral country has witnessed a chequered history, from early invasions of Germanic tribes to the medieval Babenberg rulers. During 600 years of Habsburg rule it rose to the rank of a world power, finally becoming the Austrian Republic in 1919. Today, Austria is a forward-looking EU nation.

Prehistory and Early Middle Ages

Due to its strategic geographical location, the Austrian territory was repeatedly raided and populated by Celtic and Germanic tribes from the 7th century BC onwards. By the end of the 1st century BC, the Romans occupied the lands south of the Danube, until they were later displaced by Huns, Goths and other Germanic tribes. In the 7th and 8th centuries, Bavarian settlers held sway, converting the region to Christianity, but they were eventually crushed by Charlemagne, King of the Franks, and then the Magyars, who raided from the east.

AD 1

The year the garrison settlement of Vindobona - later Vienna - was established.

Timeline of events

15 BC

The Celtic regions of Noricum and Pannonia are overrun by the Romans.

AD 280

Roman Emperor Probus authorizes wine-growing in the Danube area.

AD 4th–7th centuries

The Great Migration of Nations results in invasions by Goths, Avars and Bavarian tribes.

739

Following the region's conversion to Christianity, Salzburg becomes a centre for missionary activity and forms a bishopric.

The Babenbergs

In 995, German King Otto I eventually defeated the Magyars and restored Charlemagne's margravate, which was centred on Melk. His successor, Otto II, handed it as a fief to Leopold I of the Franconian Babenberg family, who extended its frontiers eastwards to the Vienna Woods. The territory continued to be extended until 1156, when Austria was appointed a hereditary fief of the Holy Roman Empire. The family were elevated to Dukes of Austria, and Vienna was adopted as the capital.

Bohemian Austria

Within 100 years, the Babenberg line died out and Austria fell into the hands of Bohemian kings: initially Vaclav I, then his successor Ottokar II – one of the most powerful dukes in the empire with vast realms. His appointment was seen as a major encroachment on German territory, especially as he had his sights set on the German crown. So the German princes elected the German, Rudolf von Habsburg, to crush the growing power of Ottokar II in 1273. For the next 640 years, Austrian rule was in the hands of the Habsburg dynasty.

1 A map of the Inn valley in Innsbruck, printed in the 1600s.

2 King Otto I and his wife arriving in Austria.

3 An illustration of Rudolf I granting Bohemia and Moravia to King Ottokar II.

4 A portrait of Rudolf I, the first Habsburg ruler.

1246
The Babenberg line of rulers dies out; Austria becomes a duchy, independent of Bavaria.

787
Charlemagne (Charles the Great) deposes the last independent Bavarian prince, Tassilo III. In 803 he founds the eastern margravate (territory).

1273
German princes favour Rudolf von Habsburg in feudal elections, despite his family's then modest lands.

1278
Rudolf von Habsburg wins the Battle of Dürnkrut; Austria becomes a hereditary fief of the Habsburgs.

1363
The Habsburgs gain control over Tyrol, a centre of trade.

1

2

The Habsburg Rise to Power

Over the next three decades, the Habsburg dominion steadily grew, occasionally by conquest, but more often by means of expedient marriages and inheritances. In 1365, Rudolf IV signed a treaty with his father-in-law, Bohemian Emperor Karl IV of the Luxembourg dynasty, stating that, should one of the lines die out, the other would control both territories. In 1438, the crowns of Germany, Hungary and Bohemia thereby passed to his successor, Duke Albrecht II of Habsburg. Subsequent betrothals added Alsace, Lorraine, the Netherlands, Spain and its South American dominions to their mighty realm.

Reformation and Turkish Threat

During the Reformation, Austria became the scene of fierce religious conflicts between Catholics and Protestants, leading to the Thirty Years' War. Greater destruction, however, was wrought by the wars fought in the 16th and 17th centuries against the Turks, who twice tried to conquer Vienna. Their crushing defeat in 1683 allowed the Habsburgs to take control of the whole of Hungary, Transylvania and Croatia.

MARIA THERESA (1717–1780)

Maria Theresa became the only female ruler of the Habsburg dominion when she was just 23. Though she lost some territories, her reign dazzled Vienna. She also ensured the family succession by producing sixteen children, and strategically marrying her 14-year-old daughter, Marie Antoinette, to the French dauphin, the future Louis XVI.

Timeline of events

1519-56
The Habsburgs reach their height of power during the reigns of Karl V and Ferdinand I.

1618-45
Religious conflict during the Reformation results in the Thirty Years' War.

1701-14
War of Spanish Succession; Austria acquires Belgium, Milan and Naples.

1485
Habsburg in-fighting results in the Ottoman siege of Vienna.

1493
Habsburg power is restored, with Austria at the heart of their mighty empire. Coronation of Maximilian I.

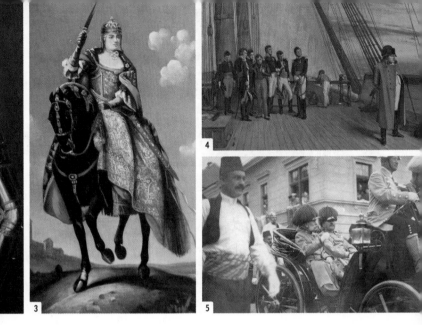

Revolution and Restoration

In the 18th and 19th centuries, a wave of revolutions swept across Europe, weakening Austria and forcing Maria Theresa's grandson Franz II to relinquish his title of Holy Roman Emperor in 1806. Following the eventual defeat of Napoleon in 1812, proceedings at the ensuing Congress of Vienna were dominated by the powerful Austrian Foreign Minister, Klemens Metternich. As a consequence, the Habsburg Empire once again became a European superpower. However, the 1848 revolution in Vienna forced the Habsburgs to flee and Ferdinand I to abdicate. Franz Joseph I eventually regained control, but of a considerably weakened empire.

The Austro-Hungarian Empire

In 1867, to ease growing tensions in Austro-Hungarian relations, Emperor Franz Joseph I signed a treaty to form the Austro-Hungarian Empire – two states united under one ruler with a joint army, finances and foreign policy. Internationally, the Empire's attention was now focused on the Balkans, where it already occupied Bosnia and Herzegovina.

1. The Battle at the White Mountain in 1620 during the Thirty Years' War.

2. Holy Roman Emperor Ferdinand I.

3. Maria Theresa riding a horse on the coronation hill at Pressburg, once the capital of Hungary.

4. Napoleon on board the HMS *Bellerophon* in 1815.

5. Emperor Franz Joseph I on a trip to Bosnia.

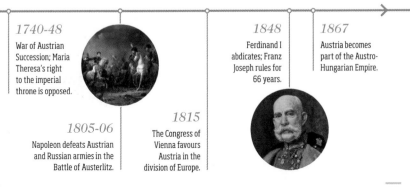

1740-48
War of Austrian Succession; Maria Theresa's right to the imperial throne is opposed.

1805-06
Napoleon defeats Austrian and Russian armies in the Battle of Austerlitz.

1815
The Congress of Vienna favours Austria in the division of Europe.

1848
Ferdinand I abdicates; Franz Joseph rules for 66 years.

1867
Austria becomes part of the Austro-Hungarian Empire.

Turn of the 20th Century

Austria's influence as a major power further declined during Emperor Franz Joseph's reign. To some he was a beacon of continuity, and his wife Sisi was the darling of Viennese society, but to others he was the relic of an obsolescent past. The revolutionary atmosphere, combined with an influx of immigrants, created an explosion of creativity: the Second Viennese School pushed musical boundaries, Sigmund Freud developed ideas of psychoanalysis, and the Secession Movement forged a unique brand of Jugendstil with their art and architecture.

World War I

In 1908, Austria-Hungary annexed Bosnia-Herzegovina, leading to tensions with Serbia, who pursued their own expansionist aims. The resulting assassination of the Habsburg heir, Franz Ferdinand, in 1914 brought about World War I. Germany declared itself on Austria's side while Russia, France and England sided with Serbia. The Austro-Hungarian Empire collapsed in 1918 and, one year later, the first Austrian Republic was declared.

1 Franz Ferdinand's assassination in Sarajevo. ↑

2 Reserve forces in Vienna in 1914.

3 War memorial, Vienna.

4 The Danube canal in present-day Vienna.

Did You Know?

By constitutional amendment, nuclear power is banned in Austria, with emphasis placed on renewable energy.

Timeline of events

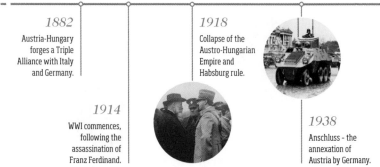

1882
Austria-Hungary forges a Triple Alliance with Italy and Germany.

1914
WWI commences, following the assassination of Franz Ferdinand.

1918
Collapse of the Austro-Hungarian Empire and Habsburg rule.

1938
Anschluss – the annexation of Austria by Germany.

World War II

Post-war, the defeated Austrian Empire was dismembered. Struggles for control of the new Austrian republic gave rise to radical ultra-German nationalist sentiment and the emergence of the National Socialist Party led by Austrian-born Adolf Hitler, Chancellor of Germany from 1933. Anschluss – Austria's integration into the Third Reich in 1938 – was greeted with approval by most of the population. Following Germany's surrender at the end of the war, Austria came under Allied control until 1955, when it became a sovereign state again.

Austria Today

As a member of the EU, this now neutral nation has flourished economically, but in recent years old political divisions have re-emerged. The far-right Freedom Party (FPÖ) has been part of government coalitions from 2000, and elections in 2013 saw a sharp rise in their support. Following the nationalist government leader Sebastian Kurz's fall from grace in 2019, Austria appointed Brigitte Bierlein to lead an interim government.

↑ Composer Arnold Schoenberg, who led the Second Viennese School

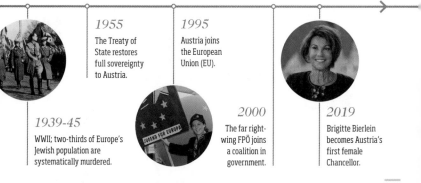

1955
The Treaty of State restores full sovereignty to Austria.

1995
Austria joins the European Union (EU).

1939-45
WWII; two-thirds of Europe's Jewish population are systematically murdered.

2000
The far right-wing FPÖ joins a coalition in government.

2019
Brigitte Bierlein becomes Austria's first female Chancellor.

EXPERIENCE
VIENNA

The lavish façade of the Hofburg Palace

EXPLORE
VIENNA

This guide divides Vienna into four sightseeing areas: the three on this map and a chapter for sights beyond the city centre. Find out more about each area on the following pages.

ALSERGRUND

Gartenpalais Liechtenstein

Narrenturm

Roosevelt-platz

Votivkirche

Universität Wien

Volkskunde-museum

JOSEFSTADT

Rathaus-Park

Neues Rathaus

Maria-Treu-Kirche

Parlament

NORTH OF MARIAHILFER STRASSE
p96

Schmerling-platz

Naturhistorisches Museum

NEUBAU

Maria-Theresien-Platz

SPITTELBERG

Museums-Quartier Wien

MARIAHILF

Esterhazy-Park

AUSTRIA

VIENNA ▪

MARGARETEN

Donaukanal

Augarten
Park

LEOPOLDSTADT

Praterstern

Schlick-
platz

W. Kienzl-
Park

Karmeliter-
platz

Börse-
platz

SCHOTTEN-
VIERTEL

Morzin-
platz

Nestroy-
platz

Altes
Rathaus

Ruprechts-
kirche

Schweden-
platz

Donaukanal

WIDMER-
VIERTEL

Am
Hof

Julius-Raab-
Platz

WEISSGERBER

Burgtheater

INNER CITY
p72

STUBEN-
VIERTEL

Minoriten-
kirche

Stephans-
platz

Michaeler-
platz

Volks-
garten

Neuer
Markt

Stephansdom

Dr-Karl-
Lueger-platz

(MAK) Museum für
Angewandte Kunst

Hundertwasserhaus

Franziskaner-
Platz

Hofburg
Complex

Albertina-
Platz

Stadtpark

Burggarten

Kunsthistorisches
Museum

Staatsoper

Beethoven-
Platz

ERDBERG

Künstlerhaus

Theater an
der Wien

Karlsplatz

Schwarzenberg-
platz

LANDSTRASSE

Resselpark

Naschmarkt

Wien Museum
Karlsplatz

Karlskirche

Schwarzenberg
Palais

WIEDEN

Lower
Belvedere

Botanischer
Garten

SOUTH OF
THE RING
p118

Belvedere
Garten

Upper
Belvedere

Schweizer
Garten

Südtiroler-
platz

Belvedere 21

HUNGELBRUNN

0 metres   500

0 yards   500

N

GETTING TO KNOW
VIENNA

Vienna is a compact and easy-to-navigate city composed of 23 districts *(Bezirke)*, all of which have their own distinctive character. Famous sights are clustered in the centre, encircled by the grand Ringstrasse boulevard, but there are visitor-friendly enclaves to discover all over the city.

INNER CITY

PAGE 72

The winding cobbled streets of the Innere Stadt – city centre – are Vienna at its most splendid. The beating heart of Austria since the 13th century, it remains hugely atmospheric, its spacious squares buzzing with activity. Both history and fine art fans are in for a treat, with the gorgeous Gothic Stephansdom cathedral dominating the area and the magnificent Hofburg complex providing an insight into the opulent lifestyle of the Habsburgs. In between palace and church hopping, the area's most historic coffee houses and sublime green spaces make for a welcome recharge.

Best for
Historic atmosphere, Habsburg splendour and coffee houses

Home to
Stephansdom, the Hofburg Complex

Experience
Whiling away the hours in a classic coffee house

NORTH OF MARIAHILFER STRASSE

The Ringstrasse with its 19th-century grandeur is a destination in itself, but it's also home to some of the city's most compelling cultural sights, as well as the Austrian parliament. Both the Kunsthistorisches and Naturhistorisches museums hold Habsburg treasures beyond compare, while the MuseumsQuartier is a draw for modern and contemporary art fans as well as a lively hub for an afternoon pitstop. To the west, Spittelberg's vibrant student-thronged streets are among the most picturesque in all of Vienna. In contrast to the student vibe, this is also where you'll find the Sigmund Freud Museum – dedicated to the iconic intellectual who taught at the university. At night, head to the Burgtheater for world-class theatre.

Best for
Museums and galleries, evening concerts and cheap eats

Home to
Burgtheater, MuseumsQuartier Wien, Kunsthistorisches Museum

Experience
A wander around Freud's old haunts and intellectual hangouts

$\rightarrow$

SOUTH OF THE RING

This densely populated but leafy and effortlessly elegant area is dominated by the Belevedere, one of the world's finest Baroque palaces. Taking in the majestic Karlsplatz and the gloriously decorated Secession building, this is Vienna at its most grandiose. If all this splendour gets too much, grab a bite to eat the Naschmarkt, the city's liveliest daily market, overlooked by Otto Wagner's Jugendstil apartments. Shoppers also flock to the city's main retail zone here, clustering around the pedestrianized Mariahilfer Strasse, with its many boutiques, department stores and cafes.

Best for
Eating and drinking, museum hopping and shopping

Home to
Karlskirche, Belvedere

Experience
Bartering for one-of-a-kind souvenirs at the Naschmarkt

BEYOND THE CENTRE

So compact is Vienna (and so well served by public transport) that few places require much effort to get to, even those beyond the city centre. Top of the list is Schönbrunn, the summer residence of the Habsburgs and one of the finest royal palaces in the world. The Hundertwasserhaus, all curving irregularity and bright colour, is an expression of sheer architectural exuberance in contrast to the stately palace. On the east bank of the Danube, and as emblematic of Vienna as any palace, the Prater and its Ferris wheel remain a quintessential Viennese experience.

Best for
Rococo palaces, green spaces and military history

Home to
Zentralfriedhof, Schönbrunn Palace, Hundertwasserhaus

Experience
A bird's-eye view of Vienna from the top of the Prater's Wiener Riesenrad (Ferris wheel)

←

1 Admiring mumok's collection of modern art.

2 A family at the Prater.

3 A lively performance at the Burgtheater.

4 Relaxing in the Burggarten.

2 DAYS

in Vienna

Day 1

Morning MuseumsQuartier Wien *(p102)* is one of the largest urban complexes of contemporary art and culture in the world. Devote your morning to the Leopold Museum, particularly the Secession and Art Nouveau exhibition on the ground floor. If you are with the kids, the ZOOM Kindermuseum next door is an exciting place for them to explore. Alternatively, marvel at mumok's collection of modern art, with masterpieces by Warhol, Picasso and Yoko Ono. After, relax in the grand courtyard; known as "Vienna's living room", it is open around the clock.

Afternoon For lunch, have a picnic and recharge your batteries in the nearby Burggarten, and make a quick visit to the Schmetterlinghaus (Butterfly House) to view the collection of butterflies. Then head to the Ringstrasse's palatial Kunsthistorisches Museum *(p104)* to enjoy the astonishing array of fine art and antiquities. Much of the collection is derived from those of Habsburg monarchs, accumulated over centuries.

Evening A bar hop through the city centre is a great way to discover Vienna's fabulous nightlife, and there is no better place to get things under way than with a perfectly mixed cocktail at the American Bar *(p93)*. Sky Bar *(www.steffl-vienna.at/ de/skybar)* on Kärntner Strasse has some of the best views of the Stephansdom. Meanwhile, renowned jazz bar Porgy & Bess *(porgy.at)* is well suited to late-night drinks with music into the small hours.

Day 2

Morning A gentle tram trip around the Ringstrasse is a pleasant way to start the day, and from the city centre, line D will drop you off right outside the Belvedere Palace *(p124)*. So stunning is the symmetry of the palace and its gardens that many visitors simply admire the building and move on, but make time to see the plentiful treasures housed inside. The Klimt Collection features an extensive array of Jugendstil art, including Klimt's famous *The Kiss*.

Afternoon For lunch, make for the top deli Lingenhel Käserei *(www.lingenhel. com)*, on Landstrasser Hauptstrasse, a great place to stock up on fabulous salami and cheese. Suitably refuelled, make for the great green Prater *(p145)*. The park was once an imperial hunting ground and its tree-lined avenues and verdant meadows are perfect for leisurely strolls. Kids will love the miniature railway and funfair. No visit to Vienna would be complete without a spin on the Prater's Wiener Riesenrad Ferris wheel, with its fabulous views across the city.

Evening Take the tram back to the city centre, to the Museum and Town Hall Quarter, and savour an early supper at upmarket Restaurant Vestibül *(p111)*, which serves delicious classic fare with a contemporary twist, like decadent lobster *Currywurst*. Catch a modern show (many are subtitled in English) at the magnificent Neo-Classical Burgtheater *(p100)* to round off the day.

Kaffeehaus Institutions

There's nothing like sipping a frothy coffee and enjoying the cosy hum of a Viennese coffee house. A place of everyday elegance, this is where history is made and debates settled, where locals linger over the papers or chat with friends. Menus feature complicated brews, newspapers are fastened in wooden holders, and smartly dressed waiters bring a glass of tap water to accompany every coffee – it's a highly ritualized affair. Head to Café Landtmann (www.landtmann.at) for outdoor seating and an extensive cake list. Café Central (p85) serves Austrian classics, while Café Prückel's (www.prueckel.at) 1950s-style interior, designed by Oswald Haerdtl, is particularly Instagram-friendly. This is traditional Vienna at its best.

> **Did You Know?**
>
> Coffee beans were introduced to Vienna by its Turkish invaders in the 17th century.

→

Perusing the lengthy menu at Café Central

VIENNA FOR
COFFEE CULTURE

Like the Parisian bistro or London pub, the *Kaffeehaus* is a Viennese institution. Whether it's indulging in a leisurely Wiener Melange at a sumptuous traditional coffee house or sipping a flat white in a hip "Third Wave" café, there are plenty of ways to get your caffeine fix in this city.

THE ORIGINAL SACHER

Forget schnitzel, Vienna's culinary gift to the world is the Sachertorte, a chocolate cake created by pastry chef Franz Sacher in 1832. Franz's son Eduard opened Hotel Sacher (p127) in 1876, where the "original", secret-recipe Sachertorte can be tasted. The cakes at rival bakery Demel (www.demel.com) are just as delicious.

A Slice of History

Coffee with cake is a classic combination to be enjoyed throughout Central Europe, and Vienna is no exception, with sweet treats at every café. Enjoy the famous chocolate cake at lavishly decorated Café Sacher (p127). Kaffee Alt Wien (www.kaffeealtwien.at) is renowned for tempting crisp Apfelstrudel, a Viennese staple served with sweet vanilla custard.

Slices of Sachertorte with fresh cream ↑

TOP 5 TRADITIONAL COFFEES

Schwarzer (or Mocca)
Espresso, served as a *Kleiner* (single) or *Grosser* (double).

Wiener Melange
A milky coffee topped with foam.

Einspänner
Espresso topped with whipped cream.

Maria Theresa
Black coffee served with orange liqueur and whipped cream.

Turkische
Thick, dark and very sweet, this drink is served in a copper pot.

The "Third Wave"

In recent years, small stylish "Third Wave" coffee shops have sprung up across the city, with a new generation of baristas revitalizing classic coffee. Leading the pack are tiny Kaffeemodul (*www.kaffeemodul.at*) and trendy Kaffemik (*www.kaffmik.at*), where you can sip delicious beverages brewed from freshly roasted beans in sleek surrounds. Café Espresso (*www.espresso-wien.at*), meanwhile, has a distinct American diner feel.

← The sleek, modern interior of laid-back coffee shop Kaffemik

Intellectual Hangouts

Once the meeting place of writers and free thinkers, the grand Viennese coffee house can still draw a clever crowd. Café Prückel offers live classical music and is popular with locals playing games of bridge. Quaint Kleines Café (*Franziskanerplatz 3*) attracts a loyal clientele of thespians and artists, along with university students sipping *Schwarzers* and idling on their laptops.

→ Locals relaxing in Franziskanerplatz outside Kleines Café

VIENNA
AFTER DARK

Vienna doesn't go to sleep when the sun goes down: this 24-hour city serves everything from classic cocktails to happening hops, crowded clubs to jiving jazz venues, magic musicals to brilliant burlesque. Whatever entertainment keeps you awake at night, you're sure to find it here.

TOP 4 VIENNESE DANCE CLUBS

Sass
 Karlsplatz 1
An opulent space with mellow vibes.

Cabaret Fledermaus
Spiegelgasse 2
An eclectic mix of music in stylish surrounds.

Flex
Augartenbrücke 1
An established venue in a disused metro tunnel.

DonauTechno
Karlschweighofergasse 10
Expect pumping techno and crazy light shows.

Feel the Beat

In Vienna, clubs offer both tectonic techno beats and quirky and eye-catching designs. The massive Pratersauna nightclub (*www.pratersauna.tv*), housed in an old spa, draws crowds all year; its pool is open in warmer months. In summer, outdoor clubs pop up on the Danube embankment and DJs spin tunes by the floating bar Badeschiff's (*www.badeschiff.at*) pool long into the night.

↑ Dancing to the light-up beats at the iconic Pratersauna club

All of Wien's a Stage

From Broadway musicals to underground comedy, Vienna's stages entertain year round. There are big productions at the Raimund Theatre and Ronacher *(www.musicalvienna.at)*, dramas at the venerable Burgtheater *(p100)* and Theater an der Wien *(p127)*, great stand-up comedy at Casa Nova *(www.casanova-vienna.at)* or burlesque and drag shows at Volkstheater's *(p115)* Rote Bar.

←

The cast of *Mary Poppins* performing at glitzy Ronacher theatre

VENTURE OUT OF VIENNA

Austrian nightlife does not stop in Vienna. For those seeking a taste of rural Austria, the city's surrounding villages certainly hold their own in the party department. In the summer, discos and bars are in abundance around Austria's lakes. All the best late nights culminate in a snack at a *Würstel* stand, where crowds congregate alongside late-night truck drivers.

Jumping Jazz Clubs

Jazz is big news in Vienna, and the eclectic Porgy & Bess *(www.porgy.at)* attracts famous international acts and a crowd of music lovers. Jazzland *(www.jazzland.at)* is the oldest jazz club in the city, dating back to 1972, and is the place to see Austrian greats. It's also one of the venues for the JazzFloor festival, which brings together acts from around the world each November.

←

Acts playing in a former church crypt at Jazzland

By the Glass

Here, sophisticated bars sit cheek by jowl with casual taprooms and microbreweries. For high-end drinks seek out minimalist Ebert's Cocktail Bar *(p115)*, or for cocktails with a fine view try Sofitel Hotel's Das LOFT *(www.dasloftwien.at)*. The beer scene is booming: try a brew at 7 Stern Bräu *(www.7stern.at)* or at Beaver Brewing Tour *(www.beaverbrewing.at)*.

→

The colourful ceiling by Pipilotti Rist at Das LOFT

INNER CITY

The ancient quarter of Vienna's Innere Stadt, or "inner city", was first occupied over 2,000 years ago by the Romans, who were drawn to the area by its valuable resources, among them gold. Established around AD 100, this military settlement was known across the Roman Empire as Vindobona. It was destroyed by the Huns in 403, and little trace of the Roman garrison survives.

The most profound influence on the quarter was made by its subsequent inhabitants and early Habsburg rulers, with its winding lanes following the compact arrangement of medieval settlements. The ancient soul of Vienna still dominates the skyline – the Gothic Stephansdom. A parish church had stood on this site since the 12th century, but the foundation stone of the cathedral was laid by Duke Rudolf IV, "the Founder", in 1359. What began in the 13th century as a modest city fortress, the Hofburg or "Castle of the Court" grew over the centuries into the extensive palace that marks the heart of this stately quarter. For some 650 years, the palace was the nexus of the vast Habsburg empire. The winter residence of the Habsburgs, it had a profound effect on the nearby quarters. Neighbouring streets are lined with dwellings built by the nobility in order to be close to the seat of Austro-Hungarian imperial power.

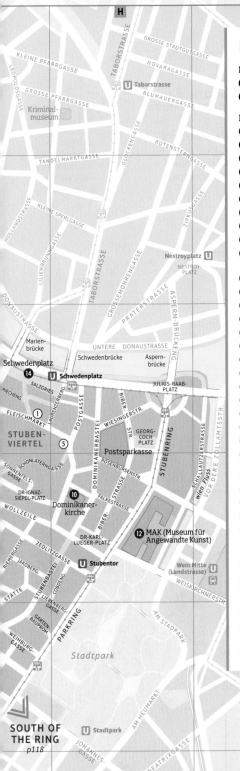

INNER CITY

Must Sees

① Stephansdom
② The Hofburg Complex

Experience More

③ Michaelerplatz
④ Mozarthaus Vienna
⑤ Graben
⑥ Peterskirche
⑦ Deutschordenskirche
⑧ Franziskanerkirche
⑨ Volksgarten
⑩ Dominikanerkirche
⑪ Altes Rathaus
⑫ MAK (Museum für Angewandte Kunst)
⑬ Jewish District
⑭ Schwedenplatz
⑮ Ruprechtskirche
⑯ Maria am Gestade
⑰ Freyung
⑱ Dom Museum
⑲ Uhrenmuseum
⑳ Am Hof
㉑ Hoher Markt
㉒ Kapuzinerkirche
㉓ Winterpalais des Prinzen Eugen
㉔ Minoritenplatz
㉕ Kärntner Strasse
㉖ American Bar

Eat

① Griechenbeisl
② TIAN Wien
③ Wrenkh
④ Café Central
⑤ Beim Czaak

Drink

⑥ Esterhazykeller
⑦ Palmenhaus

Shop

⑧ Grimm Bakery
⑨ Demel
⑩ Lobmeyr

SOUTH OF THE RING
p118

① Ⓜ️ 🏛️

STEPHANSDOM

📍G4 🏠Stephansplatz 1 Ⓤ Stephansplatz 🚌1A, 2A, 3A
🕐9-11:30am & 1-4:30pm Mon-Sat, 1pm-4:30pm Sun & hols
🌐stephanskirche.at

Situated in the very centre of Vienna, Stephansdom is the spiritual heart of the city, and its chief place of worship. Its soaring towers, impressive crypt and ornately carved altars make this Gothic cathedral the capital's most iconic sight.

A church has stood on this site for over 800 years. It is thought that its first iteration was constructed on the ruins of an ancient Roman cemetery. The first Romanesque building on this plot was consecrated by the Bishop of Passau in 1147; following its destruction, a second was erected in 1230. All that remains of this Romanesque church are the Riesentor (Giant's Doorway) and Heidentürme (Heathen Towers). The Gothic nave, choir and side chapels are the result of a rebuilding programme in the 14th and 15th centuries, while some outbuildings, such as the Lower Vestry, are 18th-century Baroque additions.

230,000

Glazed tiles cover Stephansdom's roof, depicting the coats of arms of Vienna and Austria.

🔍 HIDDEN GEM
The Catacombs

Under the cathedral, vast catacombs hold the bones of Vienna's plague dead in a mass grave and bone house, along with urns containing the internal organs of members of the Habsburg dynasty.

The North Tower's construction ended in 1511. In 1578 it was topped with a Renaissance cap.

A flight of steps leads to the 18th-century catacombs.

The 13th-century Giant's Doorway and Heathen Towers allegedly stand on the site of an earlier heathen shrine.

The 15th-century Pilgrim's Pulpit

Main entrance

Singer Gate was once the entrance for male visitors. A relief above the door depicts scenes from the life of St Paul.

← The magnificent Gothic Stephansdom, first consecrated in 1147

The 137-m- (450-ft-) high Gothic spire, or Steffl, houses stairs that visitors can climb to reach a viewing platform.

THE PUMMERIN BELL

The North Tower's Pummerin or "Boomer" bell is a potent symbol of Vienna's turbulent past. The original was cast from melted-down cannons abandoned when the Turks fled Vienna in 1683. In a fire of 1945, the bell crashed down through the cathedral roof. In 1952, a new, even larger bell was cast using the remains of the old one.

The cathedral roof's fine glazed tiles were carefully restored after bomb damage during World War II.

↑ The cathedral's imposing Gothic and Romanesque exterior, brightly uplit

↑ Grand nave leading to the High Altar depicting the martyrdom of St Stephen

Southeastern entrance

Lower Vestry

The grand Hofburg entrance, Michaelertor, surmounted by a dome ↑

② 🗺 Ⓜ 🖼 🏛

THE HOFBURG COMPLEX

📍 E4 🏛 Michaelerplatz 1 Ⓤ Stephansplatz, Herrengasse 🚋 D, 1, 2, 71
🚌 1A to Michaelerplatz 🌐 hofburg-wien.at

The vast Hofburg, Vienna's former imperial palace, is a lavish complex of buildings in the city centre. The seat of Austrian power since the 13th century, the complex has been developed over the years by successive rulers all anxious to leave their mark. The result is a range of architectural styles, from Gothic to late 19th-century historicism. The Neue Burg (New Palace) is the most recent and grand section. Today the Hofburg houses the office of the Austrian president, museums and galleries, the Austrian National Library, and the Spanish Riding School.

① Josefsplatz

📍 F4 🏛 Augustinerstrasse Ⓤ Stephansplatz, Herrengasse 🚋 D, 1, 2, 71 🚌 1A, 2A

Surrounded on three sides by the Hofburg Palace, this

Did You Know?

The oldest surviving part of the Hofburg is the Schweizertrakt, which dates back to the 13th century.

pleasant square offers fine views of the Baroque architecture of the complex. At the centre is an equestrian statue (1807) of Emperor Joseph II by Austrian sculptor Franz Anton Zauner, which was modelled on that of Marcus Aurelius on Rome's Capitoline Hill. Despite his reforms, Joseph II was a true monarchist, and loyalists used the square to gather.

Facing the Hofburg are two interesting palaces. No 5 is the Pallavicini Palace (1783–4), a blend of Baroque and Neo-Classical styles. It was a key location in the renowned Viennese film noir *The Third Man (p46)*, as the home of

Harry Lime's impressive apartment block. No 6 is the 16th-century Palffy Palace.

② Burggarten

📍 E5 🏛 Burgring/Opernring Ⓤ Karlsplatz 🚋 D, 1, 2, 71 🕐 Apr–Oct: 6am–10pm daily; Nov–Mar: 6:30am–7pm daily

These lovely landscaped gardens, planted with a variety of trees and wide herbaceous borders, make for a pleasant place to relax after exploring the surrounding palaces.

③ 🖼️ 🗺️

Burgkapelle

📍E4 🏠Hofburg, Schweizerhof 🚇Herrengasse ⏰10am–2pm Mon & Tue, 11am–1pm Fri 🚫Public hols 🌐hofmusikkapelle.gv.at

From the Schweizerhof, steps lead up to the Burgkapelle (Court Chapel), also known as the Hofmusikkapelle. This is the oldest part of the palace complex, originally built in 1296 but modified 150 years later. The chapel's interior reveals its medieval origins, with beautiful Gothic carvings and statuary in canopied niches. The large bronze crucifix (1720) above the altar is by the court jeweller Johann Känischbauer. On Sundays, you can hear the Wiener Sängerknaben, the **Vienna Boys' Choir**, performing High Mass.

Vienna Boys' Choir
🎟️ ⏰Jan–Jun & Sep–Dec: 9:15am Sun (book via chapel website)

Viktor Tilgner's Mozart Memorial (1896) stands just inside the Ringstrasse entrance.

The Hofburg Complex, in the centre of Vienna
↓

Anton Dominik von Fernkorn designed this monument to Prince Eugene (1865).

②

⑥
⑤
④
⑦
①
③
⑧
⑨

N
↓

The curved façade of the Michaeletrakt

The red and black Schweizertor (Swiss Gate) leads to the Schweizerhof.

Classical statuary on display at the Neue Burg's Ephesos Museum

④

Neue Burg

⚑E5 ⌂Neue Burg Heldenplatz ⓊVolkstheater, Herrengasse 🚊D, 1, 2, 71 ◷9am–6pm daily ⓦkhm.at

This massive, curved structure situated on Heldenplatz was added to the Hofburg Complex between 1881 and 1913. The Neue Burg (New Palace) embodies the last gasp of the Habsburg Empire as it strained under aspirations of independence from its domains, when the personal prestige of Emperor Franz Joseph was all that seemed able to keep it intact. It was not quite the perfect moment to embark on an extension to the Hofburg, but the work was undertaken nevertheless, and the Neue Burg was built to designs by the Ringstrasse architects Karl von Hasenauer (1833–94) and Gottfried Semper (1803–79). Five years after its completion, the Habsburg Empire ended.

Today the Neue Burg is home to the reading room of the National Library, and as well as a number of museums that are all under the direction of the KHM-Museumsverband. Ancient finds excavated from the Greek and Roman site of Ephesus in Turkey are on display at the **Ephesos Museum**. The **Sammlung Alter Musikinstrumente** houses Renaissance musical instruments, with impressive pianos that belonged to Beethoven, Schubert and Haydn, and the world's oldest surviving claviorgan (1596). The weapons collection at the **Hofjagt und Rüstkammer** is astonishing both in its size and the workmanship of its finest items: filigree inlay on swords, medieval ceremonial saddles and jewelled Turkish and Syrian maces. The core collection comprises the personal armouries of the Habsburgs. The **Weltmuseum Wien** galleries offer an exploration of travel, anthropology and ethnography, with exhibits from across the globe.

> The Neue Burg wing of the Hofburg embodies the last gasp of the Habsburg Empire as it strained under aspirations of independence from its domains.

Ephesos Museum

⚙ ◷10am–6pm Tue–Sun (to 9pm Thu) ⓦkhm.at

Sammlung Alter Musikinstumente

⚙ ◷10am–6pm Thu–Tue ⓦkhm.at

Hofjagt und Rüstkammer

⚙ ◷10am–6pm Thu–Tue (to 9pm Fri) ⓦkhm.at

Weltmuseum Wien

⚙☺ ◷10am–6pm Thu–Tue (to 9pm Fri) ⓦweltmuseumwien.at

---

⑤

Augustinerkirche

⚑F5 ⌂Augustinerstrasse 3 ☏(01) 5337099 ⓊStephansplatz 🚌1A, 2A ◷7am–6pm Mon–Fri, 8am–7pm Sat & Sun

The Augustinian Church has one of the best-preserved 14th-century Gothic interiors in Vienna; only the modern chandeliers strike a jarring note. Its Loreto Chapel, dating back to 1724, contains the silver urns that preserve the hearts of the Habsburg family. Here too are the tombs of Maria Christina, daughter of Maria Theresa, and Leopold II. Both lie empty; the royal remains are in the Kaisergruft (p92). The church is also celebrated for its music, including Masses by Schubert or Haydn held here on Sundays.

---

⑥

Albertina

⚑F5 ⌂Augustinerstrasse 1 ⓊKarlsplatz, Stephansplatz ◷10am–6pm daily (to 9pm Wed & Fri) ⓦalbertina.at

Once hidden away at the Opera end of the Hofburg the Albertina palace is now a very distinctive, modern landmark. Its raised entrance has a controversial free-standing diving-board roof by Austrian architect Hans Hollein. The palace once belonged to Maria Christina and her husband, Duke Albert of Sachsen-Teschen, after whom the gallery is named.

Today the Albertina houses a collection of priceless prints, over 65,000 watercolours and drawings, and some 70,000 photographs. Highlights include works by Dürer, Michelangelo and Rubens. Other temporary exhibitions feature paintings on loan. The permanent Batliner Collection is one of the most significant collections of Modernist art in Europe, comprising over 500 works including pieces by Monet, Degas and Picasso.

---

⑦ 🎨 Ⓜ
Prunksaal

📍E4 🏛Josefsplatz 1
Ⓤ Herrengasse 🚋 1A
🕐 10am–6pm daily (to 9pm Thu) 🌐 onb.ac.at

Commissioned as the court library by Karl VI, the State Hall, or Prunksaal, of the National Library was designed by Johann Bernhard Fischer von Erlach in 1719, and is the largest Baroque library in Europe today. The collection

---

📷 PICTURE PERFECT
Prunksaal

One of Vienna's best ceiling frescoes can be found in the dome of the Prunksaal of the Austrian National Library. You might have to lie on the floor to get the best shot.

---

includes the personal library of Prince Eugene, as well as tomes taken from monastic libraries closed during the religious reforms of Joseph II. Paired marble columns frame the domed main room, and walnut bookcases line the walls. Spanning the vaults are frescoes by the Baroque painter Daniel Gran, restored by Franz Anton Maulbertsch. The fine statues, including the likeness of Karl VI in the hall, are the work of Paul Strudel (1648–1708) and his brother Peter (1660–1714). The National Library also spans the **Papyrus Museum**, which documents ancient Egyptian life, and the Esperanto and Globe museums at the nearby Mollard Clary Palace.

Papyrus Museum
🎨 🏛 Neue Burg, Heldenplatz, 1010 🌐 onb.ac.at

---

⑧ Ⓜ 🏛
State Apartments and Treasury

📍E4 🏛Reichskanzleitrakt and Amalienburg

The **State Apartments** are housed in two separate sections of the Hofburg, and include rooms once occupied by Emperor Franz Joseph, Empress Elisabeth (or Sisi), and Tsar Alexander I. The rooms belonging to Sisi, now the **Sisi Museum**, are the prettiest and most interesting, full of her assets. The **Imperial Treasury** holds treasures amassed during centuries of Habsburg rule, including the crown of the Holy Roman Emperor.

State Apartments and Sisi Museum
🏛 Michaelerkuppel
🕐 9am–5:30pm daily (Jul & Aug: to 6pm)

Imperial Treasury
🏛 Schweizerhof 🕐 9am–5:30pm Wed–Mon

↓ The marble and gilded walnut interior of the Baroque Prunksaal

⑨ ⟨⟩ ⟨M3⟩ ⟨□⟩ ⟨🛍⟩

SPANISH RIDING SCHOOL

📍E4 🏛Michaelerplatz 1 ⓊHerrengasse 🚌1A, 2A to Michaelerplatz
🕐Times and performances vary, check website 🌐srs.at

Vienna's famous Lipizzaners are perhaps the only horses in the world to live in an emperor's palace. It's a fitting home for these noble creatures, whose performances are a timeless delight for visitors.

The origins of the Spanische Reitschule (Spanish Riding School) are obscure, but it is believed to have been founded in 1572 to cultivate the classic skills of *haute école* horsemanship. The Habsburgs bred and trained horses from Spain, thus giving the school its name. Today, 70- or 90-minute demonstrations, ranging across three levels of complexity and formality, some accompanied by Viennese music, are performed in the opulent Winter Riding School, which dates from 1729. The gracious interior is lined with 46 columns and adorned with elaborate plasterwork, chandeliers and a coffered ceiling. At the head of the arena is the court box. Spectators sit here or watch from upper galleries.

↑ One of the riders, as immaculately turned out as his horse

THE LIPIZZANER HORSES

The stallions that perform their athletic feats on the sawdust of the Winter Riding School take their name from the stud farm at Lipizza near Trieste in Slovenia, which was founded by Archduke Karl in 1580. Today the horses are bred on the Austrian National Stud Farm at Piber *(p203)* near Graz. Lipizzaner horses were originally bred by crossing Arab, Berber and Spanish horses, and are re-nowned for their grace and stamina. They begin learning the complex sequences of steps at the age of three.

① The Riding School occupies the former residence of the Emperor Maximilian.

② The emperor Karl VI commissioned the Winter Riding School building.

③ Equestrian statue of Joseph II in the school courtyard.

Did You Know?

Riders entering the arena must always doff their hats to the portrait of Karl VI, to show respect.

Horses and riders in perfect step, ready to go through their paces ↑

EXPERIENCE MORE

③ Michaelerplatz

⚑E4 **Ⓤ**Herrengasse, Stephansplatz **🚌**1A, 2A

Michaelerplatz faces the impressive Neo-Baroque Michaelertor (Michael's Gate), which leads through the Michaelertrakt to the Hofburg's inner courtyard (p78). On both sides of the doorway are 19th-century fountains that represent the empire's land and sea power.

Opposite is the grand **Michaelerkirche**, once the parish church of the court and one of the oldest Baroque churches in the city. Its oldest parts date from the 13th century; according to legend, the church was built in 1221, but its present form dates from 1792. The porch is topped by Baroque sculptures (1724–5) by Italian sculptor Lorenzo Mattielli, and depicts the Fall of the Angels. Inside are Renaissance and 14th-century frescoes, and a vividly carved and gilded organ (1714). The

Michaelerplatz with its church and Michaelertor ↓

Did You Know?

Michaelerkirche's fine gilded pipe organ is the largest in Vienna.

main choir (1782), replete with cherubs and sunbursts, is by sculptor Karl Georg Merville.

Off the north choir is the crypt, where well-preserved bodies in their burial finery are displayed in open coffins.

Beside the Michaelerkirche is the domed Michaelertrakt, an extravagant wing of the palace. It was finished in 1893, complete with gilt-tasselled statuary representing imperial Austria's land and sea power.

At the centre of the famous square there is a viewing spot for an excavation of a Roman encampment, as well as medieval foundations.

Michaelerkirche
🏠Michaelerplatz 1
🕐7am-10pm Mon-Sat, 8am-10pm Sun & public hols **🌐**michaelerkirche.at

④ Mozarthaus Vienna

⚑G4 **🏠**Domgasse 5 **Ⓤ**Stephansplatz **🚌**1A, 2A, 3A **🕐**10am-7pm daily **🌐**mozarthausvienna.at

Mozart and his family lived in a seven-room apartment on the first floor of this building from 1784 to 1787. A significant number of his masterworks were composed here, including the exquisite Haydn quartets, a handful of piano concertos and The Marriage of Figaro.

The building was restored in 2006 to commemorate the 250th anniversary of Mozart's birth. It contains exhibitions on two of the upper floors, the original apartment that he and his family occupied, and the Bösendorfer Saal, where concerts and events are held.

⑤ Graben

⚑F4 **Ⓤ**Stephansplatz **🚌**1A, 2A

Facing No 16 on this pleasant pedestrianized street is the Joseph Fountain by Austrian

↑ The lavishly decorated interior of the Peterskirche

sculptor Johann Martin Fischer. A little further along is his identical Leopold Fountain; both were constructed in 1804. No 13, the clothing shop Knize, is by the renowned architect Adolf Loos. The Ankerhaus by Otto Wagner *(p126)*, at No 10, is topped by a studio once used by Wagner himself and, in the 1980s, by Friedensreich Hundertwasser *(p140)*. Just off the Graben at No 19 Tuchlauben is the **Neidhart Fresco House**, a charming exhibition space that displays medieval frescoes.

Neidhart Fresco House

🏠 Tuchlauben 19 🕐 1–6pm Tue–Sun 🌐 wien museum.at

6

Peterskirche

📍 F4 🏠 Petersplatz 6
☎ (01) 53364330
Ⓤ Stephansplatz 🚌 1A
🕐 7am–8pm Mon–Fri, 9am–9pm Sat, Sun & hols

A church has stood here since the 12th century, but the oval structure you see today dates from the early 18th century. A number of architects collaborated on the design, notably Gabriele Montani. The interior is amazingly lavish, culminating in an exuberant, eye-catching pulpit (1716). The richly clothed skeletons on the right and beneath the altar are the remains of early Christian martyrs originally deposited in the catacombs in Rome. Frescoes inside the dome by painter J M Rottmayr depict the Assumption of the Virgin.

In 1729, Italian sculptor Lorenzo Mattielli designed the sculpture of St John of Nepomuk, which sits to the right of the choir. This priest earned his sainthood by being tortured and then thrown into the Vltava River in Prague in 1393, after he refused to reveal the secrets of the confessional to King Wenceslas IV; his martyrdom by drowning later became a favourite subject of artists.

EAT

Griechenbeisl

This traditional *Beisl* (bistro) is the city's oldest guest house, once frequented by Beethoven and Brahms.

📍 G3 🏠 Fleischmarkt 11
🌐 griechenbeisl.at

€€€

TIAN Wien

Expect fresh flavours and innovative vegetarian dishes at this modern Michelin-starred eatery.

📍 G5 🏠 Himmel-pfortgasse 23
🌐 tian-restaurant.com

€€€

Wrenkh

This is one of the city's best restaurants, serving mostly vegetarian dishes in sleek surrounds.

📍 G3 🏠 Bauernmarkt 10
🌐 wrenkh-wien.at

€€€

Café Central

Enjoy a Grand Café experience at this Vienna institution where the likes of Freud and Loos once sipped their coffee.

📍 E3 🏠 Herrengasse 14
🌐 cafecentral.wien

€€€

Beim Czaak

Opened in 1926, this authentic, rustic *Beisl* serves tasty Austrian fare in traditional dining rooms.

📍 H3 🏠 Postgasse 15
🌐 czaak.com

€€€

7
Deutschordenskirche

G4 **Singerstrasse 7** **Stephansplatz** **1A, 2A, 3A** **Times vary, check website** **Sun, Mon & public hols** **deutscher-orden.at**

This church belongs to the Order of Teutonic Knights, a chivalric order established in the 12th century. The building is 14th-century Gothic, and though restored in the 1720s in Baroque style by Austrian architect Anton Erhard Martinelli, it retains some Gothic elements such as its pointed arched windows. Numerous coats of arms of Teutonic Knights and memorial slabs are displayed on the walls. The Flemish altarpiece is from 1520 and incorporates panel paintings and carvings of scenes from the Passion beneath a number of delicate traceried canopies.

In 1807, Napoleon abolished the Order of Teutonic Knights in East Prussia. The knights opted to move their headquarters to Vienna, bringing the order treasury with them. Situated just off the courtyard, the treasury now serves as a museum, with various fine collections acquired by its Grand Masters over the centuries. The starting point is a room housing a large coin collection, medals and a 13th-century enthronement ring. A second room contains chalices and Mass vessels worked with silver filigree, while a third displays maces, daggers and ceremonial garb. The museum also has some striking Gothic

→

Madonna and Child statue in the Deutschordenskirche

paintings and a Carinthian carving of St George and the Dragon (1457).

8
Franziskanerkirche

G4 **Franziskanerplatz 4** **Stephansplatz** **1A, 2A, 3A** **6:30am-noon & 2-5:30pm Mon-Sat, 7am-5:30pm Sun** **wien.franziskaner.at**

During the 14th century, the Franciscans took over this church, which was originally built by wealthy citizens as a "house of the soul" for prostitutes wishing to reform. The present church was built in South German Renaissance style in 1601–11.

Its façade is topped by an elaborate scrolled gable with obelisks. The Moses Fountain in front of the church was the work of the Neo-Classicist Johann Martin Fischer in 1798.

The interior is in full-blown Baroque style and includes a finely modelled pulpit dating from 1726, and richly carved pews. A dramatic high altar by Andrea Pozzo rises to the full height of the church. Only the front part of the structure is three-dimensional – the rest is trompe l'oeil. Look out for the 1725 *Crucifixion* by Carlo Carlone among the works of art in the side altars.

Tucked away just behind the high altar is Vienna's oldest organ. Designed in 1642, the organ is beautifully painted, with a focus on various religious themes and subjects. If you would like to take a look, it is usually necessary to ask a passing monk for permission. However, performances are given every Friday at 2pm (from April to October).

9
Volksgarten

E4 **Dr-Karl-Renner-Ring** **Herrengasse** **D, 1, 2, 71** **2A** **Apr-Oct: 6am-10pm daily; Nov-Mar: 6:30am-7pm daily**

The elegant Volksgarten was created after Napoleon's destruction of the city walls, and was opened to the public soon after its completion in 1820. Its splendid formal and rose gardens are matched in grandeur by the statuary and monuments, notably the Temple of Theseus (1823) by Peter von Nobile. Other highlights include Karl von Hasenauer's monument to the Austrian poet Franz Grillparzer and the fountain memorial to the assassinated Empress Elisabeth (1907) by Viennese sculptor Hans Bitterlich.

10
Dominikanerkirche

H4 **Postgasse 4** **(01) 5124332** **Stephansplatz, Schwedenplatz** **2A** **7am-6pm daily**

Dominican monks came to Vienna in 1226, and by 1237 they had built a church here. In the 1630s, Antonio Canevale designed the present church, with its majestic Baroque façade. The central chapel on the right has swirling Rococo grilles and candelabra, and the beautiful organ above the west door is clad in mid-18th century casing. The frescoes on the barrel-vaulted ceiling are especially masterful.

The magnificent main hall of the MAK and its many treasures (inset) ↑

① ⑪ ⑫

Altes Rathaus

▣ F3 ▣ Wipplinger Strasse 8 Ⓤ Stephansplatz 🚋 1 🚌 1A, 3A ⊙ Times vary, check website Ⓦ doew.at

This building at Wipplinger Strasse was once owned by the brothers Otto and Haymo of Neuburg, who conspired to overthrow the Habsburgs in 1309. The property was confiscated by Prince Friedrich the Fair and donated to the city. Over the following centuries the site was expanded to form the complex of buildings that until 1883 served as the city hall, or Rathaus.

The entrance of the Altes Rathaus (old town hall) is festooned with ornamental ironwork. In the courtyard stands the 1741 Andromeda Fountain, the last work of the sculptor Georg Raphael Donner. The fountain depicts Perseus rescuing Andromeda.

A door from the courtyard leads to the Salvatorkapelle (St Saviour's Chapel), the former Neuburg family chapel and the only surviving building of the original medieval town house. It has since been enlarged and renovated, but retains its fine Gothic vaults. The walls are lined with marble tomb slabs, some from the 15th century. The chapel has an exquisite Renaissance portal, facing Salvatorgasse. Dating from 1520 to 1530, it is a rare example of Italianate Renaissance style.

Today the old town hall houses the District Museum. Of much greater interest is the Archives of the Austrian Resistance, devoted to the memory of those who risked their lives opposing National Socialism in Austria, in the years 1934–45.

⑫ 🏛️ 🖼️ 🍴 🏺

MAK (Museum für Angewandte Kunst)

▣ H4 ▣ Stubenring 5 Ⓢ Landstrasse Ⓤ Stubentor 🚋 2 🚌 1A, 74A ⊙ 10am–6pm Tue–Sun (to 10pm Tue) 🗓️ 1 Jan, 25 Dec Ⓦ mak.at

The Museum of Applied Arts houses an extensive collection of modern and antique furniture, textiles, glass, carpets, East Asian art and Renaissance jewellery. It is also host to interesting multimedia exhibitions. The basement houses the MAK Design Lab, MAK Forum and MAK Gallery, while the permanent collection is found largely on the ground floor, including the Asia and Carpet and Textiles collections. The impressive arcaded Main Hall houses temporary exhibitions. Visit on Tuesday evenings for reduced admission.

📷 **PICTURE PERFECT**
Urania

This Art Nouveau observatory on the east side of Julius-Raab-Platz, just south of MAK, has a distinctive dome that is visible from afar. It is best captured in the evening, when it reflects the city lights.

13 🤍 🗗

Jewish District

📍 G3 Ⓤ Schwedenplatz, Herrengasse 🚌 1A, 2A, 3A

A tangle of narrow streets west of Rotenturmstrasse makes up the earliest Jewish quarter in Vienna. Today, the Jewish District is a busy area of clubs, bars and restaurants, but during the Middle Ages,

VIENNA'S JEWISH COMMUNITY

A Jewish community has existed in Vienna since the 12th century. In 1421, almost the entire population was killed, forcibly baptized or expelled. By the late 19th century, the city's cultural life was dominated by Jewish people, only for them to be decimated during the Holocaust. Today, there are around 15,000 Jews residing in Vienna, just 10 per cent of pre-World War II numbers.

Judenplatz was the site of the Jewish ghetto, with a synagogue, the remains of which can be seen under the square.

Behind the former town hall stands Kornhäuselturm, a tower named after renowned architect Josef Kornhäusel. In the 1820s Kornhäusel designed the **Stadttempel** at No 4 Seitenstettengasse, the only synagogue in Vienna to survive the Holocaust.

In 1895, the world's first **Jewish Museum** was founded here, but it has since moved to two separate locations at Dorotheergasse and Misrachi-Haus on **Judenplatz**. Besides the remains of a 500-year-old synagogue and a monument to Austrian victims of the Holocaust, the Misrachi-Haus is home to a revealing exhibition on the pogrom of 1421.

Stadttempel

🏛 🚪 Seitenstettengasse 4 🕐 For tours at 11:30am and 2pm Mon–Thu 🌐 ikg-wien.at

Jewish Museum Judenplatz

🏛🗗🚪 Judenplatz 8 🕐 10am–6pm Sun–Thu, 10am–5pm Fri 🚫 Sat 🌐 jmw.at

14 🍴 🗗

Schwedenplatz

📍 G3 Ⓤ Schwedenplatz

Schwedenplatz, the Swedish Square, is one of Vienna's busiest spots. The area under Schwedenbrücke on the banks of the Danube is buzzing with pleasure boats, snack and ice cream stands and buskers providing entertainment.

In Laurenzberg, on the south side of Schwedenplatz, remains of the old town wall can be seen, with a metal ring that was used to tie up horses and an old sign with traffic regulations. At Fleischmarkt 11, steep, narrow steps lead down to the wine bar Griechenbeisl (p85), which claims to be the oldest restaurant in the city. You are welcomed by a board showing the *Lieber Augustin*; from the entrance hall you can see down to a small cellar where his statue is on display. The story of Augustin, a piper, goes back to the times of the Great Plague in Vienna. One night, he slumped into the gutter in a drunken stupor. When undertakers mistook

← Riverboats and cafés lining the Danube Canal, close to Schwedenplatz

him for dead and threw him into a plague pit, he woke up and terrified them by singing: "O du lieber Augustin…" (Oh, dear Augustin). Today, tourists wishing to return to Vienna throw a coin into the cellar.

15

Ruprechtskirche

☑ G3 ⌂ Ruprechtsplatz ⬡ Schwedenplatz 🚋 1, 2, N 🚌 1A, 2A, 3A ⬡ 10am-noon Mon-Fri, 3-5pm Mon, Wed, Fri ⬡ ruprechtskirche.at

St Ruprecht's is cited as the oldest church in Vienna, with origins in the 11th century. Venerating Vienna's medieval patron saint of salt merchants, Rupert of Salzburg, the church overlooks the salt wharfs on the Danube Canal. At the foot of the main tower, a statue portrays Rupert with a tub of salt. The interior of the church betrays its frequent restorations: the chancel has two panes of Romanesque stained glass; the choir dates from the 13th century; and the vaulted south aisle was added in the

15th century. If you are not attending a service, you are expected to make a donation.

---

16 🅜

Maria am Gestade

☑ F3 ⌂ Salvatorgasse 12 ☎ (01) 53395940 ⬡ Stephansplatz 🚌 2A ⬡ 7am-7pm daily; tours by appt only

One of the city's oldest sights is this lofty Gothic church with its 56-m- (180-ft-) high steeple and immense choir windows. There are records of the church from as early as 1158, but the present building dates from the late 14th century, with restoration evident from the 19th century. The church has had a chequered history, and Napoleon's troops used it as an arsenal during their occupation of Vienna in 1809. Inside, the nave piers are enlivened with Gothic canopies which shelter statues from various periods: Medieval, Baroque and Modern. The choir contains High Gothic panels (1460) depicting the Annunciation,

the Crucifixion and the Coronation of the Virgin. Behind the high altar the windows feature medieval stained glass, which has been carefully restored with surviving fragments. Tucked away on the north side of the choir is a chapel with a painted stone altar from 1520. The main parts of the interior are visible from the front entrance, but to walk around inside you need to make an appointment.

⑰ Freyung

📍 E3 🚇 Herrengasse

This square derives its name from the right of sanctuary (*frey* is an old word for "free") granted to any fugitive seeking refuge in the Schottenkirche (Scottish Church), now at No 6. The priory church, known as the "chest-of-drawers house", was founded by Irish Benedictine friars, who came to Vienna in 1177. No 4 is the elegant **Palais Kinsky** (1713–16), famous for its High-Baroque architecture. Next door is the 1546 Porcia Palace, one of the oldest palaces in Vienna. Opposite is the Austria Fountain, whose four figures symbolize the major rivers of the Habsburgs' lands.

Facing the Freyung is the Palais Ferstel, which dates from 1860. This Italian-style palazzo is home to the glass-roofed Freyung Passage. Lined with elegant shops and restaurants, this luxury arcade is a fine example of a civilized urban amenity. Enter the arcade from the Freyung side and follow the passage to a small courtyard: here you'll find a statue of the lissome mermaid of the Danube. The passage also has a secret entrance into one of Vienna's finest coffee houses, the iconic Café Central (*p85*).

Palais Kinsky

🕙 10am–5pm Mon–Fri

🔲 **PICTURE PERFECT**
Freyung Passage

This elegant 19th-century shopping arcade provides some atmospheric camera fodder, its illuminated, barrel-vaulted ceilings an impressive sight in the evening. The lovely seasonal decorations will add an extra dimension to your shot.

⑱

Dom Museum

📍 G4 🏛 Stephansplatz 6 🚇 Stephansplatz 🚌 1A, 2A, 3A 🕙 10am–6pm Wed–Sun (to 8pm Thu) 🌐 dommuseum.at

The Cathedral Museum, or Dom und Diözesan-museum as it is sometimes known, reopened in 2017 after four years of renovation. All of the old treasures are on display, including 16th- and 17th-century carvings and personal gifts from Duke Rudolf IV to the cathedral. His shroud is housed here, along with a well-known portrait of him by a Bohemian master dating from the 1360s. Added to the museum since the renovation are a number of Modernist and contemporary paintings and sculptures, and galleries now include an extensive collection of modern pieces, including works by Chagall and Klimt. The creative displays juxtapose the old with the new, the purpose being to show a continuity in underlying religious themes across the ages, expressed in changing styles and also in materials as varied as paint, glass and metal.

⑲

Uhrenmuseum

📍 F3 🏛 Schulhof 2 🚇 Stephansplatz 🚌 1A, 2A, 3A 🕙 10am–6pm Tue–Sun 🚫 1 Jan, 1 May, 25 Dec 🌐 wienmuseum.at

You don't have to be a clock fanatic to enjoy a visit to this fascinating clock museum. Located in the beautiful former Obizzi Palace (1690), the museum contains a fine collection of timepieces and gives a comprehensive account of the history of chronometry through the ages, and of clock technology from the 15th century through to the present day.

There are more than 3,000 exhibits, some of which were accumulated by an earlier curator, Rudolf Kaftan, while others belonged to the novelist Marie von Ebner-Eschenbach. On the first floor you can see the mechanisms of tower clocks from the 16th century onwards, alongside painted clocks, grandfather clocks and pocket watches. On the other floors are huge astronomical clocks and intriguing novelty timepieces, with many dating from the Beidermeier and belle époque eras.

← Dining in the elaborate Renaissance-style arcades of Freyung Passage

A major highlight is the Cajetano clock, an elaborate astronomical clock created by David Cajetano, which dates from the 18th century. It has 150 gears and wheels, and over 30 readings and dials that show the dates of solar and lunar eclipses and the movement of the planets.

At every full hour, each of the museum's three floors resounds in a cacophony of clocks striking, chiming and playing music. All of them are carefully maintained to keep the correct time.

⑳ Am Hof

⑦ F3 Ⓤ **Stephansplatz, Herrengasse** 🚌 **1A, 2A, 3A**

The name of this square (which means "by the Court") refers to the medieval princes' residence nearby. This later housed the mint, the royal military chancery, and today a bank.

The main architectural gem on the square is the **Kirche am Hof** (Church of the Nine Angel Choirs), built in the late 14th century by Carmelite Friars and rebuilt after the fire of 1607. It is adorned with a Baroque façade crowned with a triangular pediment featuring Our Lady, Queen of Angels. The dissolution of the Holy Roman Empire was proclaimed from the church's terrace on 6 August 1806.

In front of the church is the Mariensäule (Column of Our Lady), commissioned by Ferdinand III to commemorate the end of Swedish occupation during the Thirty Years' War. The building at No 14 is the Collalto Palace, where, in 1762, the six-year-old Mozart gave his first performance.

Kirche am Hof

🏠 Schulhof 1 📞 (01) 5338394 🕐 4:30–6pm Mon–Sat, 7am–7pm Sun

㉑ Hoher Markt

⑨ G3 Ⓤ **Stephansplatz, Schwedenplatz** 🚌 **1A, 2A, 3A**

Hoher Markt is the oldest square in Vienna. In medieval times, it hosted fish and cloth markets, as well as executions.

Today the ruins of a former Roman garrison, Vindobona, lie beneath the square at the fantastic **Römermuseum**. Discovered after World War II, its ancient foundations show groups of houses bisected by straight roads leading to the town gates. It seems probable that they were 2nd- and 3rd-century officers' houses. Exhibits of pottery, reliefs and tiles supplement the ruins.

In the centre of the square is the Vermählungsbrunnen (Nuptial Fountain), also known as the Josefsbrunnen. This was built between 1729 and 1732 to honour a promise by Leopold I to celebrate the safe return of his son Joseph from the Siege of Landau.

Linking two buildings on the square is the bronze and copper Ankeruhr (Anker Clock), set atop the Uhrbrücke (Clock Bridge). Noon is the best time to visit, when all of the clock figures are on glorious display.

Römermuseum

♿ 🕐 9am–6pm Tue–Sun & hols 🚫 1 Jan, 1 May, 25 Dec 🌐 wienmuseum.at

↑ The Column of Our Lady in front of the Kirche Am Hof in the Am Hof square

22

Kapuzinerkirche

📍F5 🏛Tegetthostrasse 2
📞(01) 5337099
Ⓤ Stephansplatz 🚌2A
🕐9am–6pm daily

Set back from the pleasant
pedestrianized shopping
street of Kärntner Strasse,
Neuer Markt square is home
to the Capuchin church,
consecrated in 1632. Beneath
the church and monastery are
the vaults of the **Kaisergruft**,
the imperial crypt, founded in
1619 by the Catholic Emperor
Matthias. Here lie the remains
of 145 Habsburgs, including
Maria Theresa.

The poignant tomb of Franz
Joseph is flanked by those of
his wife Elisabeth and their
son Rudolf. The last reigning
Habsburg, Empress Zita, died
in 1989 and her remains are
also buried here. The crypt is
tended by resident guardians,
the Capuchin monks.

Kaisergruft

🕐10am–6pm daily (to 9pm
Thu) 🌐kapuzinergruft.at

DRINK

Esterhazykeller

This ancient cellar
offers a great selection
of Austrian wines and
classic hearty food.

📍F3 🏛Haarhof 1, 1010
🌐esterhazykeller.at

€€€

Palmenhaus

This brasserie
overlooking the
Burggarten is perfect
for a refreshing
glass of wine.

📍F5 🏛Burggarten 1,
1010 🌐palmenhaus.at

€€€

23

Winterpalais des Prinzen Eugen

📍F5 🏛Himmelpfortgasse
4–8 Ⓤ Stephansplatz 🚋2
🚌1A, 2A, 3A 🔒To public

The sumptuous and elegant
Winter Palace was commissioned in 1694 by Prince
Eugene of Savoy, one of
the most brilliant military
commanders of his day. The
task was entrusted to Johann
Bernhard Fischer von Erlach,
and later to his rival Johann
Lukas von Hildebrandt in
1702, both of whom were
among the foremost Baroque
architects of their time.

The result is an imposing
town mansion, complemented
by one of the most magnificent
Baroque edifices in Vienna.
Maria Theresa purchased the
palace for the state in 1752
and it was home to the Ministry
of Finance from 1848 to 2006.
In 2018, the palace was closed
to the public indefinitely.

24

Minoritenplatz

📍E4 Ⓤ Herrengasse
🚋1, 71, D 🚌1A, 2A

At No 1 Minoritenplatz is the
Baroque-style former State
Archives building, built behind
the Bunderskanzleramt in
1902. There are a number of
palaces around the square. At
No 3 is Dietrichstein Palace,
dating from 1755, an early
building by Franz Hillebrand.
It now contains the offices
of the Federal Chancellor and
the Foreign Office. No 4 is
the side of the Liechtenstein
Palace, which has its frontage
on Bankgasse, and the mid-
17th century Starhemberg
Palace is at No 5. Now housing
ministry offices, it was once
the residence of Count Ernst
Rüdiger von Starhemberg, a
hero of the 1683 Turkish siege.

At No 2 is the ancient
Minoritenkirche, established
here by the Minorite friars in

↑ Gothic interior of
the Minoritenkirche
in Minoritenplatz

around 1224, although the
present structure dates from
1339. The tower acquired its
unusual pyramid shape during
the Turkish siege of Vienna in
1529, when a shell sliced the
top off the steeple. During the
1780s the Minoritenkirche was
restored to its original Gothic
style, when Maria Theresa's
son, Joseph II, made a gift of
the church to Vienna's Italian
community. The church retains
a fine west portal (1340) with
statues beneath traceried
canopies; the carvings above
the doorway are modern. The
church interior is unexpectedly
bright and airy, and contains a
mosaic copy of Leonardo da
Vinci's *Last Supper*. Napoleon
Bonaparte commissioned the
Italian artist Giacomo Raffaelli
to execute this work, and it
was his intention to substitute
it for the original in Milan and
to move the real painting to
Paris. Following Napoleon's
downfall at Waterloo in 1815,
Raffaelli's version was bought
by the Habsburgs. In the south
aisle is a painted statue of the
Madonna and Child, dating

→

Traffic-free Kärntner
Strasse, full of shoppers
and coffee seekers

from around 1350, while at the same spot in the north aisle is a faded fragment of a 16th-century fresco of St Francis of Assisi.

Minoritenkirche
🕐 9am–6pm daily
🌐 minoritenkirche-wien.info

25
Kärntner Strasse

📍 F4 Ⓤ Stephansplatz

Kärntner Strasse was once the main road running south to Kärnten (Carinthia), hence its name. Today, the view down the street is blocked at its Ring end by the silhouette of the opera house, and at the Stock-im-Eisen-Platz end by the modern Haas-Haus, which reflects the spires of the Stephansdom. At Stock-im-Eisen-Platz there is a wooden block into which every passing apprentice ironworker used to drive a nail, in the hope that it would ensure his safe return.

No 37 on the street is the **Malteserkirche**, otherwise known as the Church of Saint John the Baptist. This church was founded by the Knights of Malta, who were invited to Vienna early in the 13th century by Leopold VI. The interior still has its lofty Gothic windows and vaults.

> The restored interior of the American Bar has retained Loos' carefully constructed detail, such as under-lit tables, glass cabinets and mahogany panelling.

At No 26 is **J&L Lobmeyr** *(p89)*, a unique shop founded in 1823 which houses hand-crafted glassware. There is a small museum on the third floor, with pieces on display by Josef Hoffmann, the founder of the Arts and Crafts studio Wiener Werkstätte. Around the corner, at No 5 Johannesgasse, is the superb Questenberg-Kaunitz Palace, which dates from the early 18th century.

Today, the pedestrianized Kärntner Strasse is one of Vienna's most fashionable and expensive shopping streets. Here, you can shop at one of many exclusive boutiques, eat and drink in busy restaurants, bars and outdoor cafés, and listen to street musicians or just watch others stroll by.

Malteserkirche
🕐 7am–7pm daily
📞 (01) 5127244

J&L Lobmeyr
🕐 9am–5pm Mon–Fri
🌐 lobmeyr.at

26
American Bar

📍 F4 🏠 Kärntner Strasse 10 Ⓤ Stephansplatz 🕐 Noon–4am daily 🌐 loosbar.at

Beneath a garish depiction of the Stars and Stripes is this tiny bar designed by architect Adolf Loos in 1908. Loos drew his inspiration from a sojourn in New York between 1893 and 1896. After a spell as one of the go-to spots in the city for a Manhattan, the bar closed during World War II and languished for many years. In the 1980s, something of a nightlife renaissance took hold in the city, and interest in cocktail bars was rekindled.

The restored interior of the American Bar has retained Loos' carefully constructed detail, such as under-lit tables, glass cabinets and mahogany panelling. Mirrors create the illusion of a spacious interior, and onyx and marble panels reflect the soft lighting.

A SHORT WALK
OLD VIENNA

Distance 2 km (1 mile) **Time** 20 minutes
Nearest U-Bahn Stephansplatz

This part of the inner city retains its compact medieval layout of cobbled lanes, winding alleys and spacious courtyards. The influence of the Church is still evident here. As you stroll, you'll notice remains of orders such as the Dominicans, the Teutonic Knights and the Jesuits. Dominating the area is the 137-m- (450-ft-) high spire of Stephansdom, the heart of Vienna for centuries. Despite its ancient origins, there's plenty of activity in this quarter. Stephansplatz throngs with visitors all day, and bars and restaurants buzz with people long into the night.

↑ Great Gothic Stephansdom seen from Stephansplatz

Much of the **Dom Museum** *(p90) collection was donated by Duke Rudolf IV.*

Stephansdom
(p76) *took centuries to build and is rich with medieval and Renaissance monuments.*

FINISH

STEPHANS-PLATZ

START

STOBELGASSE

A remarkable treasury of objects collected by German aristocrats lies alongside the Gothic **Deutschordenskirche** *(p86).*

SINGERSTRASSE

BLUTGASSE

Courtyards like this are typical of the tenement houses on **Blutgasse.**

GRÜNANGERGAS

Mozarthaus Vienna
(p84) *is where the composer lived from 1784 to 1787.*

Grünangergasse *and pretty* **Domgasse** *are full of intriguing houses with unique details.*

Did You Know?

Stephansdom's tallest tower is affectionately known as *Alter Steffl* – which translates as "Old Steve".

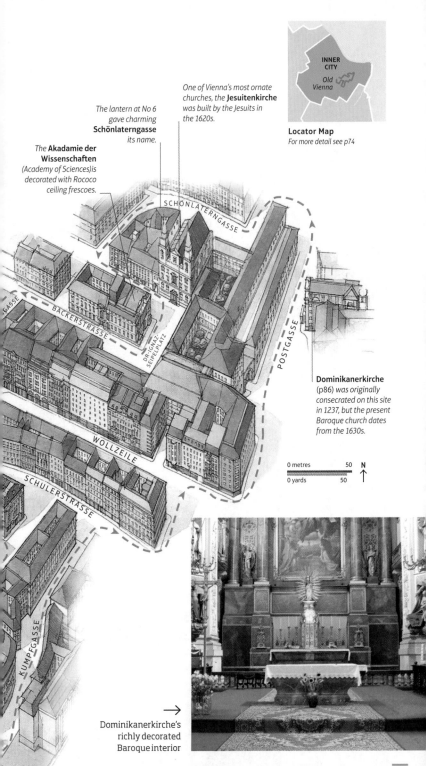

The **Akademie der Wissenschaften** (Academy of Sciences) is decorated with Rococo ceiling frescoes.

The lantern at No 6 gave charming **Schönlaterngasse** its name.

One of Vienna's most ornate churches, the **Jesuitenkirche** was built by the Jesuits in the 1620s.

Locator Map
For more detail see p74

INNER CITY

Old Vienna

SCHÖNLATERNGASSE

BÄCKERSTRASSE

DR IGNAZ SEIPELPLATZ

POSTGASSE

Dominikanerkirche (p86) was originally consecrated on this site in 1237, but the present Baroque church dates from the 1630s.

WOLLZEILE

SCHULERSTRASSE

KUMPFGASSE

0 metres   50

0 yards   50

N

→ Dominikanerkirche's richly decorated Baroque interior

NORTH OF MARIAHILFER STRASSE

This quarter is bordered by the wide imperial boulevard of the Ringstrasse, linking the city's most important cultural and political institutions. Commissioned by Franz Joseph and completed in the 1880s, the Ringstrasse's construction hailed a new age of grandeur in Vienna, despite the dwindling power of the Habsburgs. It was around this time that the Kunsthistorisches and Naturhistorisches museums, which house vast collections amassed by generations of Habsburg monarchs, were opened to the public. The Burgtheater, originally constructed in 1741 by Maria Theresa, who wanted to have a theatre next to her palace, was also restored in Renaissance style. The former imperial stables, commissioned in 1713 by Emperor Karl VI, were transformed into exhibition spaces in 1918 after the fall of the Habsburg Empire. In 2001, the MuseumsQuartier opened on this site, after an investment of €150 million, and is today a contemporary equivalent of the Habsburgs' fine cultural institutions, with its superb collection of modern art and architecture.

NORTH OF MARIAHILFER STRASSE

Must Sees
1 Burgtheater
2 MuseumsQuartier Wien
3 Kunsthistorisches Museum

Experience More
4 Neues Rathaus
5 Parlament
6 Universität Wien
7 Votivkirche
8 Josephinum
9 Sigmund Freud Museum
10 Dreifaltigkeitskirche
11 Narrenturm
12 Spittelberg
13 Theater in der Josefstadt
14 Palais Trautson
15 Volkskundemuseum
16 Maria-Treu-Kirche
17 Naturhistorisches Museum
18 Mariahilfer Strasse
19 Volkstheater

Eat
1 Amerlingbeisl
2 Justizcafé
3 Restaurant Vestibül

Drink
4 Dachboden
5 Eberts Cocktail Bar
6 Café Phil

Stay
7 K+K Hotel Maria Theresia
8 Sans Souci

❶ ⊘ ⊘ ⊘

BURGTHEATER

📍E3 **🏛Universitätsring 2** **Ⓤ Schottentor** **🚋 D, 1, 71**
⏰ For performances and guided tours (Jul & Aug: guided tours only)
🚫 Good Friday, 24 Dec **🌐 burgtheater.at**

A noted patron of the visual arts, the empress Maria Theresa also loved music, plays and the opera. In the 1730s she commissioned a theatre to be built conveniently next to her palace, and on 14 March 1741, the Burgtheater, or Court Theatre, opened its doors for the very first time.

The Burgtheater is one of the most prestigious stages in the German-speaking world and stages a diverse range of plays performed by its famed in-house ensemble. The original building of Maria Theresa's reign adjoined the Hofburg, but in the 19th century the theatre gained a magnificent new home among the architectural jewels that stud the Ringstrasse, and today's construction by Karl von Hasenauer and Gottfried Semper was completed in 1888. A bomb devastated the building in 1945, but subsequent restoration was so seamless that today the damage is barely visible.

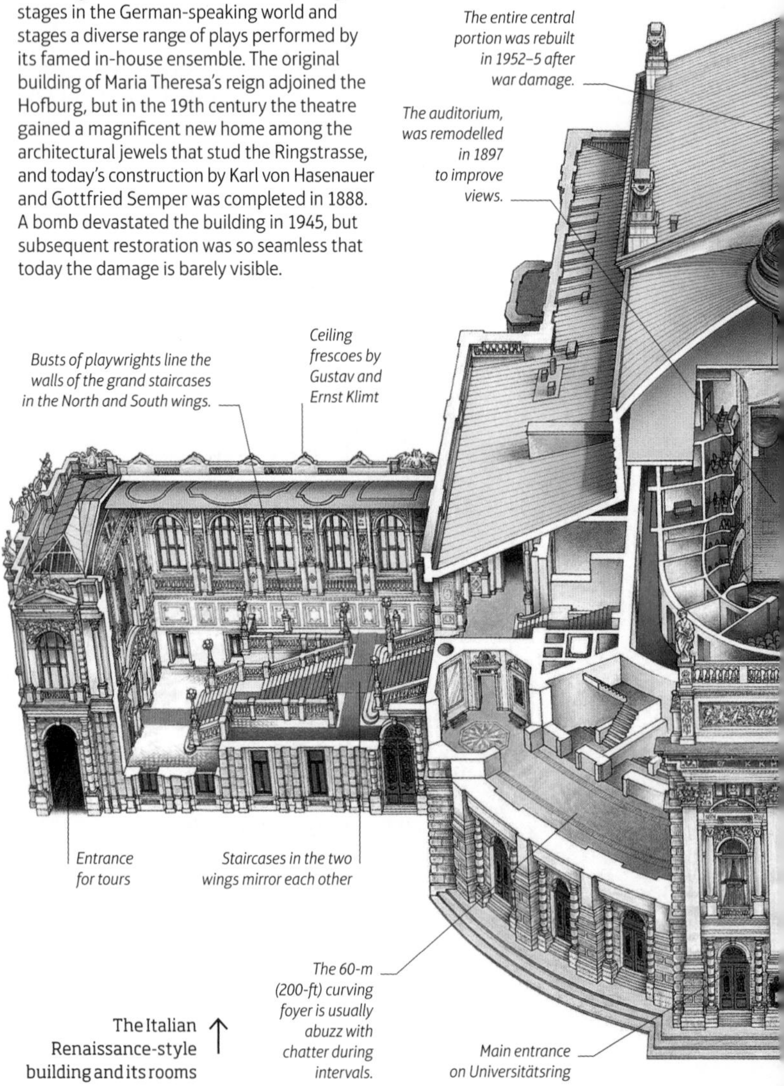

The entire central portion was rebuilt in 1952–5 after war damage.

The auditorium, was remodelled in 1897 to improve views.

Busts of playwrights line the walls of the grand staircases in the North and South wings.

Ceiling frescoes by Gustav and Ernst Klimt

Entrance for tours

Staircases in the two wings mirror each other

The 60-m (200-ft) curving foyer is usually abuzz with chatter during intervals.

Main entrance on Universitätsring

The Italian Renaissance-style building and its rooms ↑

Timeline

1741
▽ Maria Theresa founds the Burgtheater in a building next door to the Hofburg.

1750–76
△ Joseph II reorganizes the theatre and promotes it to the status of a national theatre.

1874
Work on the present building begins on the Ringstrasse.

1888
The Burgtheater opens on 14 October in the presence of the Emperor Franz Joseph and his family.

1945
▶ World War II fire destroys the auditorium.

1955
Theatre reopens with Grillparzer's *King Ottokar*.

→ The two imposing staircases, decorated with frescoes on theatrical themes

Only the two wings escaped bomb damage during World War II.

The façade is crowned by a frieze depicting Bacchus, god of drama, with his wife Ariadne and an energetic entourage.

Did You Know?

The Burg's revolving stage system, Europe's largest, enables sets to be changed in 40 seconds.

2 🏷️ 🎿 🍴 🖥️ 🛍️

MUSEUMSQUARTIER WIEN

📍D5 🏠Museumsplatz 1 🚇Museumsquartier, Volkstheater 🚊49 to Volkstheater 🚌48A to Volkstheater ⏰Visitor and ticket centres: 10am–7pm daily; for individual museum opening times check website 🌐mqw.at

The vibrant MuseumsQuartier Wien is one of the largest cultural centres in the world. The complex houses a diverse array of facilities, from art museums to a venue for contemporary dance to a children's creativity centre.

The MuseumsQuartier once housed the stables for Emperor Franz Joseph's horses. In 1918, after the fall of the Habsburg Empire, the buildings were transformed into an exhibition space to house the Wiener Messe's trade fairs. In 1986, modern and contemporary art galleries were constructed, including the popular mumok, the Kunsthalle Wien and the Leopold Museum, and further

renovations were completed in 2001. Today, the MQ, as it is called, hosts 60 institutions, and its courtyard offers pleasant cafés and outdoor seating where you can relax and soak up the atmosphere.

This is an ideal starting point for any trip to Vienna, since many other attractions are also nearby. It is advisable to stop off first at the MQ Point Info-Tickets-Shop, in the Fischer von Erlach Wing, to obtain a programme detailing all events and exhibitions in the complex.

Museum Guide

ZOOM Kindermuseum

▶ This lively centre offers an unconventional approach to the world of the museum for kids - its aim is to encourage learning through play and exploration for children aged 12 and under. The ZOOM Lab is for older children, while younger ones can take a dip in the ZOOM Ocean with their parents.

Q21

Over 50 cultural initiatives have turned Q21 into Vienna's centre for contemporary applied arts. The attractions for the public, which are on the ground floor, include fashion, design, book and music shops, an exhibition space for art schools and large event halls.

Tanzquartier Wien

The Tanzquartier Wien is Austria's first dedicated performance and study venue focusing solely on modern dance. It offers facilities for dancers, and hosts dance and other shows for the public.

mumok (Museum of Modern Art Ludwig Foundation Vienna)

◀ One of the largest European collections of modern art, mumok's range of acquisitions include American Pop Art, Fluxus, Nouveau Réalisme, Viennese Actionism, Arte Povera, Conceptual Art and Minimal Art. Galleries are split chronologically over five levels, two of them underground. There is also a cinema, a library and a studio.

Architekturzentrum Wien

This centre is committed to showcasing new architectural work to the public. Its permanent exhibition's focus is diversity in 20th-century architecture. Each year, four to six temporary exhibitions examine links between modern architecture and architecture throughout history.

Leopold Museum

▶ The vast Leopold Collection of Austrian Art was compiled over five decades by Rudolf Leopold. Highlights of the exhibition space, which spans five floors, include the Egon Schiele collection and many fine Expressionist Austrian paintings. On the ground level, an exhibition on Secessionism and Art Nouveau includes pieces by Gustav Klimt, Richard Gerstl and Oskar Kokoschka.

Kunsthalle Wien

This striking red-brick building is a home for innovation and creativity, showing international and contemporary art. Exhibits emphasize cross-genre and cross-border arts, including experimental architecture, video, photography and film, plus new media.

← Relaxing and socializing in the MQ's impressive main courtyard

3

KUNSTHISTORISCHES MUSEUM

📍 E5 🏛 Maria-Theresien-Platz Ⓤ MuseumsQuartier, Volkstheater
🚊 D, 1, 2, 71 🚌 57A 🕐 10am–6pm Tue–Sun (to 9pm Thu) 🌐 khm.at

This astonishing institution attracts over 1.5 million visitors each year. Its opulent galleries house vast collections of fine art and antiquities, based largely on those accumulated over the centuries by generations of Habsburg monarchs.

When the Ringstrasse was built by Emperor Franz Joseph, a pair of magnificent buildings, designed by architects Karl von Hasenauer and Gottfried Semper, were erected in the Italian Renaissance style. The symmetrical Kunsthistorisches Museum (KHM) and Naturhistorisches Museum *(p114)* would house the collections of imperial art and natural history, which, until the late 19th century, had been held in the Belvedere and Hofburg palaces. The KHM's lavishly decorated interiors, with ornate cupolas and sweeping Neo-Classical stairways, create a fitting setting for the treasures housed here. The Habsburg monarchs were enthusiastic patrons and collectors, and many of the works on display here, particularly the old masters, are among the most spectacular in the world.

1891

The KHM was opened, displaying the Habsburgs' private treasures to the public.

THE APOTHEOSIS OF THE RENAISSANCE

Part of the museum's extravagant decorative scheme, a fabulous trompe l'oeil ceiling painting above the main staircase depicts *The Apotheosis of the Renaissance* (1890). The work of Hungarian painter Michael Munkácsy, it shows Leonardo, Michelangelo and Titian, all presided over by Pope Julius II.

↑ Fine classical statuary exhibited in the collection of Greek and Roman antiquities

→ Visitors admiring Renaissance paintings in the Picture Gallery

↑ The Italian Renaissance-style KHM overlooking Maria-Theresien-Platz

Exploring the Kunsthistorisches Museum

The museum's displays are spread over three floors, and are so large that they cannot be fully appreciated in one visit. On the ground floor, the ancient civilizations of Egypt, Greece and Rome are chronicled in their full splendour. The Kunstkammer, or Viennese chamber of curiosities, also on the ground floor, is known as a "museum within a museum", with its collection of rare Renaissance and Baroque treasure. The first floor contains the Picture Gallery, a unique collection of 16th-, 17th-, and 18th-century European paintings amassed by Habsburg monarchs, with masterworks of Renaissance and medieval art including pieces by Pieter Bruegel the Elder, Rembrandt and Dürer. On the second floor is one of the largest coin collections in the world.

You can seek refreshment during your visit in the café in the central Cupola Hall, which is decorated in spectacular Renaissance fashion, with marble archways and a fine mosaic floor. Many prominent artists were employed to decorate the museum's interior. Keep an eye out for the especially ornate gilded frescoes by Gustav Klimt, which adorn the archways of the grand central staircase.

> **The ancient civilizations of Egypt, Greece and Rome are chronicled in their full splendour.**

↑ Caravaggio's *Madonna of the Rosary* (1601) hanging in the Picture Gallery

↑ An ancient faïence hippopotamus from the Egyptian Collection

→ Inspecting displays of sarcophagi and mummies in the Egyptian Collection

Top Collections

Picture Gallery

▷ The collection focuses on old masters from the 15th to the 18th centuries and largely reflects the personal tastes of its Habsburg founders. Venetian and 16th- and 17th-century Flemish paintings are particularly well represented, and there is an excellent display of works by Dutch and German artists.

Egyptian and Near Eastern Collection

Five specially decorated rooms adorned with Egyptian friezes and motifs provide the perfect setting for the bulk of the museum's collection of Egyptian and Near Eastern antiquities. The collection was founded by the Habsburg monarchs, though most of the items were acquired in the 19th or 20th century. This collection holds over 17,000 objects, with funerary art from Ancient Egypt and treasures from Babylon and Arabia.

Greek and Roman Antiquities

▷ Part of the museum's Greek and Roman collection is housed in the main building, with other finds displayed in the Hofburg (p78). The main gallery at the KHM (Room XI) is decorated in the style of an Imperial Roman villa, complete with a mosaic of Theseus and the Minotaur and ancient Greek and Roman statuary. Other rooms house stunning early Greek sculpture, the Austria Romana collection, and Etruscan, Byzantine and Coptic pieces. There is also a very fine collection of Roman cameos, jewellery, pottery and glass.

Kunstkammer Wien

The curators call this "the cradle of the museum". Here, the personal prizes of Habsburg collectors Rudolf II and Archduke Leopold William are housed in their "wonder rooms". These were originally chambers of artifacts and natural wonders that were intended to represent the sum total of human knowledge of the day. In addition to sculpture, these princely treasuries contained precious items of master craftsmanship, exotic and highly unusual novelties, and scientific instruments.

Coins and Medals

▽ Tucked away on the second floor is one of the most extensive coin and medal collections in the world. Once again, the nucleus of the collection came from the former possessions of the Habsburgs, but it has been added to by modern curators and now includes many 20th-century items. Only a fraction of the museum's 600,000 pieces can be seen in the three exhibition rooms. Room I gives an overview of the development of money, including coins from Ancient Greece and Rome, examples of Egyptian, Celtic and Byzantine money, and medieval, Renaissance and European coins, as well as Austrian currency from its origins to the present.

THE OLD MASTERS

The fine collection of old masters at the KHM is near unparalleled. The extensive Picture Gallery is filled with works by the Flemish masters, including about a third of all surviving pieces by Pieter Bruegel the Elder, including his renowned painting *Tower of Babel*. The Italian masters are well represented here too, with staggering works by Caravaggio, Titian and Tintoretto.

EXPERIENCE MORE

4

Neues Rathaus

D3 **Friedrich-Schmidt-Platz 1** **Rathaus** **D, 1, 71, D** **For tours at 1pm Mon, Wed & Fri; groups by appointment** **wien.gv.at**

The New Town Hall, which lies in an attractive park, is the seat of the Vienna City and Provincial Assembly. Built in 1872–83 to replace the Altes Rathaus (p87), its design is unashamedly Neo-Gothic in style. The architect, Friedrich von Schmidt, was chosen by the city in a competition for the best design.

Its huge central tower is topped by a statue of a knight in armour, one of Vienna's symbols. The most attractive feature of the building is the lofty loggia, with its delicate tracery and curved balconies.

> **INSIDER TIP**
> **Free Tours of the Rathaus**
>
> Take a free tour of the Neues Rathaus, which reveals controversies and the city's lesser-known political secrets (www.wien.gv.at).

Around all four sides are Neo-Gothic arcades, together with statues of Austrian worthies. Inside, at the top of the first of two grand staircases, is the Festsaal, a ceremonial hall that stretches the length of the building.

5

Parlament

D4 **Dr-Karl-Renner-Ring 3** **Volkstheater** **D, 1, 2, 71** **Times vary, check website** **parlament.gv.at**

Today's assembly hall of Austria's two-chamber parliament originally served as the location of the highest legislative body of the Austrian part of the Austro-Hungarian Empire. An imposing Neo-Classical building, Parlament took ten years to build and was completed in 1883 to designs by the Dutch architect Theophil Hansen.

A gently sloping ramp at street level leads to the main portico, which is modelled on a Greek temple. Both the ramp and the pediment are adorned with carved marble figures of Greek and Roman historians, scholars and statesmen. The relief depicts the Emperor Franz Joseph handing the constitution to the representatives of the 17 peoples of the empire. The magnificently decorated state apartments and conference rooms can be visited on a guided tour.

The side wings have four bronze chariot groups, each driven by Nike, the Greek goddess of victory. Another statue of Nike is held aloft by Pallas Athena, the goddess of wisdom, whose statue is the main feature of the fountain in front of the central portico. It is flanked by allegorical figures of Law Enforcement (left) and Legislation (right). In this splendid setting, on 11 November 1918, after the collapse of the Habsburg Empire,

> **Did You Know?**
>
> Austria's Federal President can veto bills and dissolve parliament - but to date never has.

parliamentary deputies proclaimed the formation of the Republic of German-Austria, renamed the Republic of Austria in 1919.

6

Universität Wien

🔲 D3 🏠 Universitätsring
Ⓤ Schottentor 🕐 Times vary, check website
🌐 univie.ac.at

Founded in 1365 by Duke Rudolf IV, Vienna University is the oldest university in the German-speaking world. Its present home, designed by Heinrich von Ferstel in Italian Renaissance style, was completed in 1883.

From the entrance hall, huge staircases lead up to the university's ceremonial halls. In 1895, Gustav Klimt was commissioned to decorate the hall, but the degree of nudity portrayed proved unacceptable to the authorities. Klimt returned his fee and took back the paintings, but they were destroyed during World War II. A spacious courtyard lined with stern busts of the university's most distinguished professors, is located in the centre of the building. Among the figures on display are those of the founder of psychoanalysis Sigmund Freud (p110) and philosopher Franz Brentano.

↑ Baptismal font in the Votivkirche, bathed in the light of stained-glass windows

7

Votivkirche

🔲 D2 🏠 Rooseveltplatz 8
📞 (01) 4061192 Ⓤ Schottentor 🚋 D, 1, 71 🕐 9am-1pm daily, 4-6pm Tue-Sat

After a Hungarian nationalist tried to assassinate Emperor Franz Joseph I on 18 February 1853, a collection was made to fund the construction of a new church opposite the Mölker-Bastei, where the attempt had been made. Work began in 1856, and many of the chapels are dedicated to Austrian regiments and military heroes. The finest monument is the Renaissance sarcophagus of Niklas Salm, who commanded Austria's forces during the 1529 Turkish siege, in the chapel just west of the north transept.

8

Josephinum

🔲 D2 🏠 Währingerstrasse 25/1 Ⓤ Schottentor 🚋 37, 38, 40, 41, 42 🕐 4-8pm Wed, 10am-6pm Fri & Sat 🚫 Public hols 🌐 joseph inum.ac.at

Designed by Austrian-French architect Isidor Canevale and built in 1783–5, this building once housed the Military Surgical Institute. Now part of the Medical University of Vienna, it also houses the university's historic medical collections. The main attraction here is the collection of life-sized anatomical wax models, commissioned by Joseph II to teach human anatomy to his army surgeons.

← The Athenebrunnen fountain in front of the Parlament building

Photographic displays illustrating Freud's career at the Sigmund Freud Museum ↑

9 🚲 Ⓜ 🛍️

Sigmund Freud Museum

📍E1 🏠Berggasse 19
Ⓤ Schottentor 🚋D 🚌40A
🕐10am–6pm daily
🌐freud-museum.at

Freud's former apartment at Berggasse 19 differs little from any other 19th-century apartment building in Vienna, yet it is now one of the city's most famous addresses and something of a shrine. The father of psychoanalysis Sigmund Freud lived, worked and received patients here

FREUD'S THEORIES

Having coined the term "psychoanalysis" in 1896, Sigmund Freud (1856–1939) has exerted a lasting influence on medicine and culture. According to Freud, the unconscious psyche, driven by instincts and impulses, is the engine behind conscious and unconscious action. An imbalance in this system, Freud suggested, could lead to serious emotional disorders and even severe mental disturbance.

from 1891 until his departure from Vienna in 1938. There are more than 420 items of memorabilia on display, including letters and books, furnishings, photographs documenting Freud's long life and various antiquities. Unique films depicting the Freud family in the 1930s are shown in a video room with a commentary by Anna Freud. The flat was quickly abandoned when the Nazis forced Freud and his family to leave Vienna, but it has fortunately been successfully preserved as a museum to his life and work, and is also home to an extensive library. The museum is closed for major refurbishment until summer 2020, during which time a temporary exhibition is being staged at Berggasse 13.

10

Dreifaltigkeitskirche

📍C2 🏠Alser Strasse 17
📞(01) 4057225 Ⓤ Rathaus
🚋43, 44 🕐8–11:30am
Mon–Sat, 8am–noon Sun

Built between 1685 and 1727, the Church of the Holy Trinity is a typical Baroque structure, with a twin-tower façade. It contains an altarpiece (1708) in the north aisle by the painter Martino Altomonte,

and a beautiful crucifix in the south aisle from the workshop of Veit Stoss.

It was to this church that the composer Ludwig van Beethoven's body was brought when he died in 1827. Following the funeral service, which was attended by many of his contemporaries (including composer Franz Schubert and playwright Franz Grillparzer), the cortège conveyed his coffin to its final resting place, the cemetery in Währing, on the city outskirts. The following year, the church was given three new bells, for which Schubert composed the choral piece *Glaube, Hoffnung und Liebe* (Faith, Hope and Love).

11

Narrenturm

📍C1 🏠Spitalgasse 2
📞(01) 52177606
Ⓤ Schottentor 🕐10am–6pm Wed, 10am–1pm Thu & Sat 🔒Public hols

Once the city's Allgemeines Krankenhaus (General Hospital), founded by Joseph II, the Narrenturm (Fools' Tower) is a former asylum designed by Isidor Canevale. The circular tower now houses the Museum for Pathological Anatomy, with a reconstructed apothecary's shop and models. The few rooms open to the public show only a fraction of what is one of the world's most comprehensive pathology and anatomy collections, but tours explore further areas.

Spittelberg

☑ C5 Ⓤ Volkstheater

Often described as the "village in the city", Spittelberg is the oldest and most colourful part of this part of Vienna. In the 17th century, the cluster of streets between Siebenstern-gasse and Burggasse, centred on Spittelberggasse, was Vienna's first immigrant worker district. Its inhabitants were mainly craftsmen, merchants and servants from Croatia and Hungary, brought here to work at the court.

The area was rediscovered in the 1970s and the city authorities restored the buildings. Today, it is a district of restaurants, cafés and boutiques, all of which keep the cobbled streets buzzing into the early hours. It hosts a fantastic Christmas market,

and a regular **Arts and Crafts Market** between April and November. Among the stalls with woodcarvings, tie-dyed fabrics and silver jewellery, waiters from the local bars negotiate the busy crowds; there are dozens of bars in this small area, which contains just 138 houses. The number of bars may change from one week to the next, but the bustling, festive party atmosphere can be experienced almost every evening. The Spittelberg area also has several small art galleries, and artists display their work in the restaurants.

The beautifully restored **Amerlinghaus** at No 8 Stiftgasse, in which the painter Friedrich Amerling (1803–87) was born, now serves as the area's cultural and community centre, and provides a venue for exhibitions and events.

A little further along, between Siebensterngasse and Mariahilfer Strasse, is an enclosed area around former barracks now housing the Military Academy, and the Stiftskirche, topped with an onion-shaped cupola, which serves as a garrison church.

Its walls are lined with fabulously expressive late-Baroque reliefs.

Arts and Crafts Market
◉ ⓐ ⓐ Spittelberggasse
☑ Apr–Jun & Sep–Nov: 10am–6pm Sat; Jul & Aug: 2–9pm Sat
Ⓦ spittelberg-markt.at

Amerling haus
Ⓨ ☑ 2–10pm Mon–Fri
Ⓦ amerlinghaus.at

EAT

Amerlingbeisl
This traditional *Beisl* (bistro) is a well-kept secret, serving delicious seasonal mains, snacks and alpine breakfasts in a lovely dining room.

☑ C5 ⓐ Stiftgasse
Ⓦ amerlingbeisl.at

€€€

―――

Justizcafé
A celebrated canteen perched high in the Palace of Justice. You'll need to pass through security to enter, but hearty mains and fabulous vistas await.

☑ D4 ⓐ Schmerling-platz 10 Ⓦ justizcafe.at

€€€

―――

Restaurant Vestibül
This upmarket restaurant in the Burgtheater serves traditional dishes with a modern twist.

☑ E3 ⓐ Universitäts-ring 2 Ⓦ vestibuel.at

€€€

←
Children playing in the pleasant Spittelberggasse in the heart of Spittelberg

↑ The rich interior of the 19th-century Theater in der Josefstadt

14
Palais Trautson

📍 C4 🏛 Museumstrasse 7
Ⓤ Volkstheater 🚋 49
🚌 48A 🔒 To the public

The Baroque Trautson Palace was built between 1710 and 1712 for Johann Leopold Donat Trautson (the first Prince of Trautson), to a design by Johann Bernhard Fischer von Erlach. The palace remained a possession of the noble Trautson family until it was acquired by Maria Theresa, Archduchess of Austria and the Queen of Hungary and Bohemia, in 1760. She then donated it to the Royal Hungarian Bodyguard, which she had founded.

The Neo-Classical façade, with rows of Doric columns, is heavily ornamented. Its finest sculptures, including that of Apollo playing the lyre, tower above the first-floor windows. The palace has a beautiful staircase, decorated with carvings of the Sphinx and columns of male figures who support the ceiling, by the sculptor Giovanni Giuliani. The gardens, designed by Jean Trehet, are placed, unusually, on the right side of the palace.

In 1961, the Austrian state bought the palace from Hungary to establish the Ministry of Justice, which is based here to this day. There is no public access.

13
Theater in der Josefstadt

📍 C3 🏛 Josefstädter Strasse 26 Ⓤ Rathaus
🚌 13A 🚋 2 🔒 For performances 🌐 josefstadt.org

This intimate theatre, one of the oldest still standing in Vienna, has enjoyed an illustrious history. Founded in 1788, the theatre was rebuilt by Joseph Kornhäusel in 1822, and has been in operation ever since, accommodating ballet, opera and theatre performances. Ludwig van Beethoven composed his overture *The Consecration of the House* for the reopening of the theatre, conducting it himself at the celebratory gala.

In 1924, the directorship of the theatre was given to Max Reinhardt, an outstanding theatre director and reformer, who supervised its further restoration and introduced an ambitious modern repertoire as well as magnificent productions of classic drama. He transformed what was once a middle-of-the-road provincial theatre into the most exciting stage in the German-speaking world.

The theatre is worth a visit to view its interior alone. As the lights slowly dim, the crystal chandeliers float gently to the ceiling. The programme offers excellent productions of Austrian plays, with an emphasis on comedy, classics and the occasional musical.

→ Neo-Classical sculptures perched atop Palais Trautson

THE VIENNESE BALL SEASON

There's little more quintessentially Viennese than a ball, a Habsburg-era tradition that continues to thrive to this day. Between November and February hundreds of grand and elegant balls take place across the city, although things reach a climax during the carnival season (Jan–Feb). Some of the most famous annual balls include the Hunters' Ball (Jan), the Vienna Red Cross Ball (Nov) and the New Year's Eve Ball at the Hofburg.

15 ⚡ Ⓜ 🖥 🏛
Volkskundemuseum

📍 C3 🏛 Laudongasse 15–19
Ⓤ Rathaus 🚌 13A 🚊 3, 33
🕐 10am–5pm Tue–Sun (to
8pm Thu) 🚫 1 Jan, Easter
Mon, 1 May, 1 Nov, 25 Dec
🌐 volkskundemuseum.at

Near a quiet park stands the charming Austrian Folklore Museum. Founded in 1895, in 1917 it moved to the former Schönborn Palace, built in 1706–11 to designs by Johann Lukas von Hildebrandt as a homely two-storey mansion, and altered in 1760 by court architect Isidor Canevale. The building has a rather imposing façade with statues running along its top.

The folk museum is a reminder that Vienna has a history beyond imperialism. With artifacts ranging from the 17th to 19th centuries, the museum's exhibits reflect the culture and daily life of people living in Austria and its neighbouring countries. The fine collection includes furniture, textiles and ceramics, household and work tools, religious objects, and two complete living rooms that illustrate the lifestyles, customs and rituals of the various regions.

On Lange Gasse, a couple of blocks along in the direction of Josefstädter Strasse, you will pass the Alte Backstube, at No 34. This old bakery is one of the most charming town houses in Vienna. It was built in 1697 by the jeweller Hans Bernhard Leopold and was in continuous use until 1963. The rooms have been lovingly restored, retaining the old baking ovens, and house a traditional restaurant and café, as well as a small baking museum where you can view baking equipment from the early 18th century.

→

The ornate façade of
Maria-Treu-Kirche, with
plague column in front

16
Maria-Treu-Kirche

📍 B3 🏛 Jodok-Fink-Platz
Ⓤ Rathaus 🚌 13A 🚊 2
🕐 For services and by appt
🌐 mariatreu.at

Maria-Treu-Kirche (Church of Mary the Faithful) was designed by Johann Lukas von Hildebrandt in 1716, and later altered by Matthias Gerl in the 1750s. It didn't acquire its present form until the 19th century, when the elegant twin towers were added.

The church, as well as the adjacent monastic buildings, was founded by fathers of the Piarist order, one of whose main aims is education; they also founded a primary and a secondary school next door. The homely cellar of the former monastery is now a restaurant.

The interior of the church is one of the best preserved in Vienna. Its Baroque ceiling frescoes (1752–3), the work of the great Austrian painter Franz Anton Maulbertsch, are quite magnificent. These depict scenes from the life of the Virgin Mary and events from both the Old and New Testaments. In one of the

chapels, to the left of the presbytery, you can see an altarpiece of the Crucifixion, also painted by Franz Anton Maulbertsch. The Chapel of Our Lady of Sorrows contains a *pietà* (a sculpture or painting of the Virgin Mary holding Christ's dead body) known as Our Lady from Malta, which was brought here by the Knights of Malta.

In front of the church is a striking Baroque pillar, topped with a statue of the Madonna (1713), one of many such columns erected in Vienna as thanksgiving at the end of the plague era. This column commemorates the plague epidemic of 1713, the last one to occur in Vienna.

Did You Know?

Nominally, 74 per cent of Austrians claim to be Roman Catholic, but church attendance is one-third of this.

← Dinosaurs at the Natur-historisches Museum and its stately façade *(inset)*

the diversity of animal life and includes specimens of now-extinct creatures as well as birds, butterflies and beetles from every corner of the globe.

17 🛈 🛈 🛈 🛈 🛈

Naturhistorisches Museum

📍D5 🚇Maria-Theresien-Platz 🚇Volkstheater
🚋D, 1, 2, 46, 49, 71 🚌48A
🕙9am-6:30pm Wed-Mon (to 9pm Wed) 🚫1 Jan, 25 Dec 🌐nhm-wien.ac.at

Occupying opposite sides of Maria-Theresien-Platz are two identical buildings. One is an art museum (Kunsthistorisches Museum, p104), the other the Natural History Museum, whose exhibits range from fossils of the very first life on Earth to a spectacular display on interstellar travel.

The museum's palatial, late 19th-century home was purpose built to be a splendid setting for vast royal collections, amassed to satisfy the imperial passion for discovery and knowledge. The institution remains one of Europe's foremost facilities for research in the earth and life sciences.

The museum displays cover two floors. To the right of the entrance are rooms devoted to gemstones and mineralogy. Here you will find the world's largest and oldest collection of meteorites, as well as fabulous imperial jewellery pieces. To the left of the entrance the displays chart human evolution and examine prehistoric life. Some of the world's largest casts of dinosaur skeletons are on display there, as well as the museum's diminutive superstar, the carved Stone Age figurine known as the Venus of Willendorf.

The first floor is dedicated to

RINGSTRASSE

The 5.3-km (3.3-mile) Ringstrasse, ordered by Emperor Franz Joseph in 1857, took over 50 years to build. Lined with palaces and institutions such as the Kunsthistorisches Museum and Natur-historisches Museum, the boulevard was intended as a grand show of imperial power in the capital of the Habsburg Empire. A spin around it is one of the highlights of any trip to the city.

18

Mariahilfer Strasse

📍C6 🚇Zieglergasse, Neubaugasse

Mariahilfer Strasse is one of the longest, and widest, streets in Vienna, a main artery running west from the town centre to Schönbrunn.

Cyclists and shoppers on the pedestrianized, tree-lined Mariahilfer Strasse ↑

The section connecting Getreidemarkt (the Grain Market) and Westbahnhof (the western railway station) is also one of the busiest pedestrianized shopping streets in Vienna. Here you will find many of Vienna's largest department stores and its best window displays. Shopping tends to be better value here than on Kärntner Strasse (p93), but it is still more costly than at the mall complex at the Meidling train station, or further out in the Favoriten district.

Mariahilfer Strasse took its name from the Baroque-style Mariahilfer Kirche. Dominated by two towers with large steeples, the church is named after a 16th-century cult of the Virgin Mary. Its façade is an austere pyramidal structure, rising to a bulbous steeple, and there are lively Rococo reliefs set in its walls. In front of the church stands a monument to the composer Joseph Haydn, who lived at this address for 12 years. No 45 is the longest and most famous double-exit house in Vienna, and the birthplace of popular Austrian playwright Ferdinand Raimund (1790).

19
Volkstheater

D5 **Neustiftgasse 1** **Volkstheater** **1, 2, 46, 49, 71, D** **48A** **volkstheater.at**

Combining classic and modern drama with Viennese plays, the Volkstheater (People's Theatre) was, for many years, a staging post for directors and actors on their way from the provincial theatres to the renowned Burgtheater. Today, the Volkstheater presents many plays for the first time, or for the first time in the German language.

The Volkstheater was built in 1889 by the Austrian architects Ferdinand Fellner and Hermann Helmer. They strove to employ the latest in theatre technology, including electric lighting throughout, and many theatre designers later copied their work. The auditorium, with more than 1,000 seats, is one of the largest in a theatre devoted to German-language drama, and is a great example of Viennese *fin-de-siècle* architecture. In front of the theatre stands a statue (1898) of the dramatist Ferdinand Raimund.

DRINK

Dachboden
High up in the 25hours Hotel, this rooftop bar provides great views of the city, with good drinks and tasty tapas.

C4 **Lerchenfelder Strasse 1–3** **25hourshotel.com**

Eberts Cocktail Bar
This stylish, minimalist cocktail bar is staffed by expert bartenders and mixologists from the bartending school next door.

D7 **Gumpendorfer Strasse 51** **Sun–Wed** **eberts.at**

Café Phil
This hip bookshop-café comes alive after hours with excellent drinks and trendy DJs.

E6 **Gumpendorfer Strasse 10** **phil.info**

A SHORT WALK

AROUND THE TOWN HALL

Distance 2 km (1 mile) **Time** 20 minutes
Nearest U-Bahn Rathaus

The most prestigious buildings in Vienna were erected in the second half of the 19th century, on Ringstrasse *(p114)*, at the command of Emperor Franz Joseph. As you stroll through the area you'll come across the Neues Rathaus (New Town Hall, seat of the town administration), the immense Parlament (the seat of Austria's upper and lower houses), the magnificent buildings of the university, and the Burgtheater. The square in front of the town hall, with its adjacent park, is Vienna's largest open-air arena, serving as a stage for theatre and concert performances, and in the summer for vast film screenings.

The **town hall forecourt** *turns into a vast and popular Christmas market in December, selling gifts and decorations.*

LIEBIGGASS

RATHAUSSTRASSE

EBENDORFERST

The Neo-Gothic **Neues Rathaus** *(p108), modelled on Brussels' town hall, is the seat of the Vienna City and Provincial Assembly.*

START

Arkadenhof, *the courtyard of the town hall, serves as a concert venue in summer.*

LICHTENFELSGASSE

REICHSRATSTRASSE

The main decorative feature inside the Neo-Classical **Parlament** *(p108) building is the stylized Austrian eagle.*

BARTENSTEINGASSE

STADIONGASSE

1,575

The number of rooms in the impressive Neues Rathaus.

DR-KARL-RENNER-RING

0 metres 100
0 yards 100

N

The **Universität** (p109) *courtyard is surrounded by arcades lined with busts of its professors.*

Locator Map
For more detail see p98

Around the Town Hall

NORTH OF MARIAHILFER STRASSE

FINISH

Statue of Liebenberg *honours the gallant mayor of Vienna during the Turkish siege of the town in 1683.*

REICHSRATSSTRASSE

GRILLPARZERSTRASSE

UNIVERSITÄTSRING

Pasqualati house *at Mölker-Bastei No 8 was the home of Ludwig van Beethoven in 1804–8 and again in 1810–15. It was here that he composed many of his works. Today, the house is a museum.*

Café Landtmann, *opened in 1873, is the coffee house of the affluent middle classes, and was once Sigmund Freud's favourite haunt.*

*The high panel above the centre of the **Burgtheater** (p100) exterior features a frieze depicting a Bacchanalian procession.*

→
Trams on the Ringstrasse, passing the fine Burgtheater

SOUTH OF THE RING

For decades, Vienna had been under threat and siege from the Ottoman Empire, but in 1683, the Turks were defeated at the Battle of Vienna by the Habsburgs' imperial forces. With the Ottoman threat abated, in the following decades the imperial court turned its energy towards regeneration of the city, and as a result the southeastern suburbs are shaped by 18th-century Baroque architecture. The Belvedere was the summer residence for Prince Eugene of Savoy, the military commander whose strategies had helped vanquish the Turks, while the Karlskirche was commissioned to honour St Charles Borromeo, patron saint of the plague, following Vienna's deliverance from one of the last great outbreaks that had decimated the population in 1713.

From the early 1800s this mercantile centre, including the sprawling Naschmarkt, expanded as imported goods flowed in from across the empire, arriving via the Danube canal. In the 19th century, the Wien river was paved over and the market sprawled further, extending along the Linke Wienzeile. In the north of the district, the Staatsoper, completed in 1869, was the first major building on Emperor Franz Joseph's Ringstrasse boulevard. At the turn of the 20th century, controversial monuments of Jugendstil architecture sprang up, including Joseph Maria Olbrich's Secession Building.

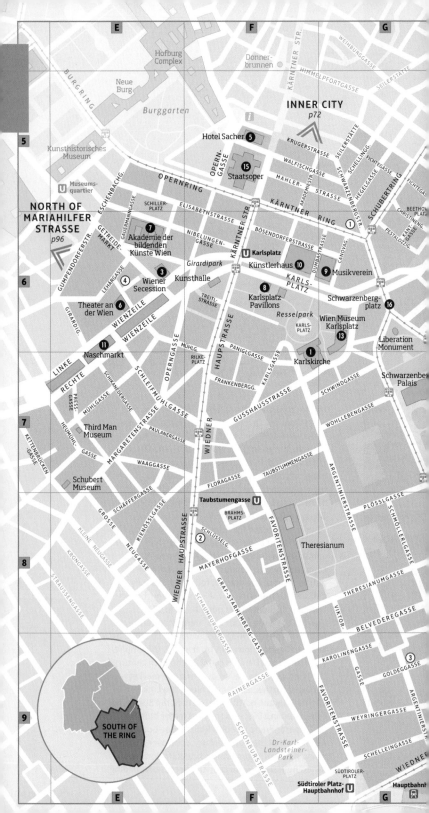

SOUTH OF THE RING

Must Sees
① Karlskirche
② The Belvedere

Experience More
③ Wiener Secession
④ Botanischer Garten
⑤ Hotel Sacher
⑥ Theater an der Wien
⑦ Akademie der bildenden Künste Wien
⑧ Karlsplatz Pavillons
⑨ Musikverein
⑩ Künstlerhaus
⑪ Naschmarkt
⑫ Stadtpark
⑬ Wien Museum Karlsplatz
⑭ Belvedere 21
⑮ Staatsoper
⑯ Schwarzenbergplatz

Eat
① Café Schwarzenberg
② Restaurant Entler
③ Café Goldegg

Stay
④ Hotel Beethoven Wien

❶ ⌖ Ⓜ

KARLSKIRCHE

📍F7 🚇Karlsplatz, A-1040 🚇Karlsplatz 🚌4A
🕐9am–6pm Mon–Sat, noon–7pm Sun & hols 🌐karlskirche.at

This eclectic church, a fine example of Baroque craftsmanship, sits proudly on the edge of the Resselpark. Its façade draws influence from the porticos of ancient Greece, Rome's Trajan's column and Oriental minarets. The interior is no less spectacular, with abundant frescoes and a richly gilded altar.

During Vienna's plague epidemic of 1713, Emperor Karl VI vowed that as soon as the city was delivered from its plight he would build a church dedicated to St Charles Borromeo (1538–84), a former Archbishop of Milan who was celebrated for the help he gave plague sufferers. The epidemic would claim more than 8,000 lives in Vienna. The following year, the Emperor announced a competition to design the church, which was won by the architect Johann Bernhard Fischer von Erlach. The result

was the Karlskirche (St Charles' Church). The church's two huge columns are decorated with scenes from the life of St Borromeo. A statue of the saint stands atop the Classical portico, designed by Lorenzo Mattielli. Building took almost 25 years, and the interior was embellished with carvings and altarpieces by leading architects Daniel Gran and Martino Altomonte.

↑ Henry Moore's *Hill Arches* (1973) in the pond in front of the Karlskirche

Internal stairway (closed to public)

Two Chinese pavilion-inspired gatehouses lead to side entrances.

JOHANN BERNHARD FISCHER VON ERLACH

Many of Vienna's finest buildings were designed by Fischer von Erlach (1656–1723). The Graz-born architect studied in Rome, and then moved to Vienna, where he became the court architect and a leading exponent of Baroque style. His designs include Karlskirche, the Salzburg University church and the initial plans for Schönbrunn Palace. He died before the Karlskirche was finished; the cathedral was completed by his son, Joseph Emanuel, in 1737.

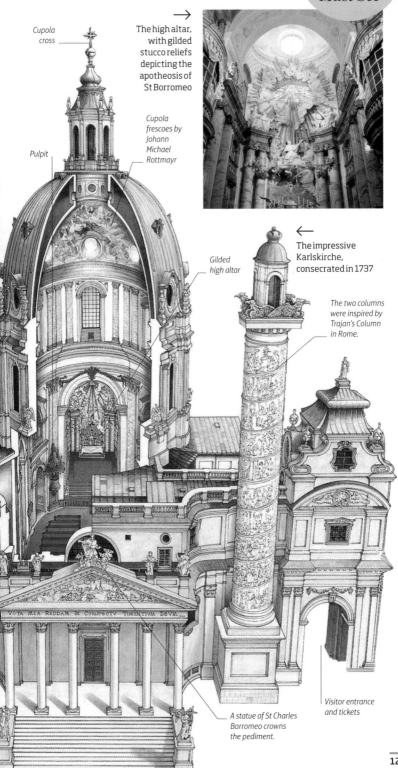

Cupola cross

→ The high altar, with gilded stucco reliefs depicting the apotheosis of St Borromeo

Cupola frescoes by Johann Michael Rottmayr

Pulpit

Gilded high altar

← The impressive Karlskirche, consecrated in 1737

The two columns were inspired by Trajan's Column in Rome.

VOTA MEA REDDAM IN CONSPECTV TIMENTIVM DEVM.

Visitor entrance and tickets

A statue of St Charles Borromeo crowns the pediment.

2 ⊛ ⊛ ⊛ ⊛ ⊛

THE BELVEDERE

◉ H8 ⌂ Upper: Prinz-Eugen-Strasse 27; Lower: Rennweg 6 ⑤ Upper:
Quartier Belvedere ⑪ Upper: Südtirolerplatz ⊞ Upper: D, O, 18; Lower: D,
71 ⊟ Upper: 69A ⏱ 10am–6pm daily (to 9pm Fri) ⓦ belvedere.at

The Belvedere was built as the summer residence of Prince Eugene
of Savoy, the military commander whose tactics helped defeat the
Turks in 1683. Everything here reflects glory, from the magnificence
of the palace interiors to the carefully landscaped gardens.

The Baroque main gate (1728) by Arnold and Konrad Küffner

Situated on a gently sloping hill, the
Belvedere consists of two palaces
built by Johann Lukas von Hildebrandt,
linked by a formal garden designed in
the French style by Dominique Girard.
Standing at the highest point of
the garden, the Upper Belvedere
(completed in 1723) is the larger
and grander of the two, with a more
elaborate façade than the Lower
Belvedere. In addition to the impressive
interiors, the building now houses an
Austrian art collection. Building of the
Lower Belvedere was completed first,
in 1716. It is now used for themed
exhibitions and incorporates the
Orangery and the palace stables.

The ornate façade of the Upper Belvedere

Water flows from an upper basin over five shallow steps in the Upper Cascade.

Exploring the Garden

The garden is laid out
on three levels, each
conveying a complicated
series of classical allusions:
the lower part represents
the domain of the Four
Elements, the centre is
Parnassus and the upper
section Mount Olympus.

Statues of nymphs and goddesses in the Lower Cascade

Entrance to the Lower Belvedere from Rennweg

Lower Belvedere north façade

Triumphal gate to the Lower Belvedere

KLIMT AT THE BELVEDERE

A place of pilgrimage for Klimt
fans, the Belvedere holds the
largest collection of the Viennese
artist's work, some 24 oil paintings,
and one of his sketchbooks. The
museum's undisputed highlight is
the artist's most famous painting,
The Kiss (1907–8), an instantly
recognizable gilded image.

① Girard, a master of hydraulics, designed the impressive cascades and fountains that divide the garden levels.

② Maria Theresa added gilded panelling to the Lower Belvedere's Gold Cabinet.

③ A guard of honour of clipped topiary can be seen on the way to the Lower Belvedere.

Entrance to the Upper Belvedere and gardens from Prinz-Eugen-Strasse.

Statues of sphinxes, their lion bodies representing strength and their human heads intelligence.

Did You Know?

Literally meaning "beautiful views", a belvedere is a building that commands fine prospects.

Privy Garden, the prince's private space

Orangery

Palace Stables

Entrance to the Orangery

↑ The Belvedere palace and its geometrically designed gardens

EXPERIENCE MORE

3 〰️ 〰️ 🏛️

Wiener Secession

📍E6 🏠Friedrichstrasse 12
Ⓤ Karlsplatz 🚋D, 1, 2, 71
🕐10am– 6pm Tue–Sun
🚫1 May, 1 Nov, 25 Dec
🌐secession.at

The Secession Building (1897) remains a unique statement of intent made by some of the most avant-garde artists to have lived and worked in Vienna. Its combination of geometric forms with flowing, Art Nouveau design laid the cornerstone for the distinctive Jugendstil architectural style.

Architect Joseph Maria Olbrich designed this striking, almost windowless building – topped with a filigree globe of entwined laurel leaves – as a showcase for the Secessionist artists, including Otto Wagner, Gustav Klimt, and Koloman Moser, who broke away from Vienna's traditional art scene. The Secessionist motto, emblazoned in gold on the façade, states, "To every age its art,

---

OTTO WAGNER (1841–1918)

The most prominent architect at the turn of the 20th century, Wagner was the foremost representative of the Austrian Secession. His most outstanding works include the Majolikahaus *(p129)*, train stations, the Post Office Savings Bank building and the Kirche am Steinhof *(p146)*.

---

to art its freedom". Inside, Gustav Klimt's *Beethoven Frieze* (1902) is its best-known feature and one of the finest works of the movement. Running along three walls, it depicts interrelated groups of figures and is thought to be a critique of Beethoven's Ninth Symphony.

Arthur Strasser's extraordinary statue of Mark Antony in his chariot (1899) flanks one side of the building.

4

Botanischer Garten

📍H8 🏠Rennweg 14
🚋Rennweg, Unterest Belvedere 🕐10am–dusk daily 🌐botanik.univie.ac.at/hbv

Vienna University's beautifully landscaped Botanical Garden was created in 1754 by Maria Theresa and her physician Van Swieten for the cultivation of medicinal herbs. Extended and opened to the public in the 19th century, it remains a centre for the study of plant sciences and is part of the university's Institute of Botany. It is divided into a number of themed areas, including the Flora of Austria and an Alpine Garden. The two towering sequoia trees are a highlight, as well as the huge display of carnivorous plants. In all there are more than 12,000 species on display from across six continents.

⑤ Hotel Sacher

♀ F5 **⌂ Philharmoniker-strasse 4** **Ⓤ Karlsplatz**
ⓦ sacher.com

Hotel Sacher is one of the "must-see" sights in Vienna. It was founded by the son of Franz Sacher, who created the famous Sachertorte in 1832. Although this cake is now sold in almost every café around the city, this is its true home, and you can treat yourself to a slice in the hotel's Café Sacher Wien.

The hotel came into its own under Anna Sacher, the founder's daughter-in-law, who ran the hotel from 1892 until her death in 1930. She collected autographs,

360,000

Sachertorten are produced by Hotel Sacher each year.

↑ The elegantly decorated Blaue Bar in the luxurious Hotel Sacher

and, to this day, a vast white tablecloth signed by Emperor Franz Joseph I is on display. During her time, the Sacher became a venue for the extra-marital affairs of the rich and noble. It is now a discreetly sumptuous hotel with red velvet sofas, draped curtains and stylish furniture.

⑥ Theater an der Wien

♀ E6 **⌂ Linke Wienzeile 6**
Ⓤ Karlsplatz **🚌 59A**
⊘ For performances and guided tours twice a month **ⓦ theater-wien.at**

The Theatre on the Wien River, one of the oldest theatres in Vienna, was founded in 1801 by Emanuel Schikaneder. A statue above the entrance shows him playing Papageno in the premiere of Mozart's *The Magic Flute*. Schikaneder, who had written the libretto for this opera, was the theatre's first director. The premiere of Beethoven's *Fidelio* was staged here in 1805, and for a while the composer lived in the theatre. Many plays by prominent playwrights such as Kleist, Grillparzer and

← The Wiener Secession, as breathtaking today as when it first opened

Nestroy, and many Viennese operettas were premiered here too, including works by Strauss Jr, Zeller, Lehár and Kalman. Today it hosts popular operas, dance performances and classical concerts along with lectures and symposiums.

⑦ Akademie der bildenden Künste Wien

♀ E6 **⌂ Schillerplatz 3**
Ⓤ Karlsplatz **🚋 D, 1, 2, 71**
⊘ For renovations
ⓦ akademiegalerie.at

Vienna's Academy of Fine Arts was built in 1872–6 by the Danish architect Theophil Hansen as a school and museum. In 1907, Adolf Hitler applied to be admitted to the academy but was refused a place on the grounds that he lacked talent.

The teaching academy is closed to visitors until 2020. Its small but exquisite collection of fine art, which includes several late Gothic and early Renaissance works, and Hieronymus Bosch's *Last Judgment*, is in the meantime on display at the Hofburg Quarter's **Theatermuseum**.

Theatermuseum

⌂ Lobkowitzplatz 2
⊘ 10am–6pm Wed–Mon
ⓦ theatermuseum.at

Karlsplatz Pavillons

📍F6 🚇Karlsplatz
ⓊKarlsplatz ⏰Apr-Oct:
10am-6pm Tue-Sun & hols
🚫1May 🌐wienmuseum.at

The master of Jugendstil, Otto Wagner *(p126)* was responsible for designing and engineering many elements of Vienna's light urban railway system, the Stadtbahn, in the late 19th century. A few of his stations remain to this day – it is worth taking a look at the stations in Stadtpark, Kettenbrückengasse and Schönbrunn – but none can match this stylish pair of railway exit pavilions (1898–9) alongside Karlsplatz. The patina-green copper roofs and fine ornamentation complement Karlskirche beyond. Gilt patterns are stamped onto the white marble cladding and eaves, with repetitions of Wagner's beloved sunflower motif. The greatest impact is made by the elegantly curving lines of the building's roof.

Today the western pavilion holds an exhibition devoted to Wagner's revolutionary work. It covers his most important designs, including the Kirche am Steinhof *(p146)* and the revolutionary Stadtbahn, as well as his theories of design, which were quite radical for the time. The eastern pavilion houses a café.

Musikverein

📍G6 🚇Bösendorferstrasse 12 ⓊKarlsplatz
🚋D, 1, 2, 62, 71 🚌2A, 4A, 59A ⏰For concerts and guided tours (1pm Mon-Sat)
🌐musikverein.at

Next to the Künstlerhaus is the Musikverein, headquarters of the Society of the Friends of Music. It was designed in 1867–9 by Theophil Hansen in a mixture of styles, employing terracotta statues, capitals and balustrades.

The Musikverein is home to the world-famous Vienna Philharmonic Orchestra, which gives regular performances here. Tickets are sold by subscription to Viennese music lovers, but some are available on the day. The concert hall, seating almost 2,000, has excellent acoustics, and the decor is superb. The balcony is supported by vast columns; the gilded ceiling shows nine muses and Apollo; and lining the walls are the statues of various famous musicians.

NEW YEAR'S DAY CONCERT

Since the late 1930s, at 11:15am on every New Year's Day, families across Austria switch on the TV for one of the annual musical highlights: the Vienna Philharmonic Orchestra's New Year's Day concert at the Musikverein. It only features Austrian composers and music by the Strauss family is always included on the programme.

The best-known annual event here is the New Year's Day concert, which is broadcast live around the world.

Künstlerhaus

📍F6 🚇Karlsplatz 5
ⓊKarlsplatz 🚋D, 1, 2, 62, 71
🚌2A, 4A, 59A ⏰Times vary, check website
🌐k-haus.at

Commissioned by the Vienna Artists' Society as an exhibition hall for its members, the Künstlerhaus (Artists' House) was completed in 1868. The

←

Lamplight accentuating the ornate features on the Musikverein's façade at night

society favoured grandiose, academic styles of painting in tune with the historicist Ringstrasse architecture which was also being developed around that time. The Artists' House itself is typical of this style. Designed by August Weber (1836–1903) to resemble a Renaissance *palazzo*, it is decorated with marble statues of the masters of art, including Albrecht Dürer, Michelangelo, Raphael, Peter Paul Rubens, Leonardo da Vinci, Diego Velázquez and Titian, symbolizing the timeless value of art.

The Künstlerhaus has been undergoing renovation work for several years, during which time exhibitions have been housed at Künstlerhaus 1050 on Siebenbrunnengasse. It is expected to reopen in the spring of 2020.

Naschmarkt

⑨ E6 **Ⓤ Karlsplatz, Kettenbrückengasse**
🚌 59A **🕐 6am–6:30pm Mon–Sat (to 6pm Sat)**
🌐 naschmarkt-vienna.com

Vienna's liveliest market has a huge variety of stalls and some of the best snack bars in the city. In the western section of the market, you'll find flowers, farm produce and wine, as well as cakes, bread and meats. Held each Saturday, the lively flea market throws together professional antique dealers with pure junk peddlers, and makes for a fun morning activity. There are certainly bargains to be had here, but it pays to be vigilant as no returns are accepted.

Nearby, at Kettenbrückengasse No 6, by the U-Bahn, is the simple flat where Franz Schubert died in 1828. Today this is the **Schubert Museum** (signposted as the "Schubert Sterbewohnung"). This tiny flat, housing a piano and a meagre scattering of personal effects, is perhaps the most haunting of all memorials to the great classical composer.

Overlooking Naschmarkt, at Linke Wienzeile Nos 38 and 40, are the remarkable Wagner Apartments, designed by Otto Wagner in 1899. No 38 is bedecked in gilt ornamentation, while No 40 – known as Majolikahaus, after the glazed pottery used to weather-proof the walls – is wrapped with subtle floral patterns.

Schubert Museum
📞 (01) 5816730 **🕐 10am–1pm, 2–6pm Wed & Thu**
🚫 1 Jan, 1 May & 25 Dec

↑ Inspecting the fresh produce on display at the lively Naschmarkt

12

Stadtpark

H5 **Parkring** **(01) 40008042** **Stadtpark, Stubentor** **Wien Mitte** **2** **3A, 74A** **24 hours**

Vienna's first and largest public park opened in 1862 when the old city walls were demolished. On the Weihburggasse side of the park stands one of the most photographed sights in Vienna, the gilded bronze statue of the King of Waltz, Johann Strauss II. The park also has statues of the composer Franz Schubert, the portraitist Friedrich von Amerling and

1921

The year the Stadtpark's monument to Johann Strauss II was unveiled.

the painter Hans Makart. The park's design was inspired by English landscaped gardens: in particular, the ornamental herbaceous borders, which provide year-round colour. The Kursalon music hall hosts open-air concerts and costume balls in summer. The cosy park café **Meierei im Stadtpark** is a popular meeting place.

Meierei im Stadtpark
Am Heumarkt 2A
steirereck.at

13

Wien Museum Karlsplatz

G6 **Karlsplatz 8** **Karlsplatz** **10am-6pm Tue-Sun & hols** **1 Jan, 1 May, 25 Dec** **wien museum.at**

Visitors to the Vienna Museum are greeted by a vast model of the city from the era when the Ringstrasse *(p114)* was developed. The exhibition covers nearly 3,000 years of urban history, illustrating the lives of its first settlers; life in the Roman camp of Vindobona; the threat from Turkish invaders; and the rise of Vienna to the capital of a great empire.

The museum is strongest on the 19th century – displaying paintings as well as furniture and clothing. Perhaps the most interesting exhibits are the reconstructed apartments of the writer Franz Grillparzer and the architect Adolf Loos.

Extension and renovation work on the building will take place over the coming years to upgrade the museum into a cutting-edge space.

14

Belvedere 21

H9 **Arsenalstrasse 1** **0, 18** **69A** **11am-6pm Thu-Sun (to 9pm Wed)** **belvedere1.at**

At the south end of Belvedere *(p124)*, near to the Military Museum, is Vienna's temple to contemporary art: Belvedere 21 (also referred to as 21er Haus). Built of steel and glass, the modernist building was originally designed for the World Exhibition in 1958. It now celebrates Austrian art from 1945 to the present day, with changing exhibitions, performance art, lectures and a sculpture garden.

STAY

Hotel Beethoven Wien
Enchanting hotel that hosts art shows and concerts in the lobby.

E6 **Papagenogasse 6** **hotel-beethoven.at**

€€€

The gilded monument to Johann Strauss in Stadtpark ↑

↑ A packed auditorium at the Staatsoper, rebuilt after its destruction in World War II

⑮ 🖌 ⬛ ⬜

Staatsoper

⌖ F5 **⌂ Opernring 2, A-1010**
Ⓤ Karlsplatz **🚋 D, 1, 2, 71**
🚌 2A **🕐 Check website for performance and tour times**
🌐 wiener-staatsoper.at

The first of the buildings on the Ringstrasse (p114) to be completed, in May 1869, the State Opera House opened to the strains of Mozart's *Don Giovanni*. Built in dramatic Neo-Renaissance style, the opera house initially failed to impress the Viennese. The distressed interior designer, Eduard van der Nüll, committed suicide and, two months later, the architect, August Sicard von Sicardsburg, also died. Yet, when the opera was hit by an allied bomb in 1945, the event was a symbolic blow to the city. With a new state-of-the-art auditorium and stage, the opera house eventually reopened on 5 November 1955 with a performance of Beethoven's *Fidelio*. Its illustrious directors have included Gustav Mahler, Richard Strauss and Herbert von Karajan.

The hall is renowned for its exceptional acoustics, and some 300 performances are held every year, including premieres of new operas. For those that can't make a performance, some events are streamed live on the internet.

💬 INSIDER TIP
Standing Room Tickets

Opera tickets can be pricey and sell out far in advance. But if you're willing to queue on the day, there are often a few standing tickets for as little as €2–€4. Visit the Stehplätze ticket office 80 minutes before the performance.

Each year, on the last Thursday of Carnival, the stage is extended to create a vast dance floor for the Vienna Opera Ball (p50).

---

⑯

Schwarzenbergplatz

⌖ G6 **Ⓤ Karlsplatz** **🚋 D, 71**

The elongated Schwarzenberg Square, by far one of the city's grandest spaces, is best seen from the Ringstrasse, from where several important structures come into view together. In the foreground is an equestrian statue of Prince Karl Philipp Fürst zu Schwarzenberg, who commanded the Austrian and allied armies in the Battle of Leipzig in 1813 against the French army under Napoleon.

The Hochstrahlbrunnen (high jet fountain) was built in 1873 to mark the connection of Vienna's first Alpine water supply. The fountain is floodlit in summer. Once the focal point of the square, it now partly obscures the heroic-style Soviet monument to the Red Army that commemorates the Russian liberation of Vienna. Beyond the Russian monument is the beautiful Schwarzenberg Palace. Today, one wing of the palace is occupied by the Swiss Embassy. The present head of the Schwarzenberg family served as advisor to President Havel following the Velvet Revolution in Czechoslovakia in 1989 and was Czech foreign minister in 2007–2009 and 2010–13.

→ Monument to the Prince of Schwarzenberg on Schwarzenbergplatz

A SHORT WALK
OPERNRING

Distance 2 km (1 mile) **Time** 20 minutes
Nearest U-Bahn Karlsplatz

Between the Staatsoper and Karlskirche, two of the great landmarks of Vienna, lies an area that typifies the varied culture of the city. Here, you'll pass an 18th-century theatre, a 19th-century art academy and the Secession Building. Mixed in with these cultural monuments are emblems of the Viennese devotion to good living: the Hotel Sacher, as sumptuous today as it was a century ago; the Café Museum, still as popular as it was in the early 20th century; and the hurly-burly of the colourful Naschmarkt, where you can buy everything from oysters and exotic fruits to second-hand clothes.

The **Goethe Statue** was designed by Edmund Hellmer in 1890.

The **Schiller Statue** stands in the charming park in front of the Academy of Fine Arts.

The Italianate **Academy of Fine Arts** (p127) building is home to one of the best collections of old masters in Vienna.

ELISABETHSTRASS

SCHILLERPLATZ

NIBELUNGENGASS

MAKARTGASSE

↑ The glittering dome above the entrance to the Secession Building

Built in 1898 as a showroom for the Secession artists, the **Secession Building** (p126) houses the Beethoven Frieze by Gustav Klimt.

The **Mark Anthony Statue** (1899), outside the Secession Building, is a decadent bronze work by Arthur Strasser.

Today, the 18th-century **Theater an der Wien** (p127) is used as an opera house. It has been the venue for many premieres, among them Beethoven's Fidelio.

GETREIDEMARKT

MILLÖCKERGASSE

LINKE WIENZEILE

The **Naschmarkt** (p129) sells everything from fresh farm produce to bric-a-brac. It is liveliest early on Saturday mornings.

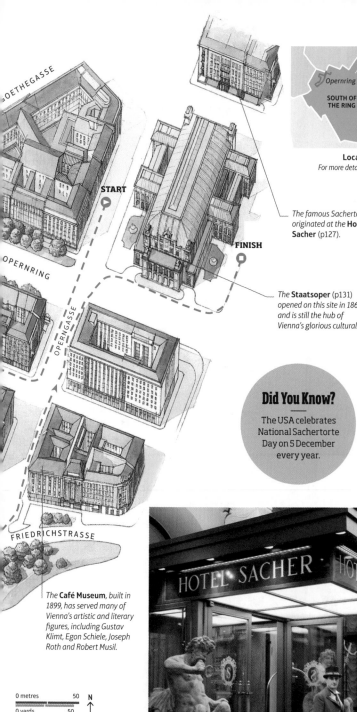

GOETHEGASSE

OPERNRING

OPERNGASSE

FRIEDRICHSTRASSE

START

FINISH

*The famous Sachertorte originated at the **Hotel Sacher** (p127).*

*The **Staatsoper** (p131) opened on this site in 1869, and is still the hub of Vienna's glorious cultural life.*

Opernring

SOUTH OF THE RING

Locator Map
For more detail see p120

Did You Know?

The USA celebrates National Sachertorte Day on 5 December every year.

*The **Café Museum**, built in 1899, has served many of Vienna's artistic and literary figures, including Gustav Klimt, Egon Schiele, Joseph Roth and Robert Musil.*

0 metres   50   N
0 yards   50   ↑

→
A smartly dressed doorman greeting patrons at the luxurious Hotel Sacher

The brightly coloured façade of the Hundertwasserhaus

BEYOND
THE CENTRE

Some of Vienna's most interesting sights, including the fascinating Hundertwasserhaus and Europe's largest cemetery, are a fair distance from the compact and historic city centre. This area is the preserve of former Habsburg hunting grounds, with parks and gardens now open to the public including the vast Prater and the peaceful Lainzer Tiergarten. Beyond the Ring sprawls Schönbrunn, a vast Neo-Classical palace and former summer home of the Habsburgs.

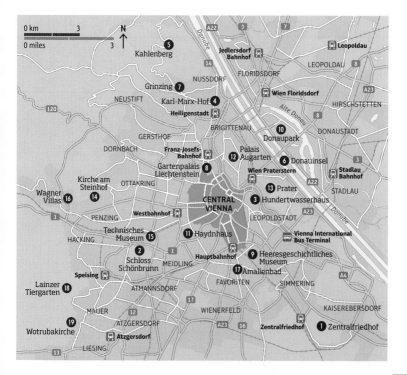

① ⓂⒶ Ⓓ

ZENTRALFRIEDHOF

🏠 Simmering Hauptstrasse 234, Tor 2 Ⓢ Zentralfriedhof, Kledering
🚌 6, 71 🕐 Times vary, check website 🌐 friedhoefewien.at

Austria's largest cemetery, and its most famous, was opened in 1874 to accommodate the deceased of the rapidly industrializing 19th-century capital. Today it contains 300,000 graves over an area of 2.5 sq km (1 sq mile).

The beautiful old Central Cemetery sits in the verdant outskirts of Vienna's Simmering district – "Central" refers to the site's significant number of graves rather than its location. The cemetery is divided into specific numbered sections: as well as the central garden of honour where VIPs are buried, there are old and new Jewish cemeteries; a Protestant cemetery; a Russian Orthodox section; and various war graves and memorials. Also here is the Bestattungsmuseum, which gives a fascinating insight into the history of Vienna's love affair with lavish burials. A pleasant way to explore the grounds is on the circulating bus.

Luegerkirche

Arcades around the Luegerkirche

The presidential vault contains the remains of Dr Karl Renner, the first President of the Austrian Republic after World War II.

Sculptor Fritz Wotruba's grave

Modernist composer Arnold Schoenberg's grave is marked with a bold cube by Fritz Wotruba.

Beethoven, Brahms Schubert and the Strausses are buried in the musicians' area.

←
The Luegerkirche (1907-10) dedicated to St Borromeo

1 Fritz Wotruba's cuboid sculpture marks the grave of Viennese composer Arnold Schoenberg.

Monument to Dr Johann Nepomuk Prix by Viktor Tilgner (1894)

2 The Russian Orthodox Chapel, completed in 1894, is still used by Vienna's Russian community.

3 A statue of Johannes Brahms marks his grave in the musicians' section.

Spectacular monuments are carved in the semicircular arcades facing the main entrance.

← The expansive Central Cemetery, divided into distinct sections

Bestattungsmuseum

The main entrance from Simmeringer Hauptstrasse

The Russian Orthodox Chapel

THE BESTATTUNGSMUSEUM

Vienna has several rather morbid attractions but none so sombre as this, the Undertakers' Museum *(bestattungs museum.at)*. Exhibits examine the ways in which death has been dealt with over many centuries by the Viennese, and explore burial rituals and customs; displays include funerary art and a 1784 folding coffin. Though small (allow around 15 minutes to see it all), it will leave a lasting impression.

The elegant Ehrenhof fountain in front of the magnificent Schönbrunn Palace ↑

2 🗡️ 🎭 🍽️ 🖥️ 🛍️

SCHLOSS SCHÖNBRUNN

🏠 Schönbrunner Schloss Strasse 47 🚇 Schönbrunn, Hietzing 🚋 10, 58, 60 🚌 10A, 56A, 56B, 58A 🕐 Times vary, check website 🌐 schoenbrunn.at

The former summer residence of the Habsburgs, the lavish Schönbrunn Palace is a masterpiece of Baroque architecture set amid exquisite landscaped grounds. Under the rule of Empress Maria Theresa, this was the glittering heart of the imperial court. Today it is one of Vienna's most spectacular and most visited sights and makes for a wonderful escape from the bustling city centre.

Schönbrunn is named after a beautiful spring that served the original hunting lodge built here in the late 16th century. Leopold I initially asked Johann Bernhard Fischer von Erlach to design a grand Baroque residence here in 1695. However, it was not until Maria Theresa employed Nikolaus Pacassi in the mid-18th century that the project was completed. The sumptuous Rococo decorative schemes devised by Pacassi dominate the state rooms, where white panelling lavishly adorned with gilded mouldings prevails. Rooms vary from extravagant – such as the Millionenzimmer, panelled in fig wood inlaid with Persian miniatures – to the rather plain state apartments once occupied by Franz Joseph and Empress Elisabeth. "Imperial" and "Grand" guided tours lead you through the palace rooms, and the state rooms open to the public are on the first floor.

💬 INSIDER TIP
Take in a Show

Puppet shows at the Marionetten Theater (www.marionetten theater.at) in the Little Court Theatre at Schönbrunn will delight children and adults alike. A version of Mozart's The Magic Flute is an undisputed highlight.

← The Great Gallery, once used for imperial banquets, hosted state receptions until 1994

→ A vast collection of tropical plants flourishes in the garden's Palm House

1696
△ Leopold I commissions J B Fischer von Erlach to design a new palace.

1705
Jean Trehet lays out the gardens.

1744–9
Nikolaus Pacassi adapts the building for Maria Theresa.

1805 and 1809
△ Napoleon uses the palace as his headquarters.

1882
△ Palm House is built.

3 🖥 🏛

HUNDERTWASSERHAUS

📍 Löwengasse and Kegelgasse Ⓤ Landstrasse 🚋 1 Hetzgasse 🚌 4A Löwengasse
🕐 Art Café: 10am–6pm daily; shopping centre: 9am–6pm daily 🚫 Building: closed to the public 🌐 Building: hundertwasserhaus.at; shopping centre: hundertwasser-village.com

A relatively recent addition to the city's architectural heritage, the 20th-century Hundertwasserhaus is Vienna's most remarkable and striking contemporary structure. This gloriously eclectic block of flats on Löwengasse divides opinion; while some love it, others think it is more like a stage set than a block of flats.

The Hundertwasserhaus is a municipal apartment block created in 1985 by the artist Friedensreich Hundertwasser, who wished to diverge from what he saw as the rather soulless modern architecture appearing in Vienna's suburbs. The result was a structure that has been controversial since its construction, with many critics dismissing it as kitsch. It features undulating floors and large trees growing from inside the rooms. Hundertwasser took no payment for the design, declaring that it was worth it to prevent something ugly from going up in its place. As a private building, its interior cannot be visited, but opposite is the Hundertwasser Village shopping centre, a bazaar of shops and cafés open to the public and a pleasant place to browse for quirky souvenirs.

> 💬 **INSIDER TIP**
> **Art Café**
>
> Grab a coffee at the Art Café on the ground floor of the apartment building (one of the few parts of the structure open to the public). It's bursting with suitably unique decor and has a friendly atmosphere.

FRIEDENSREICH HUNDERTWASSER

Born to a Jewish mother in 1928, Hundertwasser was an artist and designer whose passion for the irregular was inspired by Viennese Secessionists. In his use of colour and organic forms, he said, he hoped to realize "a more human and nature-orientated architecture". He founded the Kunst Haus Wien *(kunsthauswien.com)*, a short walk from the Hundertwasser-haus, where there are exhibits of his work.

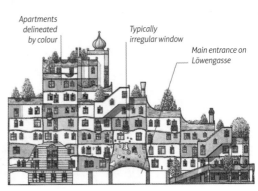

Apartments delineated by colour

Typically irregular window

Main entrance on Löwengasse

↑ The building combines elements of a mosque with features of palaces

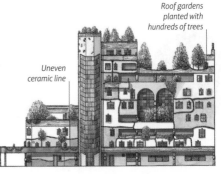

Roof gardens planted with hundreds of trees

Uneven ceramic line

↑ Roof gardens on the multilevel block are a key feature of the building's design

900
—
Tonnes of earth and grass cover the Hundertwasserhaus roof.

↑ Colour blocks and banding delineating the individual apartments

EXPERIENCE MORE

4

Karl-Marx-Hof

🏠 Heiligenstädterstrasse 82-92, Döbling ⓤ Heiligenstadt 🚋 D 🚌 5A, 10A, 11A, 38A, 39A 🔒 To the public

In the 1920s, a period known as Red Vienna, the city was governed by the Social Democratic Party of Austria, elected mainly thanks to the support of first-time women voters. The council formed the ambitious plan to build houses for its entire working population. As a result, during 1923–33 more than 60,000 new apartments were built. The programme was financed by a luxury tax imposed on wealthy citizens. Its execution was so strict that the municipal finance director, Hugo Breitner, earned himself the nickname the "financial vampire".

Karl-Marx-Hof is an immense complex of 1,382 apartments and recreational facilities, and is the most celebrated of the developments of that period. The project's architect, Karl Ehn, was a pupil of Austrian architect Otto Wagner (*p126*).

> ### Did You Know?
>
> At 1.1 km (0.75 miles) in length, Karl-Marx-Hof is the world's longest residential building.

5

Kahlenberg

🏠 1190, 10 km (6 miles) N of Vienna 🚌 38A

North of the city, on the edge of the Vienna Woods, is Kahlenberg, the highest peak in Vienna, with a television mast and the outline of a white church at the top.

It was from here, on 12 September 1683, that the Polish king, Jan Sobieski, led his troops to relieve the Viennese forces fighting for

---

⛰️ GREAT VIEW
Stefaniewarte

This 22-m- (72-ft-) high viewing tower atop the Kahlenberg soars 300 m (894 ft) above the Danube, and is one of the best vantage points in the city. On a clear day you can see Schneeberg mountain, some 70 km (43 miles) away.

---

the city. Pope Innocent III's papal legate celebrated a thanksgiving mass in the ruins of the church, which had been destroyed by the Turks.

The restored St Josefkirche on Kahlenberg is now maintained by Polish monks. Inside the church is a chapel with frescoes by the Polish artist Jen Henryk de Rosen, and a display of the coats of arms of families whose members took part in the battle.

Just behind the church is a viewing terrace and a restaurant. The views over the vineyards and the city are fabulous.

↑ The idyllic waterfront on the Donauinsel, Vienna's largest recreation area

→ Enjoying a glass of wine at a *Heurige* bar in Grinzing, overlooking the city

6 Donauinsel

Ⓤ Donauinsel, Handelskai
Ⓦ danauinselfest.at

The numerous side-arms and rivulets of the Danube river regularly flooded the town until it was first canalized between 1870 and 1875. The second period of canalization in the Vienna region began in 1972 and was completed in 1987. The New Danube, a 5-km (3-mile) canal that acts as an "overflow", dates from this period.

The wooded island created between the Danube and its canals is known as Donauinsel, or Danube Island. It is Vienna's largest recreation area and a favourite with swimmers and sunbathers. The vast park is crisscrossed by dozens of avenues, walking and cycling paths, and picnic areas with built-in barbecues, as well as nudist areas. Even water-skiing and surfing are available.

The Danube Island Festival, held each June, is the biggest free open-air festival of music and food in Europe, claiming as many as three million visitors.

7 Grinzing

Ⓗ Heiligenstadt 🚌 38A
🚋 38 to Grinzing

The quiet villages among the vineyards on the slopes of the Vienna Woods come to life during wine-making season, when large groups of tourists arrive to visit *Heurigen* – new-vintage wine taverns, typical of Vienna. At *Heurigen* inns, drinks are served at the table and food is available from self-service buffets. The most famous village is Grinzing.

On the way to Grinzing, it is worth taking the time to visit Heiligenstädter Testament-Haus at No 6 on the narrow Probusgasse – Ludwig van Beethoven's most famous home in Vienna. It was here that the great composer tried to find a cure for his worsening deafness; when he failed, he wrote a dramatic letter to his brothers, known as *The Testament* (1802).

8 Gartenpalais Liechtenstein

Ⓗ Fürstengasse 1
Ⓤ Friedensbrücke 🚌 40A
🚋 D Ⓒ For tours (by appt)
Ⓦ palaisliechtenstein.com

Completed in 1692 to designs by Domenico Martinelli in the Rococo style, the Liechtenstein family's summer palace now houses the art collection of Prince Hans-Adam II von und zu Liechtenstein. Behind the Palladian exterior, notable features include the Neo-Classical library, and the Hercules Hall and grand staircase with their magnificent frescoes. The collection ranges from the Renaissance through to the early 19th century but concentrates on the Baroque, with special focus on Rubens. The palace stands in an extensive garden.

EAT & DRINK

Hirt
Set amid its own vineyards on the Kahlenberg slopes, this *Heuriger* serves great wines and food.

Ⓗ Parzelle 165
Ⓦ heuriger-hirt.at

Weingut Schilling
This traditional *Heuriger* offers superb wines and a buffet of local delicacies.

Ⓗ Lang-Enzersdorfer Strasse 54
Ⓦ weingut-schilling.at

9

Heeresgeschichtliches Museum

Arsenal, Ghegastrasse Objekt 18 Hauptbahnhof D, 0, 18 13A, 69A 9am-5pm daily 1 Jan, Easter Sun, 1 May, 1 Nov, 25 & 31 Dec hgm.at

The impressive Museum of Army History is housed in the military complex known as the Arsenal, built as a fortress in 1856. Exhibits include fine paintings, ornate antiques and military artifacts.

To view the collection in chronological order, begin on the first floor on the left, where the exhibits detail the Turkish siege. Other rooms chronicle various 18th-century wars and Napoleon's victory over Austria. The 19th- and 20th-century displays, including heavy artillery used in World War I, are on the ground floor. There is also a "tank garden" located behind the museum.

Do not miss seeing the car in which Archduke Franz Ferdinand was assassinated, or the modern armaments used in World War I, which the murder of the Habsburg heir precipitated.

THE ASSASSINATION OF FRANZ FERDINAND

On 28 June 1914, Archduke Franz Ferdinand, heir to the Austrian throne, and his wife Sophie von Hohenberg paid a visit to Sarajevo. Gavrilo Princip, a Serbian nationalist, assassinated the couple, provoking a crisis that led to World War I. The museum houses the car in which they were killed.

Archduke Franz Ferdinand's Car

10

Donaupark

Kaisermühlen 20B 24 hrs

This wonderful park is located on an island in the Danube, northeast of the historical centre. Developed in 1964, the park features a variety of beautiful gardens, cycle lanes and cafés, and is the perfect place to escape the city. Its most obvious landmark is the **Donauturm**, a colossal tower with two revolving restaurants and an observation deck (last ride up is at 11:30pm). The park and surrounding area are incorporated into **Donau City**, a vast urban project containing the Vienna International Centre, a complex of United Nations agencies. Guided tours (cash only) of the complex run daily.

Donauturm
10am-11:30pm daily
donauturm.at

Donau City
For tours at 11am, 2pm and 3:30pm daily
unis.unvienna.org

11

Haydnhaus

Haydngasse 19 Zieglergasse 57A 10am-1pm, 2-6pm Tue-Sun 1 Jan, 1 May, 25 Dec wienmuseum.at

Haydn built this house with money that he had earned on his successful trips to London between 1791 and 1795. He lived in the house from 1797 until his death in 1809, and composed many major works here, including *The Seasons* and *The Creation*.

←

The Heeresgeschichtliches Museum's ornamented Byzantine-style façade

Strolling around the rides at Wurstelprater in the Prater ↑

The exhibits include portraits, documents and original scores as well as Haydn's clavichord, which was bought by Johannes Brahms. The museum's garden, in the middle of Mariahilfer Strasse, is open to the public.

---

12 🅜

Palais Augarten

🅐 Obere Augartenstrasse 1 🅤 Taborstrasse 🚋 5, 31 🚌 5A, 5B 🅞 Park: 6am–9pm daily 🅦 augarten.com

There has been a palace on this site since the days of Leopold I, but it was destroyed by the Turks in 1683 and then rebuilt around 1700. Since 1948 it has been the home of the world-famous Vienna Boys' Choir and is consequently closed to the public.

It is worth exploring the **Porcelain Museum** housed in the palace, which displays pieces from the Rococo and Biedermeier periods, as well as the 20th and 21st centuries. The palace also boasts the oldest Baroque garden in the city, planted in the second half of the 17th century, renewed in 1712, and opened to the public by Joseph II in 1775. The handsome entrance gates were designed by Isidor

Canevale in 1775. Beethoven, Mozart and Johann Strauss I all gave concerts in the park pavilion, behind which is the studio of early-20th-century Austrian sculptor Gustinus Ambrosi. In the distance, you can see two huge flakturms, immovable reminders of World War II. Built by German forces in 1942 as defence towers and anti-aircraft batteries, these enormous concrete monoliths could house thousands of troops and withstand the most powerful explosives.

Porcelain Museum
♿ 🅞 10am–6pm Mon–Sat 🅠 Public hols

13

Prater

🅐 Prater 🅤🅢 Praterstern 🚋 1 🚌 77A, 80A; funfair: 5, 0 🅞 Times vary, check website 🅦 prater.at

Formerly imperial hunting grounds, these woods and meadows between the Danube and its canal were opened to the public by Joseph II in 1766. Today they make up the Green Prater, a huge park area bisected by a tree-lined central avenue, the Hauptallee. Once

TOP 3 **KIDS' ATTRACTIONS AT THE PRATER**

Wurstelprater
There's plenty of fun to be had here, with dodgems, ghost trains and carousels among the many rides.

Planetarium
Kids will be enthralled by the immersive multimedia shows exploring the galaxy.

Miniature Railway
Catch the *Liliputbahn* for a pleasant 4-km (2-mile) trip through the Prater.

the preserve of the nobility and their footmen, it now attracts joggers and cyclists. At the western end of the Prater is a large amusement park, locally known as the Wurstelprater (or Clown's Prater), which dates back to the 19th century and is the oldest in the world. It is home to the iconic Wiener Riesenrad Ferris wheel, built in 1896. Access to the Prater itself is free of charge, but each ride is charged individually.

⑭ ✂️ Ⓜ️
Kirche am Steinhof

🏠 Baumgartner Höhe 1, Penzing ☎ (01) 9106011007 🚌 48A ⏰ 4–5pm Sat, noon–4pm Sun by appt

At the edge of the Vienna Woods rises the conspicuous copper dome of the Church at Steinhof. Built in 1902–7 by Otto Wagner, the church is considered to be one of the most important works of the Secession. Situated within the grounds of a large psychiatric hospital, it has a marble-clad

Kirche am Steinhof's façade, and stained glass windows *(inset)* ↑

exterior with copper nailhead ornament and spindly screw-shaped pillars, topped by wreaths supporting the porch. The light and airy interior is a single space with shallow side chapels decorated with gold and white friezes. Illumination is provided by daylight shining through the beautiful blue stained-glass windows by Austrian artist Koloman Moser.

⑮ ✂️ Ⓜ️
Technisches Museum

🏠 Mariahilfer Strasse 212, Penzing 🚋 52, 58 🚌 10A ⏰ 9am–6pm Mon–Fri, 10am–6pm Sat, Sun & hols; under-19s free 🌐 technisches museum.at

Franz Joseph I founded the Technisches Museum in 1908, using the Habsburgs' personal collections as core material, but only opened its doors to the public ten years later.

The museum documents all aspects of technical progress, from small domestic appliances to heavy industry. Exhibits include the world's first sewing machine, the oldest typewriter and the first petrol-driven car. A major section looks at computer technology and oil- and gas-refining, as well as a reconstruction of coal mine.

The Railway Museum, an integral part of the museum, houses a large collection of imperial carriages and engines.

A lighthouse at the entrance recalls the Habsburg Empire's once formidable extent, from the Tatra Mountains to the Atlantic Ocean.

⑯ ✂️ Ⓜ️
Wagner Villas

🏠 Hüttelbergstrasse 26, Penzing Ⓤ Hütteldorf 🚌 43B, 52A to Camping Platz Wien West ⏰ 10am–4pm Tue–Sun; by appt Mon

Hidden behind dense, leafy greenery, at the start of a road to Kahlenberg, stand two villas built by Otto Wagner. The oldest is stylistically midway between his earlier grand Ringstrasse works and the more decorative elements of Jugendstil. It was meticulously restored by the present owner, the painter Ernst Fuchs, who added his own colours and established the **Ernst Fuchs Museum**. The villa is now a famous meeting place for Vienna's artistic community as well as a venue for fund-raising auctions. The second villa, built some 20 years later, was completed in pure Secession style, with deep blue panels and a glass nailhead ornament. Privately owned, it can be viewed only from outside.

Ernst Fuchs Museum
🏛 ⏰ 10am–4pm Tue–Sun
🌐 ernstfuchsmuseum.at

---

❶⑦

Amalienbad

🏛 Reumannplatz 23, Favoriten Ⓤ Reumannplatz
🚌 7A, 14A, 66A, 67A, 68A
🚃 6, 67 🌐 wien.gv.at

Public baths may not seem like an obvious destination for tourists, but the Jugendstil Amalienbad (1923–6) is a fine example of a municipal authority providing essential public facilities for the local population with style and panache. Named after one

---

💬 INSIDER TIP
Bare Necessities

The entire sauna at Amalienbad is for the naked only. However, at certain times there are separate male and female sessions. Check session times in advance *(www.wien.gv.at).*

of the councillors, Amalie Pölzer, the baths were designed by Karl Schmalhofer and Otto Nadel of the city's architectural department.

The magnificent main pool, overlooked by galleries, is covered by a stained-glass roof that can be opened in minutes. There are saunas, baths and therapeutic pools, each enlivened by fabulous Secession tile decorations. The baths were damaged in World War II but have been impeccably restored.

---

❶⑧

Lainzer Tiergarten

🏛 Lainzer Tiergarten, Hietzing Tiergarten 🚃 60 to Hermesstrasse, then bus 55A ⏰ Mid-Feb–mid-Nov: 8am–dusk daily
🌐 lainzer-tiergarten.at

Take a walk through the woods and meadows of this large park and you will be transported

↑ The stylish Amalienbad main pool, with stained-glass roof and Secession tiling

---

into another world. A former imperial hunting ground, now an immense nature reserve in the Vienna Woods, the Tiergarten was opened to the public in 1923, and in 1941 the entire area was declared a nature reserve. It is encircled by a 24-km (15-mile) stone wall, protecting its herds of deer and wild boar. From the observation platform on top of Kaltbründlberg there are great views over Vienna.

A 15-minute walk along the paths from the entrance will bring you to the Hermesvilla. In 1885, Emperor Franz Joseph ordered a hunting lodge to be built here and presented it to his wife Elisabeth, in the hope that this would stop her from perpetually seeking to escape the clamour of the city. He did not succeed, but the beautiful Hermesvilla, built by Karl von Hasenauer, served as a retreat for the imperial family. The interior of the Hermesvilla is currently closed to the public.

---

❶⑨

Wotrubakirche

🏛 Georgsgasse, Mauer
🚌 60A ⏰ 2–8pm Sat, 9am–4:30pm Sun & hols
🌐 georgenberg.at

Standing on a hillside close to the Vienna Woods, this church was designed in uncompromisingly modern style in 1965 by the Austrian sculptor Fritz Wotruba (1907–75), after whom it is named. It was built in 1974–6 by Fritz Gerhard Mayr. The church is made up of a pile of uneven concrete slabs and glass panels that are its principal source of light and provide views for the congregation out onto the hills. Raw in style, the building is nonetheless compact; the church looks different from every angle and has a strong sculptural quality. The central section, consisting of 152 concrete blocks, can accommodate a congregation of up to 250.

EXPERIENCE AUSTRIA

Breathtaking Dachstein massif, Styria

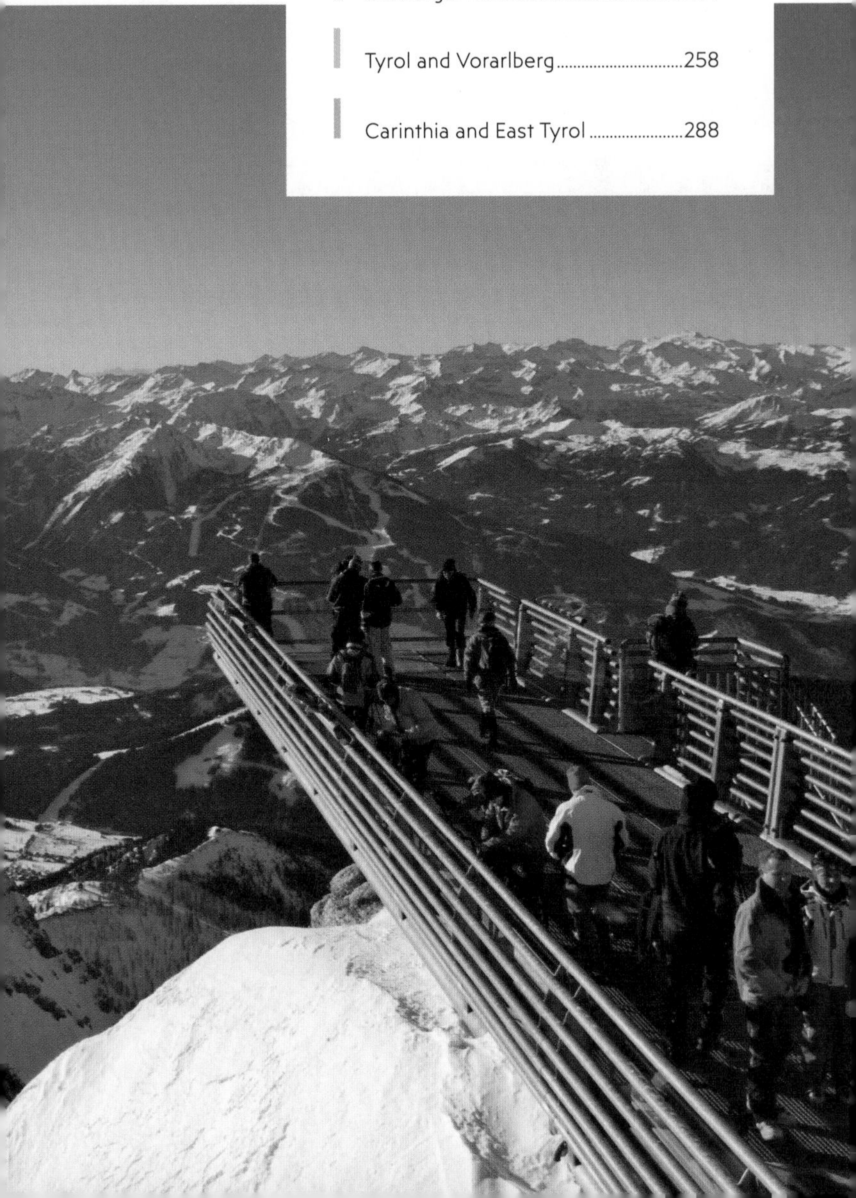

LOWER AUSTRIA AND BURGENLAND

The largest province in Austria, Lower Austria is also the oldest. During Roman times, its southern reaches belonged to the provinces of Noricum and Pannonia, while the areas north of the Danube frequently changed hands as Slavic and Germanic tribes fought over them. From AD 791, Lower Austria belonged to the Franks and, in AD 970, it was given the name Ostmark (Eastern Margravate). Today, it stretches along the Danube valley, from the German border in the west to Hungary in the east.

To the southeast of Lower Austria, from Neusiedler See down, is the narrow province of Burgenland. Historically, it was a part of Hungary, but after the Turkish wars (1529–1791) it was settled by Germans and Croats, and finally incorporated into Austria in 1921. The main town, Eisenstadt, was where the mighty Esterházy family established their seat; they continue to play an important role in the region's development today.

Following a plebiscite in 1986, the provincial capital of Lower Austria was moved from Vienna to St Pölten, making it the newest capital in Europe. This city has been the seat of the Lower Austrian government since 1997.

LOWER AUSTRIA AND BURGENLAND

❶
ST PÖLTEN

A F3 🚌🚊 **i** Rathausplatz 1; www.stpoeltentourismus.at

The capital of Lower Austria since 1986, St Pölten was the first Austrian city to be granted municipal rights, in 1159. Its fastest period of growth was during the Baroque period, when outstanding masters of that era, such as the architect Jakob Prandtauer and the painter Daniel Gran, made their home here. Apart from the beautiful Baroque centre, St Pölten also has more recent architecture to interest enthusiasts.

①
Domkirche Mariä Himmelfahrt

A Domplatz 1 **C** (02742) 353402

In the 12th century, a church dedicated to St Hippolytus stood on this site but it was rededicated to the Assumption of the Virgin Mary in 1228. Destroyed by fire in 1278, and again in 1621, the church was rebuilt in Baroque style. Deceptively plain on the outside, the interior is typical of exuberant Baroque ornamentation. Large paintings depicting the life of Jesus adorn the walls and ceiling.

The Diocesan Museum, on the first floor of the former monastery cloister, houses a collection of sculptures and paintings dating from the Gothic and Baroque periods.

Diocesan Museum

🕙 **C** (02742) 324331
⏰ May-Oct: 10am-noon, 2-5pm Tue-Fri; 10am-1pm Sat

> 💬 INSIDER TIP
> **Film am Dom**
>
> Each evening in July and August, the Rathausplatz hosts an open-air film festival with Cinema Paradiso *(cinema-paradiso.at/st-poelten)*, featuring new blockbusters, classics and Austrian films.

②
Institut der Englischen Fräulein

A Linzer Strasse 9-11
C (02742) 3521880
⏰ Church: 10am-5pm daily

The Institute of the English Ladies, founded by the English Catholic nun Mary Ward (1585–1645), established several schools in St Pölten to educate the girls of aristo-cratic families. The institute, one of the most beautiful Baroque buildings in Lower Austria, was begun in 1715 and enlarged some 50 years later. Prandtauer created the beautiful white and pink façade, punctuated by black wrought-iron grilles on the windows, with three groups of sculptures on two floors.

③
Riemerplatz

Another beautiful Baroque square, Riemerplatz is lined with exquisite buildings such as the striking Herberstein Palace. At No 41 Kremser Gasse stands Stöhr-Haus with its beautiful Art Nouveau façade. It is the work of the architect Joseph Maria Olbrich, who also designed Vienna's Secession Building *(p126)*.

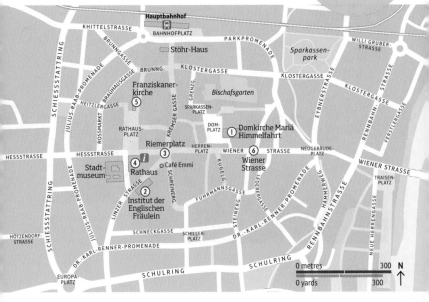

④

Rathaus

🏠 Rathausplatz 1
📞 (02742) 3333000

The present town hall was built in the 16th century by combining two Gothic buildings in a mishmash of styles. While the entire structure has been concealed behind a Baroque façade, it is worth heading inside to see the ceiling stuccowork in the Mayor's Chamber.

The town hall occupies the southern side of Rathausplatz, once considered the most beautiful square in Austria. Today, it is lined with modern buildings, and has lost some of its Baroque charm.

⑤

Franziskanerkirche

🏠 Rathausplatz

A Rococo church with a delightful pink façade, the Franciscan Church of the Holy Trinity is unusual because it has no tower. The interior, also decorated in Rococo style, features four wing paintings by a well-known Austrian Baroque artist, Martin Johann Schmidt, or Kremser Schmidt.

⑥

Wiener Strasse

Wiener Strasse, adjacent to Herrenplatz, has been a main thoroughfare since Roman times, as is still obvious today from its many inns. There are a number of interesting historical buildings in this road, including St Pölten's oldest pharmacy at No 1, dating back to 1595. Its façade, built in 1727 by Joseph Munggenast, still displays the pharmacist's original coat of arms from 1607 and the 19th-century sign "Zum Goldenen Löwen" (To the Golden Lion).

DRINK

Café Emmi
Expert baristas brew fabulous coffee in this bright, contemporary café, complete with huge windows perfect for people-watching. Many of the custom roasts can be bought by the packet to take home.

🏠 Linzer Strasse 1
🕐 Sun 🌐 kaffee bohnenmonster.at

←

The Holy Trinity fountain by the pink Franziskanerkirche in Rathausplatz

↑ The unusual structure of the Bergkirche, one of the town's iconic sights

2

EISENSTADT

🅰 G4 🚉 🚌 🛈 Hauptstrasse 21; www.eisenstadt-tourismus.at

Lying on the southern slopes of the Leitha hills, this small town is mainly associated with the Hungarian Esterházy family and their famous choirmaster, Joseph Haydn. It became the capital of Burgenland province in 1925, and from this date Eisenstadt underwent a remarkable growth. Today it is an important transport hub and wine-making centre.

①
Landesmuseum Burgenland

🅰 Museumgasse 1-5
🕐 Jan-May & Jun-Nov: 9am-5pm Tue-Sun (from 10am Sat, Sun & hols) 🌐 landes museum-burgenland.at

This museum houses a large collection of objects associated with the history and art of the Burgenland province. Its geological collection is the most fascinating, with minerals and exhibits on the local Ice Age fauna. Archaeological findings include the Drassburg Venus, items from burial mounds in Siegendorf and objects that represent the Hallstatt and Roman cultures.

② 〽
Haydn-Haus

🅰 Joseph-Haydn-Gasse 21
🕐 Apr-mid-Nov: 10am-5pm daily 🕐 Apr & May: Mon
🌐 haydn-haus.at

Joseph Haydn fans should not miss the chance to visit the house where the composer lived between 1766 and 1778. Now a small museum, it displays a number of his prized possessions. From 1761, Haydn was employed by the Esterházy family as their *Kapellmeister* (music director), and in the evenings he conducted the court orchestra for performances of his own music. Many of his compositions were first heard in Eisenstadt.

③
Bergkirche

🅰 Joseph-Haydn-Platz 1

In 1715, Prince Paul Esterházy ordered a hill to be created to the west of the castle and of Eisenstadt's centre. He then had this church built on top of that hill, dedicated to the Visitation of the Virgin Mary, with a Way of the Cross made up of 24 stations. The Passion figures are life-size. The most-visited attraction of the church, however, is the tomb of Joseph Haydn. In 1932, on the 200th anniversary of the composer's death, the **Haydnmausoleum** was built here by the Esterházys for the marble sarcophagus containing Haydn's remains.

Haydnmausoleum
〽 🕐 Apr-Oct: 9am-5pm daily

Did You Know?

The Bergkirche still houses the original 18th-century organ played by Haydn and Beethoven.

④
Domkirche

📍 Domplatz 1a

This late-Gothic church was built in the 15th century on the site of an earlier medieval structure. As with many other churches in this part of Austria, its builders were conscious of the permanent threat of Turkish invasion, and its lofty steeple contains lookout holes.

The interior is eclectically decorated. The pulpit and beautiful organ are Baroque, as are the two altar paintings by German-born artist, Stephan Dorfmeister. In 1960, the Domkirche was given cathedral status.

---

⑤
Schloss Esterházy

📍 Esterházyplatz ⏰ Times vary, check website 🌐 esterhazy.at

The star sight in Eisenstadt, the magnificent Esterházy Castle belonged to the powerful local dynasty, the Esterházy family. Built around 1390 on the site of earlier fortifications, it wasn't until the 17th century that the

Italian architect Carlo Martino Carlone transformed it into a Baroque palace. The main attraction inside is the Haydnsaal, a concert hall with amazing acoustics and superbly decorated with frescoes.

Today, the larger part of the castle is leased to the Burgenland provincial authorities. The castle is surrounded by a beautiful English-style park.

---

⑥
Franziskanerkirche

📍 Joseph-Haydn-Gasse

The Franciscan Church of St Michael, built between 1625 and 1630, is home to the crypt of the Esterházy family. There is a Diocesan Museum on the second floor, with changing exhibitions on the church and religious history.

---

⑦
Jüdischer Friedhof

📍 Unterbergstrasse

From medieval times until 1938, a Jewish settlement existed in Eisenstadt. Confined to the district of Unterberg, it played an important role

in the city's development. The two Jewish cemeteries in Eisenstadt are among the best-preserved in Austria, and worth taking the time to visit. The adjacent house, which belonged to Jewish banker Samson Wertheimer, now houses the **Österreichisches Jüdisches Museum**. With an exhibition on the area's Jewish residents, it's an informative stop after the cemeteries.

Österreichisches Jüdisches Museum
♿ 📍 Unterbergstrasse 6 ⏰ Times vary, check website 🚫 24 Dec–6 Jan 🌐 ojm.at

STAY

Parkhotel
Close to the Schloss Esterházy, this hotel offers functional and colourful rooms, some with balconies.

📍 Joseph-Haydn-Gasse 38 🌐 parkhotel-eisenstadt.com

€€€

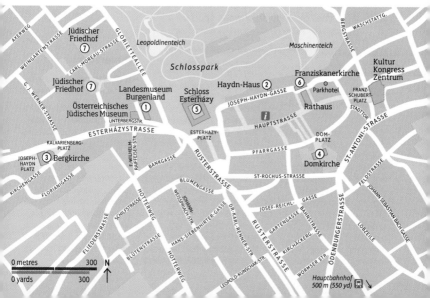

③

NEUSIEDLER SEE

🅰G4 🚆🚌 *ℹ* Neusiedlersee Tourismus; www.neusiedler see.com

The jewel of Burgenland, Neusiedler See is the largest steppe lake in Central Europe. On the border between Austria and Hungary, it covers an area of 320 sq km (124 sq miles), around which lie enchanting towns and melancholy landscapes. Densely overgrown with reeds, the banks are ideal nesting grounds for birds, while the lakeside beaches are popular for water sports.

↑ The sun setting behind Podersdorf's lighthouse and windsurfing on the popular lake *(inset)*

①
Illmitz

🅰 Frauenkirchen 🚌 *ℹ* Obere Hauptstrasse 2-4; www.illmitz.co.at

Situated amidst the marshes of the Seewinkel National Park, Illmitz is one of the sunniest towns in Austria, with 300 days of sunshine per year. It is a good base for exploring the surrounding grass- and wetlands as well as an important centre for birdwatching. Each April, during the spring migration, the national park information centre on the edge of the town hosts the Pannonian Bird Experience, which brings together twitchers from all over the world for a week of birdwatching, including special events for children. Among the more than 300 species to be spotted are spoonbills, pied avocets, curlews, pigmy cormorants and hoopoes. Outside of the migration season the information centre organizes daily tours of the park to see the flora and fauna, including herb-picking excursions. Illmitz also has a large beach popular with bathers, and an idyllic harbour where you can hire boats for short trips on the lake.

②
Podersdorf

🅰🚌 *ℹ* Hauptstrasse 4-8; www.podersdorfamsee.at

With its access to the water unencumbered by the wide band of reeds that separates other villages from the lake, Podersdorf is the most popular resort on the lake's eastern shores. Hikers and cyclists will love the protected landscape, while watersports lovers have plenty to enjoy, with swimming, boating and windsurfing facilities. The market town is also home to a pretty lighthouse.

③
Rust

🏛 **Eisenstadt** 🚌
🚉 **Conradplatz 1; www. freistadt-rust.at**

This attractive town on the western lakeshore has a perfectly preserved old town with many Renaissance and Baroque buildings and a number of cafés and places to eat. The settlement was first mentioned as Ceel in a 1317 deed issued by King Charles I of Hungary, and its name derived from the Hungarian word *szil* (elm), later translated into German as Rüster. Star sights include the town hall and the Fischerkirche, which houses Burgenland's oldest playable organ, dating from 1705, and fragments of medieval frescoes. The town is famous for its wines, especially for Beerenauslese and Ruster Ausbruch, and for the storks that nest on the old town's roofs in spring.

④
Mörbisch am See

🏛 **Eisenstadt** 🚌
🚉 **Hauptstrasse 23; www. seefestspiele-moerbisch.at**

Situated on the border with Hungary, this picturesque town produces an excellent white wine. Its charming, whitewashed houses, laden with flowers, line the main street and are known as Hofgassen. They create a truly unique atmosphere and have been UNESCO-listed since 2003.

Each July and August the town hosts the Mörbisch Operetta Festival, which brings together a rich reper-toire of classical operetta masterpieces performed by leading Austrian and international companies in front of a unique natural setting, on one of Europe's biggest and most spectacular open-air stages.

⑤
Neusiedl am See

🏛 **Neusiedl am See** 🚌
🚉 **Untere Hauptstrasse 7; www.neusiedlamsee.at**

A well-known resort and agricultural centre, Neusiedl is the largest town on the Neusiedler See. It has been devastated twice, first by the Mongols and later, in the 18th century, by anti-Habsburg Hungarians known as Kurucs. The handsome central square includes an impressive Holy Trinity monument designed by architect Elias Hügel and dedicated to the victims of the plague, which ravaged the town in the early 18th century. The ruins of the Tabor defence tower, which date from the 13th century, are worth exploring, and you should not miss the Johanneskapelle, or Hermit Church, close to the railway station. It also has a museum devoted to local fauna and flora.

DRINK

Bergwerk
This cool cellar bar and live music venue serves great white wine spritzers and has good, local beer on tap.

🏠 **Kellergasse 2, Neusiedl am See**
🕗 **8pm–4am Fri & Sat**
🌐 **gebauerkg.at**

Cafe Konditorei Kaiser
Charming café with delicious coffee and fabulous ice cream on Rust's central square. The large terrace is perfect for summer.

🏠 **Rathausplatz 15, Rust**
📞 **(02685) 60722**
🕗 **8am–7pm Fri–Wed**

The superbly vivid exterior of the yellow monastery church

④ ✍ 🚫 🍴 🛍

STIFT MELK

⊠ F3 🚌 **◷ Apr & Oct: 9am-4:30pm; May-Sep: 9am-5:30pm; Nov-Mar: guided tours only** 🛈 **Kremser Strasse 5; www.stiftmelk.at**

Perched dramatically on a high bluff overlooking the Danube, the vast yellow Melk Abbey is Austria's most magnificent Baroque monastery.

The town and abbey of Melk, the original seat of the Babenbergs, tower above the left bank of the Danube, some 60 km (37 miles) west of Vienna. In the 11th century, Leopold II invited the Benedictines from Lambach to Melk and granted them land and the castle, which the monks turned into a fortified abbey. Almost completely destroyed by fire in 1297, the abbey was rebuilt many times. A thorough remodelling of the complex began in 1702, and renowned artists of the day, including Jakob Prandtauer, helped to give the present abbey its impressive Baroque form. A guided tour of the complex, which is home to a monumental 500 rooms, is the best way to see the complex.

🔺 GREAT VIEW
See from Seegarten

Head to the small village of Seegarten, just 6 km (4 miles) northwest across the river, to appreciate the monastery in all its panoramic glory. It's a great view at night.

A spiral staircase with ornamental balustrade connects the library with the Stiftskirche, the monastery church of St Peter and St Paul.

Valuable manuscripts are held in the vast library, which is one of the most important rooms in the abbey.

The magnificent Marble Hall, decorated with a painting by Paul Troger, was once used for receptions and ceremonies.

Site Highlights

Library

▽ The impressive library holds some 100,000 volumes, including 2,000 manuscripts and 1,600 incunabula. It is decorated with a ceiling fresco by Austrian painter Paul Troger.

Crowning with the Crown of Thorns

▽ This powerful painting by the German painter Jörg Breu (1502) is exhibited in the Abbey Museum.

Crucifixes

△ The abbey holds two key crucifixes – one is Romanesque (c 1200), the other from the 14th century, containing a piece of Christ's cross.

Stiftskirche

The main altar in the Baroque monastery church features the church's patron saints, the apostles St Peter and St Paul.

The Prelates' Courtyard is surrounded by imposing buildings crowned with statues of the prophets and frescoes.

The splendid Stiftskirche has an impressive ceiling fresco by the Austrian painter Johann Michael Rottmayr.

Convent courtyard

17th-century two-tiered fountain

A grand staircase leading to the imperial apartments is adorned with putti and sculptures.

The abbey houses an important Romanesque crucifix that dates from the 13th century.

The imperial rooms are home to the vast Abbey Museum, one of the most modern abbey museums in Austria.

↑ Melk's impressive abbey, home to hundreds of amazing rooms

The Gothic Kreuzenstein Castle sitting atop a tree-covered hill near Korneuburg

EXPERIENCE MORE

5

Korneuburg

 G3 🌐 korneuburg.gv.at

Korneuburg once formed a single town with nearby Klosterneuburg, just across the river. In 1298 it became independent, and grew into an important trading and administrative centre.

Hauptplatz, the main square, is surrounded by houses with late Gothic, Renaissance and Baroque façades. Other worthwhile sights include the late Gothic St-Ägidius-Kirche (Church of St Giles) and the Rococo Augustinerkirche (Church of St Augustine), whose main altarpiece shows the sky resting on four columns, with God the Father sitting on his throne, holding the earth in his hand. The altar painting of the *Last Supper* is the work of Franz Anton Maulbertsch.

Burg Kreuzenstein, near Leobendorf village on the road to Stockerau, is a fascinating folly of a Gothic castle. Built in the 19th century by Count Johann Nepomuk Graf Wilczek, on the site of a former fortress (1140) that was almost entirely destroyed by Swedish forces during the Thirty Years' War, it holds the count's extensive collection of late Gothic art and handicrafts.

6

Wiener Neustadt

🅰 G4 🚉 🚌 ℹ️ Neunkirchner Strasse 17; www.wiener-neustadt.at

This large industrial town, some 40 km (25 miles) south of Vienna, was largely devastated during World War II, but a handful of historic buildings remain in the centre of town.

In the attractive Hauptplatz (main square) sits the part-Gothic Rathaus (town hall), which was later rebuilt in the Baroque style. Gothic houses line the northern side of the square, and St Mary's Column (1678) stands in the centre. The Cathedral of the Ascension of Our Lady was built in the 13th century. Its outstanding features include 12 wooden statues of the apostles by the columns of the central nave, and the Baroque main altar. The Brautportal (Portal of the Betrothed) dates from 1230.

Stift Neukloster was founded in 1444 by Emperor Friedrich III. His wife, Eleanor of Portugal, was buried here in 1467. You can still see the beautifully carved headstone by Niklas Gerhaert on her tomb.

The former castle, once the residence of Friedrich III, now houses the prestigious Theresian Military Academy, whose first commander was General Erwin Rommel of the Wehrmacht. In the west wing of the academy is the 15th-century St-Georgs-Kathedrale (St George's Cathedral), which houses the tomb of Emperor Maximilian I under the main

Did You Know?

The Theresian Military Academy in Wiener Neustadt is one of the oldest military academies in the world.

altar. A remnant of the old fortified city walls now houses the Reckturm (Torture Tower), a former jail and torture chamber now serving as a criminology museum, with gruesome exhibitions of instruments of torture.

---

❼

Klosterneuburg

🅰 G3 ⑤🚋🚌 ❶ Niedermarkt 4; www.klosterneuburg. net

This small town, above the Danube, to the north of Vienna, was once the main seat of the Babenberg rulers. In the early 12th century, Margrave Leopold III built his castle here, and later the collegiate church, the magnificent **Stift Klosterneuburg**, supposedly in atonement for an act of treason he had committed against Heinrich V.

The Romanesque church of the Augustinian Abbey was altered several times before it acquired its present Baroque interior, designed by Joseph Fischer von Erlach and Donato Felice d'Allio, among others, in the 17th and 18th centuries. Original features include the early Gothic cloister and burial chapel of Leopold III; the latter contains the town's greatest treasure, an altarpiece by Nicolas of Verdun, a goldsmith and master of enamel from Lorraine. The astonishing Verduner Altar, completed in 1181 after ten years' work, has 51 enamelled panels that are arranged in three horizonal layers, depicting a variety of biblical scenes. The chapel also features some fine stained-glass windows.

In the 18th century, the castle was expanded by Karl VI, who intended to build a grand complex on the same scale as

→

The glorious interior of Klosterneuburg abbey church

the Escorial palace near Madrid. The work was halted after his death in 1740.

The museum, housed on the second floor in what are known as the Archdukes' Rooms of the former imperial residence, holds a valuable collection of Gothic and Baroque sculptures.

Stift Klosterneuburg

🐾🐾 🅰 Stiftsplatz 1 🕐 May–mid-Nov: 9am–6pm daily; mid-Nov-Apr: 10am–5pm daily 🆆 stift-klosterneuburg.at

---

❽

Spitz

🅰 F3 🚋🚌 ❶ Mittergasse 3a; (02713) 2363

Spitz, a Protestant stronghold during the Reformation, is a charming town that lies at the foot of the 1,000-Eimer Berg (1,000-Bucket Mountain, so called because of the amount of wine it was said to produce). The Danube was once key to

the town's economic life, and the **Schifffahrtsmuseum** explores this history.

Another famous sight is the late Gothic Pfarrkirche. The church has a presbytery (1508), crisscross vaulting and elaborate window lacework. High above the town looms the ruin of Hinterhaus Castle, with its Gothic bulwark and Renaissance fortifications.

Schifffahrtsmuseum

🅰 Auf der Wehr 21 🕐 Apr-Oct: 10am–4pm daily 🆆 schifffahrtsmuseum-spitz.at

9

Dürnstein

AF3 **🚗🚌** **ℹ**Dürnstein 25;
www.duernstein.at

Much of the popularity of the idyllic town of Dürnstein is due to the adventures of the medieval monarch Richard I of England, known as Richard the Lionheart. On the Third Crusade, undertaken with the French king Philip August and the Austrian margrave Leopold V, Richard fell out with his fellow crusaders. On his journey home through Babenberg territories in 1192, he was imprisoned in Kuenringer castle above Dürnstein, whose ruins can still be seen today. As legend has it, the King's faithful French minstrel, Jean Blondel, discovered him with a song known only to the two of them. A large ransom was paid and Richard was released. The Babenbergs used the money to fortify Enns, Hainburg, Wiener Neustadt and Vienna, while the name of the faithful servant lives on in many of Dürnstein's establishments.

The towering silhouette of the **Stiftskirche Dürnstein** (Dürnstein Abbey) was masterminded by Provost Hieronymus Übelbacher in 1710. Building on the modest foundations of the original 1372 chapel and cloisters, Übelbacher oversaw its transformation into a Baroque treasure.

> Much of the popularity of the idyllic town of Dürnstein is due to the adventures of legendary medieval monarch Richard I of England, known as Richard the Lionheart.

The former convent of St Claire is now an inn; the Renaissance castle now serves as a hotel.

Stiftskirche Dürnstein

⊛ **A**Dürnstein **🕐**Apr-Oct: 9am-6pm Mon-Sun (from 10am Sun & hols); Nov-Mar: by appt **🌐**stiftduernstein.at

---

10 **Ⓜ**

Laxenburg

AG3 **🚌** **ℹ**Schlossplatz 7-8;
www.laxenburg.at

This small town, situated 15 km (9 miles) outside Vienna, is a favourite spot for daytrips from the capital. It began as Lachsenburg hunting lodge, around which a settlement grew. Destroyed during the Turkish siege, but restored and enlarged in the late 17th century, it became a favourite retreat for Maria Theresa and other members of the imperial family. Laxenburg was chosen as a venue for the signing of many important state treaties, including the Pragmatic Sanction, which made it possible for a woman, (specifically Maria Theresa), to accede to the throne. Today, the former imperial palace is the seat of the International Institute for Applied Systems Analysis (IIASA), and houses the Austrian Film Archives. The palace is surrounded by the meticulously landscaped English-style Schlosspark, one of the grandest such palace parks in Europe.

The park is dotted with several extravagant buildings. Of particular note is the early 19th-century Franzensburg, a mock-Gothic castle built on an island in an artificial lake. The castle was furnished with original objects collected and pillaged from all over the empire, such as the chapel's 12th-century columns from Klosterneuburg, and the ceiling of the coronation room from the Hungarian town of Eger. Guided tours are available from April to November.

↓ Sunset over the town of Dürnstein by the Danube river

⑪ Weissenkirchen

🅰 F3 🅿🚌 ⓦ weissen kirchen.at

Since 1900, this small village in the heart of the Wachau Valley has been a magnet for artists, who come to paint the magnificent scenery of the Danube gorge and enjoy the cosy inns. Today, their works hang in the **Wachaumuseum**, situated in the Teisenhoferhof, a Renaissance mansion. Sitting on a hilltop is the Pfarrkirche Mariä Himmelfahrt (Church of the Assumption of the Virgin Mary) – the "white church" from which the village takes its name. The building as its stands was put together in several phases between the 13th and 18th centuries, the larger tower being built in 1531 as a defence against Turkish invaders. The main entrance is through the western portal, which is enhanced with fine mouldings. Inside, on the rainbow arch, is a beautiful 16th-century painting of the Madonna, a product of the Danube School.

Situated between Weissenkirchen and Spitz is the small village of St Michael, which boasts another fine example

↑ The Holy Trinity plague column dominating the main square of Baden bei Wien

of a fortified church, from around 1500. A few miles beyond Spitz is Willendorf, where the famous statuette of the *Venus of Willendorf* was found. This representation of female fertility is believed to be over 25,000 years old. The figure itself is now on show at Vienna's Naturhistorisches Museum *(p114)*, while an over-sized copy stands in a field near Willendorf.

Wachaumuseum

⊛ 📞 (02715) 2268 ⏰ Apr-Oct: 10am–5pm Tue–Sun

⑫ Baden bei Wien

🅰 G4 🅿🛥🚌
ℹ Brusattiplatz 3; www. tourismus.baden.at

The spa town of Baden, on the eastern slopes of the Vienna Woods, was already well-known in Roman times, when it was called Aquae Pannoniae and Emperor Marcus Aurelius praised it for its restorative springs. As well as bathing in sulphurous water and mud to treat rheumatism, you can enjoy a dip in the soothing 36°C (97°F) hot pools. You can also sample local wines in Baden's charming restaurants.

The small town was completely rebuilt after a fire in 1812, and many of its attractive Neo-Classical town houses and Biedermeier-style villas hail from this period. The main architect at the time, Joseph Kornhäusel (1786–1860), largely shaped the look of the town.

At one time, the list of Baden visitors read like a *Who's Who* of the rich and famous, and included such luminaries as Wolfgang Amadeus Mozart, who composed his *Ave Verum* here; Franz Schubert; and Ludwig van Beethoven. It was here that he composed his Ninth Symphony. Baden was frequented by the maestros of Viennese operetta as well: Strauss (the Elder and the Younger), Lanner and Zeller. Napoleon also holidayed here with his wife Marie Louise.

> 💬 INSIDER TIP
> **Concerts at a Casino**
>
> Casino Baden *(www. casinos.at/baden)* in Baden bei Wien is one of the oldest and grandest in Europe, but it offers more than gaming: opera and classical concerts are also regularly held at the site.

EAT

Laxenburger Hof
Owned and run by the Eigner family since 1987, this quintes-sentially Austrian eatery boasts a large street terrace and serves great schnitzel alongside a terrific range of strudels.

🅰 G3 🏠 Schlossplatz 17, Laxenburg ⓦ laxen burgerhof.at

150,000

The number of books and manuscripts archived in the Stift Göttweig library.

13

Stift Göttweig

F3 **Mid-Mar-Oct: 8am-6pm daily** **stift goettweig.at**

Stift Göttweig, a Benedictine abbey, crowns a hilltop on the south bank of the Danube, near Krems. Founded in 1083, it was inhabited by Benedictine monks from St Blasien in the Black Forest from 1094. In religious circles, Stift Göttweig is referred to as the Austrian Monte Cassino – superficially, it resembles the Italian monastery in which St Benedict founded his movement.

After a devastating fire in 1718, imperial architect Johann Lukas von Hildebrandt drew up plans for an ambitious new monastery. The project was never completed, however, and the present abbey has an interesting but somewhat asymmetrical outline. In 1739, a magnificent flight of stairs, known as Kaiserstiege (imperial staircase), was added to the western section of the abbey. The stairs are lined with statues representing the four seasons and the twelve months of the year, and the ceiling is adorned with a fresco by Paul Troger, depicting the Apotheosis of Karl VI. At the top of the stairs, you will find the **Museum im Kaisertrakt** (Museum in the Imperial Wing). As well as exhibits on the history of the abbey and of Göttweig, the museum has a great collection of sculptures, paintings and music. The abbey restaurant specializes in Austrian dishes and enjoys unbeatable views of the surroundings.

Museum im Kaisertrakt

Mid-Mar-Oct: 10am-6pm daily (Jun-Sep: from 9am) **stiftgoettweig.or.at**

14

Tulln

F3 **Minoritenplatz 2; www. tulln.at**

Tulln, on the right bank of the Danube river, was the site of the Roman camp of Comagena and is one of the oldest towns in Austria. Two structures remain from that period: the 3rd-century Roman Tower, probably the oldest structure in Austria, and a milestone. The remains of the old city walls are also still preserved.

Tulln is famous as the birthplace of Egon Schiele, one of the foremost painters of the early 20th century, best known for his provocative nudes. The **Egon-Schiele-Museum**, housed in an old prison on the banks of the Danube, exhibits some 90 original works by the artist.

The former monastery, Minoritenkloster, houses Tulln's town hall, as well as the modest but engaging **Zuckermuseum**, on the top floor, which traces the history of sugar.

The Romanesque Pfarrkirche St Stephan was built in the 12th century but subsequently altered, first in Gothic, then in Baroque style. It has an alluring Romanesque portal with 12 reliefs, thought to represent the apostles. Next to the church is the 13th-century mortuary, one of the more compelling historic sites in town. It holds the impressive cemetery chapel of the Three Wise Men, combining elements of late Romanesque style with early Gothic, and featuring a beautifully decorated portal.

Egon-Schiele-Museum

Donaulände 28 **Apr-Oct: 10am-5pm Tue-Sun & hols on request** **schielemuseum.at**

Zuckermuseum

Minoritenplatz 1 **8am-3:30pm Mon-Wed, 8am-7pm Thu, 8am-noon Fri** **erleben.tulln.at**

↑ The grandiose imperial staircase and ceiling fresco of Stift Göttweig

BENEDICTINE ABBEYS

The first Benedictine abbey in Austria was founded in the 8th century, but it was not until the 11th century that the order became a major force. Its growth was linked to the importance given to the Austrian state under the rule of the Babenbergs, whose history was chronicled by the Benedictines.

Altenburg Abbey
Built in the 12th century and altered in Baroque style in the 18th century, Altenburg Abbey is adorned with statues and paintings.

Kremsmünster Abbey
This abbey *(p224)* contains a tombstone with the figure of Knight Gunther. The inscription details how his father founded the abbey in 777, following his son's death.

St Paul im Lavanttal Abbey
This fine abbey *(p299)* houses one of the most extensive Benedictine libraries, with over 40,000 volumes and manuscripts.

Stift Melk
One of the most magnificent abbeys in Austria, Melk Abbey *(p160)* affords fabulous views far across the Danube and the surrounding countryside.

① The pathway leading up to Altenburg Abbey.

② Frescoes at Kremsmünster Abbey.

③ Kremsmünster Abbey's façade.

④ Eerie crypt at St Paul im Lavanttal.

⑤ Gold leaf interior at Melk Abbey.

Blossoming pear trees on a hill by a church in Neuhofen an der Ybbs ↑

15

Neuhofen an der Ybbs

△E4 ᠁ Ⓦneuhofen-ybbs.at

Neuhofen is a small town by the Ybbs river, in the foothills of the Alps. Its centre is occupied by the Gothic Pfarrkirche Mariä Himmelfahrt (Church of the Assumption of the Virgin Mary) whose spire looms high above the main square. The town was once a stopping place for pilgrims travelling to nearby Sonntagberg, whose Baroque basilica is an important place of worship for Austrian Catholics.

The **Ostarrichi Kulturhof**, a museum of Austrian history on the outskirts of the village, is the town's top attraction.

💬 INSIDER TIP
Freibad Neuhofen

If you're looking to cool off amid gorgeous, forested surroundings, visit Freibad Neuhofen - a large outdoor pool in Neuhofen an der Ybbs, open from mid-May to late August.

The conspicuously modern red and white building was erected in 1980 to designs by Ernst Beneder, who also landscaped the surroundings in an attempt to make new and old blend in a single composition. The museum was assembled in record time, and in 1996 it was the hub of Austria's 1,000th anniversary celebrations.

The principal exhibit, from which the centre takes its name, is a facsimile of the first known document to use the term *Ostarrichi* (the original document is kept in archives in Munich). In this instrumental document, dated 1 November 996, Emperor Otto III (ruler of the German Roman Empire) presented the land around Neuhofen, known as Ostarrichi in the local language, to the Bishop of Freising in Bavaria. It was the first time that this name was used to describe the land that was controlled by the Babenbergs and which would eventually, in the 11th–12th centuries, become Austria. The Bishops of Freising had owned estates here from as early as the 9th century. The names Osterriche and Osterland, which appeared later, referred to the land east of the Enns river. It is fairly likely that originally the name referred to the entire country of Eastern Franconia. The modern name Österreich (Austria), is said to derive from Ostarrichi. According to the most widely believed interpretation, it meant "eastern territories", but an alternative view also exists: at the time when the name Ostarrichi first appeared, the area in this part of the Danube valley was still populated by Slavic tribes, and the names of many surrounding towns and villages reveal a Slavic origin. It is possible that Ostarrichi, as it was then, comes from the Slav word *ostrik*, meaning "hill".

Did You Know?

Despite its name, Neuhofen an der Ybbs does not lie directly on the River Ybbs.

→

The awe-inspiring façade and formal gardens of the 17th-century Schloss Hof

Whichever interpretation is accurate, the year 996 is recognized here as the beginning of Austrian history, and the Neuhofen Museum presents the story of the remarkable rise of a small German duchy to the heights of European power as the multi-ethnic Habsburg Empire, and the tangled web of history that, in 1918, led to the creation of the Austrian Republic.

The permanent exhibition in the Kulturhof consists of three parts. The first shows the facsimile of the original Latin Ostarrichi document coupled with a German translation and photographs. The second exhibition is devoted to the word's etymological journey, including its geographical, linguistic and political transformations. The third part of the exhibition takes a look at present-day Austria and its provinces. It illustrates how the distinct areas grew together into the Austrian Republic of today, and how each province has managed to preserve its own regional identity, as well as its unique customs, traditions, arts and culture.

Ostarrichi Kulturhof

 A Millenniumsplatz 1 **O** Mid-Apr–Oct: 9am–noon Mon, Tue, Thu & Fri; 10am–noon, 1–5pm Sat, Sun & hols **W** ostarrichi-kulturhof.at

---

16

Schloss Schallaburg

A F3 **□** **O** 9am–5pm Mon–Sun (to 6pm Sat, Sun & hols) **W** schallaburg.at

Schallaburg Castle is up there with some of the most magnificent Renaissance castles in Lower Austria. It features some early remains of its medieval Romanesque and Gothic architecture, but these are overshadowed by later additions. Particularly impressive are the lovely Renaissance courtyard and the red and white arcades. Carved terracotta atlantes support the second storey; sculptures and terracotta masks decorate the lower niches and walls of the castle. Wilhelm von Losenstein, who owned the castle when the arcades were created, was a Protestant and a humanist, a fact that is reflected in the works commissioned by him.

At the end of World War II, the castle was completely destroyed by the Russians, and it was not until 1970, when it came into state administration, that work began to return it to its former glory.

Today, Schallaburg houses Lower Austria's Cultural and Educational Centre, and serves as an excellent venue for exhibitions and lectures.

STAY

Gasthof Prinz Eugen
Homely rooms in a bright yellow *Gasthof* at the entrance to the Schloss Hof. Simply furnished but hugely comfortable.

A G3 **A** Prinz Eugen-Strasse 1 **W** amerlingbeisl.at

€€€

Goldene Krone
Relaxed, family-run guest house in a 15th-century mansion. Great value and well located for visiting both Göttweig Abbey and Dürnstein Castle.

A F3 **A** Untere Landstrasse 1, Göttweig **W** wachau-burger.at

€€€

17

Schloss Hof

A G3 **□** From Marchegg **O** 10am–6pm daily (mid-Nov–mid-Mar: to 4pm) **W** schlosshof.at

The restored Schloss Hof has long made for an appealing day trip from the capital city. In 1725 Prince Eugene of Savoy made the palace into his principal country seat and laid out a gorgeous, formal country garden that survives to this day.

Extended a generation later under Empress Maria Theresa, the palace contains state and private rooms from both these periods. The vast complex also includes an idyllic estate farm with herb gardens, craft workshops and numerous attractions for the young, including adventure paths, children's theatre and a zoo.

18

Burgruine Aggstein

F3 🚌🚃 **Mid-Mar-late Oct: 9am-6pm daily** **ruineaggstein.at**

The impressive ruins of Aggstein Castle, built into a rocky promontory high above the banks of the Danube, is a popular destination for day trips from Vienna.

Today the castle lies in ruins, but once it measured some 100 m (330 ft) in length, with tall stairs leading to the Upper Castle. Built by the notorious Kuenringers, a band of robber barons, many gruesome stories are told about the castle's early days. Its owner was said to have lain in wait for passing barges and demanded a hefty toll to grant them passage. Those who refused were imprisoned in the Rosengärtlein, a rose garden on a rocky shelf, where they would either die of hunger or jump to their death.

📷 PICTURE PERFECT
Danube Believe It

Taking a great shot of the many twists and turns of the Danube from Burg Aggstein looks easy, but it can be difficult to get the light just right. Sunset is the perfect time to try.

The castle served to repel attacks by Turks and Swedes during the 16th and 17th centuries, thus cementing its rank as one of the most important fortresses in the region.

19

Amstetten

E3 🚉🚌 **amstetten. noe.gv.at**

A major transport hub, the town of Amstetten is situated on the Ybbs River near the border with Upper Austria. Originally known as Amistein, the town witnessed the arrival

of Illyrian, Celtic and Roman settlers over time. It is the largest town in the Mostviertel region and boasts an attractive town hall, the 15th-century Church of St Stephen, with frescoes depicting the Last Judgement, and the Gothic Church of St Agatha. The **Mostviertler Bauernmuseum**, set in a former farmhouse, covers traditional country life.

Just 6 km (4 miles) southwest of town is the medieval Schloss Ulmerfeld, first recorded in the 10th century. From the 14th century until 1803, the castle belonged to the bishops of Freising. It now operates as a cultural centre with an arms collection.

Mostviertler Bauernmuseum

🚸🚸 **Gigerreith 39** **(07479) 73341** **By appt**

20

Waidhofen an der Ybbs

E4 🚉🚌 **waidhofen.at**

In the 16th century, this little town in the Ybbs valley was an important centre of iron processing and arms production. Its medieval old

The impressive ruins of Aggstein Castle, built into a hill above the river *(inset)* ↓

↑ The River Ybbs flowing through the medieval town of Waidhofen

town is dominated by church spires and two 13th-century towers, Ybbsturm and Stadtturm. These were raised by 50 m (164 ft) in 1534 to celebrate the town's victory over the Turks, and since then, the clock on the north side of Stadtturm has shown 11:45am, the exact time of victory. The **5e Museum** in Rothschild Castle tells the story of Waidhofen's history and offers state-of-the-art interactive exhibits.

Some 30 km (20 miles) southeast of Waidhofen, the **Kartause Gaming** is a former Carthusian monastery founded in 1332 by Prince Albrecht II, Duke of Austria, who is buried here. The monks' cells and the fortified walls with round turrets remain to this day. Today, the monastery is used as a hotel, a museum and as a Franciscan University campus. The Kartause's outstanding concert hall hosts the annual Chopin Festival in late summer.

5e Museum
♿🕙 ⬛ Schlossweg 2
🕐 May-Sep: 9am-1pm & 2pm-5pm Tue-Sat, 9am-1pm Sun
🌐 schloss-rothschild.at/5emuseum

Kartause Gaming
⬛ Kartause 1, off Ötscherlandstrasse 🌐 kartause-gaming.at

㉑
Krems
🅰F3 🚆🚌 ℹ Utzstrasse 1; www.krems.gv.at

During the 11th and 12th centuries, Krems, then known as Chremis, was considered a serious rival to Vienna. Today, this attractive town, together with neighbouring Stein, still attracts visitors, enchanted by the wonderous architecture of its town houses and courtyards, which give Krems a southern Italian feel. There are remains of the old town walls, but the greatest attraction is the late-Gothic Piaristenkirche, an imposing Piarist church built on the foundations of an older church. It boasts a stunning Baroque altarpiece by local artist Martin Johann Schmidt, known as Kremser Schmidt. The Pfarrkirche St Veit is the oldest Baroque church in Austria, the work of master builder Cypriano Biasino. A covered walkway connects the two churches – a convenient reason to visit both together.

The Kunstmeile Krems (Krems Art Mile) stretches from Krems's historic center to Stein's, taking in the Museumkrems, housed in the former Dominican abbey, which offers exhibits on local history and its world-famous wine and mustard making; the Kunsthalle, an exhibition house for modern and contemporary art exhibitions; and the Klangraum Krems Minoritenkirche, which specializes in contemporary music performances and sound art installations. Krems also boasts a Renaissance town hall and the vast 13th-century Gozzoburg palace.

EAT

Donauprinzessin
Good coffee, great ice cream and fabulous pizza in a traditional Lower Austrian house with a terrace.

🅰F3 ⬛ Rollfährestrasse 9, Spitz 🕐 Sun 🌐 donauprinzessin.at

Aggsteinerhof
Sensational apricot pie and cheese strudel are the picks of the menu at this traditional Austrian eatery.

🅰F3 ⬛ Aggstein 13, Aggsbach Dorf 🌐 aggsteinerhof.at

€€€

Schlosstaverne
Serves an amazing homemade goulash as well as dishes featuring local wild mushrooms.

🅰G3 ⬛ Schloss Rohrau 1, Rohrau 🌐 schlosstaverne-rohrau.at

€€€

Harrachkeller
Enjoy huge portions of homemade cooking and a good range of local wines and craft beer.

🅰G4 ⬛ Schlossgasse 8, Gemeinde Bruck 🌐 harrachkeller.at

22 Bruck an der Leitha

🅰 G4 🚌🚆 ℹ Hauptplatz 16; www.bruckleitha.at

This small town, situated 30 km (19 miles) east of Vienna, was established as a Babenberg fortress in 1230 and formed the main border between Austria and Hungary. Its present form dates mainly from the turn of the 17th century, but the remains of the medieval fortifications from the 13th century, as well as several old houses, survive in the main square today.

The most attractive feature on the square is the Baroque Pfarrkirche, built by Heinrich Hoffmann. Standing outside the church are two striking plague columns, one dedicated to the Virgin Mary and the other to the Holy Trinity. The square is also home to Bruck's handsome town hall, with a Rococo balcony and an arcaded courtyard. In Friedrich-Schiller-Gasse stands the Kapuziner-kloster, the Capuchin Friary, whose church dates from 1629.

The Prugg, a 13th-century castle with an original early Gothic turret, is by far the town's greatest architectural attraction. In 1707, Johann Lukas von Hildebrandt altered the castle in the Baroque style.

The Stadtmuseum Ungarturm, located in a 13th-century tower on Burgenlandstrasse, exhibits prehistoric and Roman finds, along with armaments and handicrafts. It also provides some background on the town's rich history.

---

23 Burg Forchtenstein

🅰 G4 🚉 Mattersburg 🚌
🏰 Melinda Esterhazy-Platz 1
🕙 Apr–Oct: 10am–6pm daily
🌐 esterhazy.at

Perched unassailably on the rocky slopes of Rosaliengebirge stands Forchtenstein Castle.

Built in the 14th century by the Mattersdorfer family and extended by the Esterházys, it played a key role in defending the Habsburg state during the Turkish raids of 1529 and 1683. Having helped to repel the Turkish threat, the fortified castle became a museum in 1815 and houses an extensive private collection of weaponry. The castle armoury exhibits arms and war trophies dating from the 16th to the 19th centuries as well as memora-bilia and pictures from the wars with Turkey, France and Prussia. Worthy of note are the painstakingly preserved murals in the inner courtyard, once serving as the castle's banqueting hall. The equestrian statue in the courtyard is of Paul, the first prince of the Esterházy family, which still owns the castle today.

The village of Raiding, 24 km (15 miles) to the south of Forchtenstein, is home to a cottage that was the birthplace of composer Franz Liszt, born here in 1811. The house is now a museum, **Liszt-Haus Raiding**. Every March, Raiding hosts the Liszt Festival in the wood-panelled concert hall next door to celebrate the composer's music.

Liszt-Haus Raiding

♿🕙 🏰 Lisztstrasse 46
🕙 Mid-Mar–mid-Nov: 9am–5pm Tue–Fri (Jun–mid-Nov: also Mon), 10am–5pm Sat, Sun & hols 🌐 liszt-haus.at

---

24 Hainburg an der Donau

🅰 G3 🚌🚆 ℹ Ungarstrasse 3; www.info.hainburg-donau.gv.at

Hainburg on the Danube was once a fortified border town of the Eastern Margravate,

←

The Baroque Pfarrkirche and Mary column in Bruck an der Leitha

↑ The historic Schloss Rohrau and a painting of Karl II from its art collection *(inset)*

and still serves as a gateway into Austria from the east. The ruins of an 11th-century castle and three substantial town gates remain from this period. The small town has many historic sights, such as the Romanesque cemetery chapel and the Rococo Mary column in Hauptplatz. By far the most enjoyable way to travel to Hainburg is along the Danube from Vienna: the marshy area around the town and to the west of Hainburg is a nature reserve, and home to rare bird species no longer seen elsewhere. The area west of Hainburg is preserved as a nature reserve.

Some 38 km (24 miles) east of Vienna is the village of Petronell-Carnuntum, where archaeologists unearthed the former capital of the Roman province of Pannonia and the remains of a military camp. The sights open to visitors in **Carnuntum Archaeological Park** include a Roman triumphal arch known as Heidentor (Heathens' Gate), public baths, a reconstructed town villa and two huge amphitheatres.

The ruins of ancient Carnuntum extend to the nearby town of Bad Deutsch-Altenburg, where many of the unearthed objects are on display in the excellent **Museum Carnuntinum**, one of the largest archaeological museums in Austria.

Carnuntum Archaeological Park

♿ 🕐 Mid-Mar–mid-Nov: 9am–5pm daily 🛈 Petronell-Carnuntum, Hauptstrasse 296; www.carnuntum.at

Museum Carnuntinum

♿ 🏛 Bad Deutsch-Altenburg, Badgasse 40–46 🕐 Mid-Mar–mid-Nov: 9am–5pm daily 🌐 carnuntum.at

Did You Know?

Rohrau has the world's oldest monument to Joseph Haydn: a bust in front of the parish church.

25

Rohrau

🄰 G3 🚌 Bad Deutsch Altenburg, Petronell

East of Vienna lies the small town of Rohrau, whose two claims to fame are the **Haydn-Geburtshaus**, composer Joseph Haydn's birthplace, and the Harrach family castle, **Schloss Rohrau**. The charming thatched farmhouse in which the composer and his brother Michael were born is now a small museum devoted to both composers. Concerts and a variety of other cultural events celebrating the work of the Hadyns are often held in the atmospheric courtyard.

The nearby stately home of Schloss Rohrau houses a beautiful private art gallery with a splendid collection of 17th- and 18th-century paintings from Spain, Italy and the Netherlands. The castle dates from the 16th century but was rebuilt in the 18th century.

Haydn-Geburtshaus

♿🕐 🕐 Apr–Oct: 10am–5pm Tue–Sun & hols 🌐 haydn geburtshaus.at

Schloss Rohrau

♿🕐 🕐 Easter–Oct: 10am–5pm Fri–Sun 🌐 schloss-rohrau.at

A DRIVING TOUR
WALDVIERTEL TOUR

Length 155 km (95 miles) **Stopping-off points** Zwettl has a useful tourist office and some good restaurants

Bitterly fought over by Germans and Slavs, who both wanted to settle here and exploit the area's natural resources, Austria's Waldviertel region is home to numerous historic sights, from abbeys built as defensive structures to the magnificent residences of the nobility built during times of peace. The wooded region became known as an idyllic spot for hunting trips and excursions, and today it is still its natural beauty and recreational facilities that make it a fantastic route for driving. Traditional crafts are also practised in the area's villages.

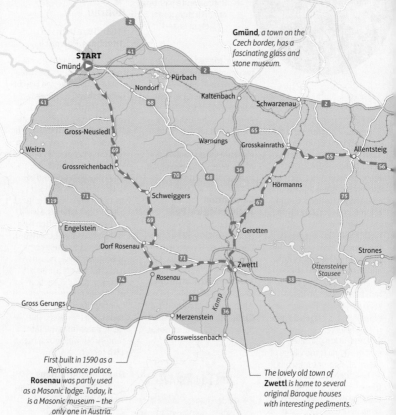

Gmünd, a town on the Czech border, has a fascinating glass and stone museum.

First built in 1590 as a Renaissance palace, **Rosenau** was partly used as a Masonic lodge. Today, it is a Masonic museum – the only one in Austria.

The lovely old town of **Zwettl** is home to several original Baroque houses with interesting pediments.

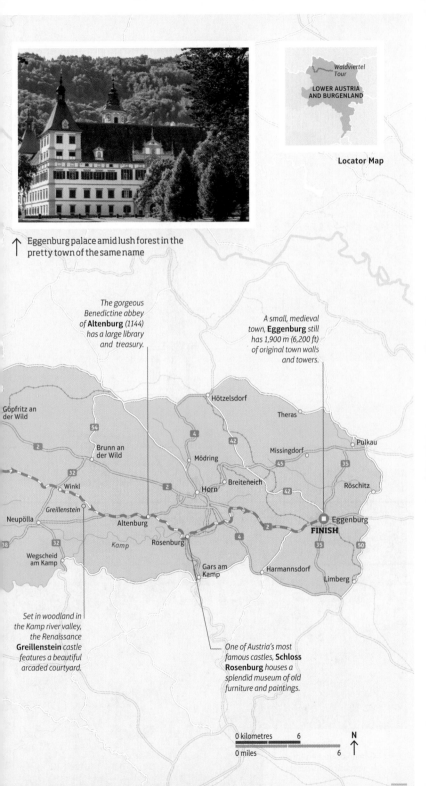

↑ Eggenburg palace amid lush forest in the pretty town of the same name

The gorgeous Benedictine abbey of **Altenburg** (1144) has a large library and treasury.

A small, medieval town, **Eggenburg** still has 1,900 m (6,200 ft) of original town walls and towers.

Göpfritz an der Wild

Hötzelsdorf

Theras

54

Brunn an der Wild

2

Winkl

Mödring

Missingdorf

Pulkau

45

Greillenstein

Horn

Breiteneich

Röschitz

Neupölla

32

Altenburg

42

35

38

Kamp

Rosenburg

2

Eggenburg
FINISH

Wegscheid am Kamp

Gars am Kamp

4

Harmannsdorf

35

50

Limberg

Set in woodland in the Kamp river valley, the Renaissance **Greillenstein** *castle features a beautiful arcaded courtyard.*

One of Austria's most famous castles, **Schloss Rosenburg** *houses a splendid museum of old furniture and paintings.*

0 kilometres   6

0 miles   6

N
↑

The Schloss Gumpoldskirchen amid verdant countryside ↑

A DRIVING TOUR
WIENERWALD

LOWER AUSTRIA
AND BURGENLAND

Wienerwald

Locator Map

Length 60 km (35 miles) **Stopping-off points** Gumpoldskirchen and Baden are home to the best restaurants.

The Vienna Woods (Wienerwald), to the west of the capital, are a favourite weekend destination for the Viennese. Crossed by numerous walking and cycling tracks, the wooded hills, covering an area of 1,250 sq km (480 sq miles), are a perfect place for recreation. A drive through the area is one of the best ways to take in the unique scenery, varied wildlife and pretty towns.

*The small, picturesque town of **Mödling**, once a retreat for artists, is situated in natural scenery of limestone rocks.*

Burg Liechtenstein in Maria Enzersdorf, built in 1166, has been altered many times and now resembles a Gothic castle.

*After the death of Crown Prince Rudolf and his lover, Mary von Vetsera, at **Mayerling** hunting lodge in 1889, Franz Joseph had it converted into a Carmelite chapel.*

*The Cistercian abbey (1133) at **Heiligenkreuz** has retained its Romanesque-Gothic character.*

Brunn am Gebirge

A21

Burg Liechtenstein

Hinterbrühl

Maria Enzersdorf

Mödling

12

17

△ Phönixberg 498 m (1,633 ft)

11

△ Steinwand 491 m (1,610 ft)

151

Alland

A21

Heiligenkreuz

Mödlingbach

11

Gaaden

△ Buchkogel 639 m (2,096 ft)

FINISH Gumpoldskirchen

Mayerling

△ Windhagberg 473 m (1,551 ft)

Siegenfeld

△ Hühnerberg 437 m (1,433 ft)

151

△ Bischofsmütze 515 m (1,689 ft)

210

Schwechat

2099

4010

Pfaffstätten

*The small wine-making town **Gumpoldskirchen** is famous for its many Heurigen (wine bars).*

△ Allandriegel 693 m (2,273 ft)

△ Blasenhöhe 653 m (2,240 ft)

△ Badner Lindkogel 582 m (1,909 ft)

Traiskirchen

△ Hoher Lindkogel 834 m (2,736 ft)

Baden bei Wien

△ Vorderer Lindkogel 666 m (2,185 ft)

210

210

17

Sooss

A2

212

START ▷ Bad Vöslau

*Poised on the southern slopes of the Vienna Woods, **Bad Vöslau** has two claims to fame: its wines and its baths.*

__Baden bei Wien__ (p165) is one of Europe's most famous spa towns.

Did You Know?

It is unknown whether Rudolf and Mary von Vetsera committed suicide or were killed at Mayerling.

0 kilometres   4

0 miles   4

N ↑

STYRIA

It was the Romans who first made Styria a wealthy region, mining iron ore in an area they called Noricum. The mineral shaped the history of the province through the centuries, and is mined, in open pits such as that at Eisenerz, to this day. Following the highs and lows of the early Middle Ages – during which time Germanic tribes supplanted early Slavic settlers, pushing them south, Styria fell into the hands of the Habsburg dynasty in the 13th century and shared in its fate and fortunes. The province was repeatedly ravaged by Hungarians and Turks, and, after having finally staved off the Turkish threat in the 17th century, also became susceptible to attacks by the French. A legacy of these times are its numerous hilltop castle strongholds and imposing fortified abbeys. While some have survived intact, others have been meticulously restored to their former splendour to capture the imagination of visitors to the region.

The construction of the Semmering Railway in 1854 ushered in a modern era, helping to make the region popular with tourists. In the early 21st century Styria received a boost to its economy following the adoption of the historic centre of Graz, the region's capital, as a UNESCO World Heritage Site in 1999.

LOWER AUSTRIA
AND BURGENLAND
p150

NIEDER-ÖSTERREICH

Annaberg

Kernhof

Wildalpen

Gusswerk

4 MARIAZELL
BASILIKA

STYRIA

Seewiesen

Mürz

MÜRZZUSCHLAG **7**

Mönichkirchen

Eisenerz

Krieglach

Aflenz
Kurort

21 EISENERZER
ALPEN

Kindberg

Feistritz

Friedberg

Trofaiach

Kapfenberg

STIFT VORAU **8**

LÉOBEN **26**

6 BRUCK AN DER MUR

Liesingtal

Birkfeld

Hartberg

Oberwart

STEIERMARK

5 FROHNLEITEN

13 PÖLLAU

Anger

Ubelbach

9 LURGROTTE

SCHLOSS
HERBERSTEIN **10**

Weiz

Pischelsdorf

Bad Waltersdorf

ÖSTERREICHISCHES
FREILICHTMUSEUM STÜBING **2**

Deutschfreistritz

Gleisdorf

ROGNER BAD
BLUMAU **14**

Gratwein

LIPIZZANER
STUD PIBER **23**

Voitsberg

Köflach

1 GRAZ

Fürstenfeld

Seiersberg

Graz Airport

SCHLOSS
RIEGERSBURG **19**

Lieboch

Kalsdorf

Gundersdorf

Wildon

Feldbach

Fehring

Raab

Stainz

BAD
GLEICHENBERG **20**

Wolfsberg

Deutschlandsberg

Leibnitz

Straden

Wies

Ehrenhausen

Mureck

BAD
RADKERSBURG
12

Eibiswald

Murska
Sobota

Lavamünd

Gornja
Radgona

Dravograd

Lenart

Maribor

Ljutomer

Slovenj Gradec

SLOVENIA

Ptuj

Ormož

Velenje

Kidričevo

Slovenska
Bistrica

Slovenske
Konjice

0 kilometres   20

0 miles   20

N

Celje

❶
GRAZ

🅐F5 ✈9 km (5.5 miles) S of city centre 🚌🚇 🚹 Graz Tourismus, Herrengasse 16; www.graztourism.at

Graz, the capital of Styria, is the second largest city in Austria. The modern city extends from the foot of Schlossberg (Castle Mountain), on both sides of the Mur river; the Altstadt (old town), with the majority of the tourist sights, is on the left bank. Famed for its universities, architecture, cultural attractions and culinary traditions, Graz is a delight.

①
Dom

🅐Hofgasse 🕐Dawn-dusk

A former castle church built between 1439 and 1464 for Emperor Friedrich III, the Dom only became a cathedral in the 18th century. It has survived almost intact to this day and still features original elements, including Gothic frescoes showing life during the plague, although most of the decorations stem from the Baroque period. Its west portal bears the emperor's coat of arms.

②
Franziskanerkirche

🅐Franziskanerplatz 🕐Times vary, check website 🌐franziskaner-graz.at

This church once belonged to the Minorite friars, but in 1515 it was handed over to the Franciscans. The interior was redesigned after World War II, and the combination of the restored vault and modern stained-glass windows with earlier details creates a very striking effect. Next to the church is a monastery with a distinctive tower.

③
Schlossberg

🅐Hofgasse

North of the Altstadt rises the 473-m- (1,552-ft-) high Schlossberg. You can reach the top by a funicular or by a 20-minute walk. The 28-m- (92-ft-) high clock tower (1561), a symbol of Graz, offers splendid views over the city. It also houses a museum.

④
Hauptplatz

The triangular square at the heart of the old town is an excellent starting point for

> 💬 **INSIDER TIP**
> **Family Thrills**
>
> Take the kids on a trip into the kingdom of fairytales on a narrow-gauge train which runs through the tunnels within the Schlossberg. Visit www.grazer maerchenbahn.at for more information.

façade decorations. To the north of the square, at No 4, is Graz's oldest pharmacy, in a house dating from 1534. In the middle of the square is the fountain of Archduke Johann, who contributed much to the city's development. The four female figures around it symbolize Styria's four main rivers: the Mur, the Enns, the Drau and the Sann.

↑ Views across Graz from its iconic Clock Tower at the top of Schlossberg

exploring the city. It is surrounded by many original town houses, including the famous Haus am Luegg, with its Renaissance and Baroque

⑤
Grazer Congress

🏠 Albrechtgasse 1
📞 (03168) 088400

Next to the town hall stands an old palace, which, in 1980, was transformed into a superb modern conference centre with facilities for arts performances. The building has two grand conference suites as well as contemporary entertainment venues furnished with state-of-the art technology. It also houses the city's largest concert hall, the Stefaniensaal.

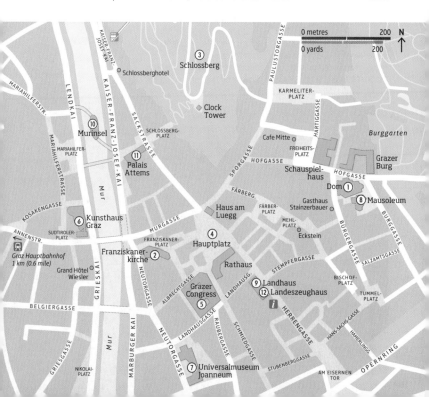

See a Sculpture

The Österreichischer Skulpturenpark (www.museum-joanneum.at/skulpturenpark), 7 km (4 miles) south of Graz, is home to 75 sculptures all designed to communicate with their natural surroundings.

⑥ ◈ ◈ ▣
Kunsthaus Graz

⌂ Lendkai ⏰ 10am-5pm Tue-Sun ◫ kunsthausgraz.at

This gallery opened in 2003 in conjunction with Graz's year as European Capital of Culture. Owing to its "biomorphous" construction using organic cellulose materials, and striking modern blue structure, it has been nicknamed the "friendly alien", and has become an attraction in itself, thanks in part to its riverside setting. Exhibitions, which change every few months, are wildly eclectic – from Japanese woodcuts to street theatre – but the main focus is on contemporary art post-1960.

⑦
Universalmuseum Joanneum

◫ museum-joanneum.at

Founded by Archduke Johann, the grandson of Maria Theresa, the Joanneum was Austria's first public museum. The memory of the archduke remains alive in Graz through this museum complex, which consists of 17 departments across 13 locations throughout Styria, each holding several exhibitions.

The **Alte Galerie** (Old Gallery), the most interesting display, is located in the Baroque Eggenberg Palace and contains some magnificent medieval paintings by Cranach, Pieter Bruegel the Younger, and Styrian 17th- and 18th-century artists. A collection of coins and medals can also be found there. The most valuable exhibit is the Strettweg chariot, which dates from the 7th century BC. In the Joanneum Quarter you'll find the excellent **Naturkundemuseum** (Natural History Museum), which provides an insight into the geological and mineralogical history of Styria. The **Neue Galerie** (New Gallery), also in this quarter, is a collection of 19th- and 20th-century paintings, drawings and sculptures.

Alte Galerie

◈ ◈ ⏣ ⌂ Eggenberger Allee 90 ⏰ Apr-Dec: 10am-5pm Tue-Sun (Nov-Dec: to 4pm)

Naturkundemuseum & Neue Galerie

◈ ◈ ⌂ Joanneumsviertel ⏰ 10am-5pm Tue-Sun

⑧
Mausoleum

⌂ Hofgasse

Commissioned by Emperor Ferdinand II (1578–1637) as a tomb for himself and his family, this small building is one of the most unusual and magnificent in Graz. The mausoleum is a prime example of Austrian Mannerism, successfully blending various different styles. It was designed by an Italian architect,

Pietro de Pomis, and completed by another Italian, Pietro Valnegro, who also built the belfry by the eastern apse. Its narrow façade, decorated with sculptures, consists of several architectural planes that create an exceptionally harmonious composition. The interior design is the work of Johann Bernhard Fischer von Erlach, who was born in Graz and began his career here.

---

⑨
Landhaus

🏠 Herrengasse 16

The Landhaus, one of the most beautiful Renaissance buildings in Styria, was once the seat of the Styrian diet. Today it is home to the provincial parliament.

The building was altered in the 16th century by the Italian military architect Domenico dell'Allio. Well worth seeing is the beautiful courtyard, with its three storeys of balustraded galleries linked by a raised walkway, and a fountain topped with a bronze cupola. In summer months it serves as a venue for festival events.

Inside the Landhaus is the Baroque Landtag conference

← The unique and wacky building that houses the Kunsthaus Graz

→ Murinsel, resembling a giant shell in the middle of the Mur river

room, which has beautifully carved doors crowned by allegorical scenes. Also worth seeing is the Knight's Hall.

---

⑩ 🖥 🏛
Murinsel

🏠 Lendkai 19
🌐 murinselgraz.at

Built in the shape of a giant shell, the Murinsel (Mur island) was designed by American artist Vito Acconci to mark Graz becoming the 2003 European Capital of Culture. It is an artificial floating island in the middle of the Mur river and is linked to both banks. Murinsel has since become one of the city's most popular visitor attractions, and a hub of Graz's cultural scene. It is often used as an exhibition space and a venue for film screenings and live music.

---

⑪
Palais Attems

🏠 Sackstrasse 17

The city's most attractive Baroque palace was built in 1702–16 to a design by Johann Joachim Carlone. The palace's main features are its monumental staircase with frescoes and stucco ornaments, and its richly ornamented façades. The uniform furnishing of the rooms, with ceiling stuccos, lovely fireplaces and tiled stoves, is testimony to the Austrian aristocracy's standard of living during the Baroque period.

(12) ⚡ 🎵 🏛

LANDESZEUGHAUS

🏠 Herrengasse 16 🕐 Apr-Oct: 10am-5pm Tue-Sun; Nov-Mar: for guided tour at 1pm Tue-Sun 📅 24 & 25 Dec 🌐 landeszeughaus.at

Housing an impressive collection of historical objects, the Landeszeughaus, or armoury, today ranks as the world's best-preserved early arsenal. Today it forms part of the Universalmuseum Joanneum, and its exceptional exhibits delight enthusiasts of weapons and armour.

The armoury was built between 1642 and 1645 as a stock of arms to be handed to the local population in the fight against the Turks. Graz was in the frontline of defence and guarded access to the threatened Austrian provinces of Styria, Carinthia and Carniola, which gave its armoury great importance.

Exploring the Armoury

The museum's beautiful Renaissance façade was designed by the Italian Antonio Solar. A Minerva statue in a niche to the right of the entrance, like the Mars statue on the left, is the work of Giovanni Mamolo. Inside the museum, the first floor is devoted to heavy guns, flintlock pistols and rifles. The second floor holds the store of armour used by infantry and cavalry units, and pistols, while the third floor displays the armour used by nobles and in tournaments. The fourth floor is devoted to staffs and edged weapons.

> The Landeszeughaus, or armoury, was built between 1642 and 1645 as a stock of arms to be handed to the local population in the fight against the Turks.

↑ A 17th-century cannon on display in the first-floor exhibition

↑ The Minerva and Mars statues gracing the armoury's exterior

Museum Highlights

Fluted Armour
△ Made in a Nuremberg workshop during the 16th century, this suit of armour is one of the earliest in the museum's extensive collection.

Helmets
△ The majority of the fine 16th-century helmets adorning the third floor ceiling were made in the Nuremberg and Augsburg workshops.

17th-century Muskets
△ These front-loading firearms, with smooth barrels, were widely used in Europe throughout the 16th and 17th centuries.

Wheel-Lock Pistol
△ This type of pistol, with a spherical barrel-end, was introduced to the German and Austrian cavalries in the 17th century.

32,000

The number of weapons, tools and suits of armour in the collection.

↑ Checking out the extensive collection of 16th-century helmets on the third floor

A SHORT WALK
GRAZ

Distance 1 km (0.5 miles) **Time** 15 minutes
Nearest tram Hauptplatz/Congress

During the Middle Ages, Graz was the seat of a minor branch of the Habsburg family, and later of Emperor Friedrich III. For centuries, Graz was also a stronghold against Turkish incursions. The chief legacy of the Habsburgs, however, is Graz's lovely Altstadt (old town), one of the best preserved in Central Europe and a UNESCO World Heritage Site. As you stroll through the narrow alleyways of this historic centre, it's easy to see why this is the heart and soul of Graz. Old and new come together as classic monuments and medieval churches stand beside hip museums and vibrant nightlife spots. The city also hosts two classical music festivals each year; check out the Styriarte if you're here in the summer, or the avant-garde Styrian Autumn if you're here later in the year.

*The **Haus am Luegg** town house at Nos 11 & 12 Hauptplatz (c 1690) has a striking façade, with Renaissance frescoes and early Baroque stuccowork.*

Hauptplatz (p182), *the old town's triangular main square, is surrounded by 17th-century town houses.*

FÄRB

HERRENGASSE

START

↑ Hanging out in Hauptplatz, the colourful centre of the old town

ALBRECHTGASSE

LANDHAUSGASSE

SCHMIED

Rathaus, *the new town hall, was built in the late 19th century on the southern side of Rathausplatz. It replaced the smaller Renaissance palace that had previously occupied the same site.*

Did You Know?

Graz has six universities and over 50,000 students.

*The inner courtyard of the **Landhaus** (p185) has three magnificent storeys of arcaded Renaissance galleries.*

| 0 metres | 100 | N |
| 0 yards | 100 | ↑ |

The impressive double spiral staircase inside **Burg** was built in 1499 on the orders of Maximilian I. He extended this vast Gothic castle built by his father, Friedrich III, who had made Graz one of his three capitals.

The beautifully carved reliquary chests in the choir of the **Dom** (p182) were originally made to hold the dowry of Paola di Gonzaga, Duchess of Mantua.

Locator Map
For more detail see p183

FINISH

HOFGASSE

The **Mausoleum** (p184), housing the tomb of Emperor Ferdinand II, is considered a perfect example of the Mannerist style of architecture.

BÜRGERGASSE

BURGGASSE

SCHLOSSERGASSE

TUMMELPLATZ

HERRENGASSE

Landeszeughaus (p186) is the largest armoury in the world that has been preserved intact.

→
Admiring the grand façade of Graz's iconic Mausoleum

❷ 🚴 🚠 🍴
ÖSTERREICHISCHES FREILICHT MUSEUM

🗺 F5 🅿 🚌 🕐 Apr–Oct: 9am–5pm daily 🌐 freilichtmuseum.at

In the Styrian village of Stübing, the compelling Austrian open-air museum provides a unique window into the past, with a collection of rural buildings covering 66 ha (24 acres) of picturesque woodland.

Founded in 1962 by the Graz humanist Professor Viktor Herbert Pöttler, this open-air museum is an impressive representation of Austria's regional architecture through the ages. The fine collection of buildings was transported here from almost every part of the country, and each dwelling, service mill and workshop has been reconstructed and preserved with original furnishings, tools and decor, to present a unique insight into the everyday life of its former inhabitants. What's more, it contributes to a fascinating overview of how working life has changed throughout the years.

Every day, the open-air museum offers activities associated with traditional customs and crafts, in which you are invited to participate. Try your hand at lace-making, or on special days sing folk songs or listen with children to classic fairytales.

WHAT ELSE TO SEE NEAR STÜBING

The small village of Stübing is the perfect spot from which to visit Stift Rein (www.stift-rein.at), the oldest Cistercian Monastery in the world and a short distance south. It was founded in 1129 and monks have lived and worked here ever since. At first glance the style is broadly Baroque, but recent renovation has revealed finds from the Gothic and Roman periods. Guided tours take place from March until December, and offer a glimpse of monastic life.

Styrian storehouse (inset) part of the Österreichisches Freilichtmuseum ↑

💬 INSIDER TIP
Adventure Day

Erlebnistag, otherwise known as adventure day, is held here every year on the last Sunday in September and combines a picnic with insights into the secrets of traditional craft skills, customs and entertainments.

↑ A step back in time with traditional garments on display in a workshop

TOP 4 BUILDINGS TO VISIT

Brenner Kreuz
A brick shrine from Ebene Reichenau in Carinthia, this little chapel houses a statue of St Florian, the patron saint of firefighters.

Grossschrotter Farmhouse
The main room in the 16th-century part of this house from Styria is the large "black room", where the entire family used to gather around the hearth and stove to cook, eat and socialize.

Bregenzer Wälderhaus
This 17th-century house is typical of the rural architecture in Bregenzer Wald (the Bregenz Forest) in Vorarlberg.

Hanslerhof Farmstead
Dating from 1660, this Tyrolean farm unites all the essential areas of a farmstead under one single roof.

Berglerhaus
This single-storey longhouse from Burgenland has a typical whitewashed and chimneyless kitchen, with a trad-itional bread oven.

③

SCHLADMINGER TAUERN

⚑D5 🚗🚌 **ℹ Schladming, Ramsauerstrasse 756;**
www.schladming-dachstein.at

This high mountain subrange lies in the middle of the Niedere
(Lower) Tauern, which extend along the Enns Valley. Rising to 2,800 m
(9,200 ft), the gentle slopes here provide excellent conditions for
downhill skiers, from the beginner to the professional.

The mountains take their name from the
small town of Schladming that lies at the foot
of the Niedere Tauern. The little town has a
rich history: once a centre of peasant revolts,
it remains to this day the centre of Austrian
Protestantism. The scenery in the vast
Schladminger Tauern is superb, excellent for
walking in summer, with an efficient bus
network, cable cars and ski lifts in winter. One
of Austria's major rivers, the Enns, separates
the Schladminger Tauern from the Dachstein
massif, the highest, most impressive peak.

Activities for all

A resort and winter sports centre, Haus, east
of Schladming, is a good starting point for
mountain walks to the nearby scenic lakes,
including Bodensee, Hüttensee and Obersee.
One of many other mountain lakes set amid
beautiful scenery is the Riesachsee, which lies
at an altitude of 1,333 m (4,373 ft) just south
of Haus. It is a perfect spot for trout fishing.
Hochgolling, rising to 2,863 m (9,393 ft), is
easy to spot from the Riesachsee. The long,
arduous climb to the peak rewards with

Did You Know?

Schladming is a
leading mountain bike
centre, and hosts the
world championships
every year.

Walking across the Dachstein ↑
suspension bridge, which
provides sweeping views

> **For a relaxing break it is worth going down to Schladming, with its tempting restaurants and cosy cafés lining the broad promenade.**

stunning views of the mountains. Rohrmoos resort, just outside Schladming, is also a good base for climbing the neighbouring Hochwurzen and Planai summits.

If you are looking for more of a challenge, you can find this in the Dachstein massif. The Dachstein peak rises to 2,995 m (9,826 ft), and the glacier is perfect for year-round skiing. The ascent by cable car from the small village of Ramsau am Dachstein *(p200)* takes you to the tops of Dachstein and Hunerkogel. Climbing instructors also give advice to rock climbers.

For a relaxing break it is worth going down to Schladming, with its tempting restaurants and cosy cafés lining the broad promenade.

↑ Hiking in the splendid scenery of the Schladminger Tauern

→ Riding on the cable car from Ramsau am Dachstein

EAT

Schattleitner
The menu here is mainly local, featuring plenty of pork and beef, and a great schnitzel.

⌂ Katzenburgweg 177, Schladming ☎ (03687) 24462 ☾ Mon

€ € €

Johann
Located in Posthotel, this homely place serves food a cut above the average. Try the chocolate soufflé.

⌂ Hauptplatz 10, Schladming ⓦ posthotel-schladming.at

€ € €

Dachstein-Gletscherbahn Panorama Restaurant
Located in the upper station of the Dachstein Gletscherbahn cable car, there are few better places to eat a fiery goulash soup or farmer's dumplings.

⌂ Winkl 75, Obertraun ⓦ derdachstein.at

€ € €

④

MARIAZELL BASILIKA

🄰F4 🄰Kardinal-Tisserant-Platz 1, Mariazell 🄲7:30am-7:30pm daily (to 9:30pm Sat); Treasury: May-Oct: 10am- 3pm Tue-Sun (to 4pm Sun & hols); during Advent: 1-5pm Thu-Sun 🅦basilika-mariazell.at

The town of Mariazell has long been a Catholic pilgrimage site for Central Europe, to which the Gothic and Baroque Basilika – the town's main attraction and Europe's most visited shrine – bears witness. Inside, you'll find a wealth of Baroque stuccowork, impressive paintings and lavish decoration.

The earliest records of a church devoted to the birth of the Virgin Mary date from 1243, but the Mariazell Basilika is believed to have been established in 1157. Originally a Gothic hall church, the building underwent Baroque style alterations in the late 17th century with help from the Swiss architect Domenico Sciassia. During the same period, the central tower was supplemented by two Baroque side towers. The treasury, home to various precious objects including a 14th-century ivory relief, is worth a visit.

Journeying to Mariazell

The basilica became famous in the 14th century, when King Louis of Hungary founded the Gnadenkapelle (Chapel of Mercy) to give thanks for his victory over the Turks. In the 17th century, the church was extended to accommodate the growing number of pilgrims, and today Mariazell continues to be the main pilgrimage centre for the Roman Catholic population in this part of Europe. Pilgrims arrive all year, but high points are Assumption (15 Aug) and the Birth of the Virgin (8 Sep).

14th-century Gothic tower

Main entrance

CARDINAL JOSEPH MINDSZENTY (1892-1975)

The Hungarian primate, imprisoned for his opposition to the communist regime, was released in the 1956 uprising. When this was crushed, he took refuge in the US Embassy in Budapest for 15 years. He later lived in Austria and was buried in Mariazell, but his body was then moved to Hungary.

↑ The imposing basilica against the dramatic backdrop of the night sky

Vault frescoes by Giovanni Rocco Bertoletti

Magna Mater Austriae, *a late-Romanesque statue of the Madonna and Child, is the main object of veneration by pilgrims.*

The monumental altar showing the Crucifixion is the work of architect Johann Bernhard Fischer von Erlach.

Gnadenkapelle, a chapel with a statue of the Virgin Mary, is said to have been founded by King Louis of Hungary and is decorated in Baroque style.

Did You Know?

Joseph Haydn wrote the Mariazeller-Messe (1782) for pilgrims to the basilica.

EXPERIENCE MORE

❺ Frohnleiten

🇦 F5 🚌🚊 **ℹ Hauptplatz 2; www.frohnleiten.or.at**

Set among gently rolling hills on the Mur river, the town of Frohnleiten is surrounded by a network of inviting rambling trails. Despite being nearly destroyed in a fire in 1763, several well-preserved buildings have survived its 700-year history. The marvellous monastery and parish church on the main square originally dates from 1677, though it was rebuilt following the 1763 fire.

Burg Rabenstein was built at the beginning of the 12th century by Lantfried de Rammenstein. Renovations took place in the 16th, 17th and 18th centuries, making the site a fascinating cross-section of history. The town has won several awards for its flower displays, and has a splendid Alpine garden with thousands of species from around the world.

A short way to the west, in Adriach, is the 11th-century St Georgskirche, with an altarpiece of the martyrdom of St George and four frescoes in the main nave by Josef Adam von Mölk.

Did You Know?

Styria is known as the "Green Heart" of Austria because of its lush forested landscape.

❻ Bruck an der Mur

🇦 F4 🚌🚊 **ℹ Herzog-Ernst-Gasse 2; www.bruckmur.at**

This small but attractive old town, at the fork of the Mürz and Mur rivers, flourished during the 14th and 15th centuries thanks to its trade with Venice. Bruck was once a town of blacksmiths, and their work can be seen on the main square, Koloman-Wallisch-Platz, where there stands an iron well (1626) sporting an intricate wrought-iron canopy. The door (1500) to the vestry of Pfarrkirche Mariä Geburt, is another beautiful example of Styrian metalwork. Also in the main square is the town hall, with an attractive arcaded courtyard, in a former ducal residence. The town's most alluring building is the late-Gothic Kornmesserhaus, built for the ironmonger Kornmess.

A small distance away, on the other side of the Mur, stands St Rupert's Church, with a superb *Last Judgement* fresco (1420). Above the town rise the ruins of Landskron fortress, whose only remaining feature is the bell tower.

❼ Mürzzuschlag

🇦 F4 🚌 **ℹ Wiener Strasse 9; (03852) 2556**

This town on the Mürz at the foot of Semmering mountain is Austria's oldest winter sports resort. Skiing here dates back to 1893, and in 1934 the town was the venue for the Nordic Games, which inspired the Winter Olympics. The town's first historic records date from 1469, when Friedrich III ordered

↑ The spire of Frohnleiten parish church overlooking the Mur river

it to be burned to the ground following a rebellion led by Count Andreas Baumkircher. Today its main sights of interest are the parish church, with a delightful Renaissance altarpiece, and its picturesque old houses, including the house of Johannes Brahms at No 4 Wiener Strasse. Also worth visiting is the **Winter Sport Museum**, which has a large collection of objects and memorabilia relating to all aspects of winter sports.

Winter Sport Museum

⌖ 🏠 Wiener Strasse 13 🕒 9am–12:30pm & 2–5pm Tue–Sun 🚫 1 Jan, Shrove Tue, 1 Nov, 24–25 Dec, 31 Dec 🌐 wintersportmuseum.com

Stift Vorau

🅰F4 🚌 ℹ Stift Vorau; www.stift-vorau.at

On a remote hill stands the 12th-century Augustinian Stift Vorau (Vorau Abbey). In the 15th century, it was turned into a fortress, and its present form is the result of alterations made throughout the 17th and 18th centuries. The main entrance is flanked by symmetrical wings on both sides, adjoining two identical towers. One wing contains the cloister; in the other wing is the magnificent fresco- and stucco-adorned library with its low barrel-vaulted ceiling. On the floor above is a cabinet of manuscripts, containing more than 400 valuable documents, including the oldest annals of poetry in the German language – the *Vorauer Handschrift* and the famous *Kaiserchronik*. The abbey church acquired its sumptuous decor in 1700–5.

The small nearby town of Vorau has an open-air museum (**Freilichtmuseum**) with a fascinating collection of typical homes and public buildings from neighbouring villages, complete with their distinctive furnishings.

Freilichtmuseum

⌖ 📞 (03337) 3466 🕒 Apr–Oct: 10am–5pm daily (Jul & Aug: from 9am)

Lurgrotte

🅰F5 🚃 🕒 Peggau: Apr–Oct: 9am–4pm daily; Semirach: times vary, check website 🌐 lurgrotte.at

The Lurgrotte is the largest and most interesting cave in the eastern Alps of Austria, with superb stalactites and stalagmites. Starting at either Peggau or Semirach, guides lead you through this world of icy wonders, along an underground stream. The largest dripstone, 13 m (43 ft) tall, is nicknamed the "Giant" (der Riese).

←

Exploring ancient dripstone formations in the caves of Lurgrotte

10 ⊘

Schloss Herberstein

🅰F5 🚌 🕐 Mar–Apr & Oct–Mar: 10am–4pm daily; May–Sep: 9am–5pm daily
🆆 herberstein.co.at

Schloss Herberstein, perched on a steep rock amid wild countryside, has remained in the hands of the Herberstein family since 1290. Since they still live in the castle, a visit feels a bit like peeping through a keyhole at history.

The medieval fortress achieved its present form in the late 16th century. Its most magnificent area is the Florence Courtyard, a delightful arcaded enclosure more reminiscent of Renaissance Italian palaces than of northern European fortresses.

> 💬 INSIDER TIP
> **Kids at Herberstein**
>
> Schloss Herberstein organizes a host of medieval-themed activities for children to enjoy throughout the summer period. Kids can learn how knights lived and join in treasure hunts around the castle.

At one time the castle was even a popular venue for knightly tournaments.

The rooms open to visitors today display a range of items relating to the Herberstein family and aristocratic life in the 18th and 19th centuries.

One of the most interesting places within the grounds is the nature reserve, **Tierwelt Herberstein**, home to an assortment of wild plants and animals. Its origins can be traced back to the 16th century, when the castle was inhabited by Count Sigmund von Herberstein, the author of pioneering works on the agriculture and geography of Eastern Europe.

Tierwelt Herberstein
⊘ 🕐 May–Sep: 9am–5pm daily; Oct–Nov: 10am–4pm daily 🆆 tierwelt-herberstein.at

11

Turracher Höhe

🅰E5 🚌 🆆 turracher hoehe.com

This small ski resort nestles high in the Nockbergen (Nock Mountains), one of Austria's most scenic Alpine ranges, on the border between Styria and Carinthia. The town makes a great base for year-round walks in the woods and mountain meadows. Nearby are the remains of an old iron-smelting plant. The blast furnace ended its operation in the early 20th century, but the remains of heavy industry stand in stark relief against the pistes and snow-covered hills of the ski resort.

12

Bad Radkersburg

🅰G5 🚊🚌 🆆 bad radkersburg.at

This spa town on the Slovenian border was founded in 1265 by the Bohemian king Ottokar. Once a fortified border post as well as an important trade centre on the Mur, today it still bears many signs of its former glory. In the main square stands the late Gothic town hall, with its octagonal clock tower topped by a belfry. The Marian, or plague column in the square dates from 1681, and the surrounding houses with their patios and shaded galleries are the former homes of noblemen and rich citizens. The house at No 9 Hauptplatz once belonged to the Von Eggenbergs, one of Styria's most powerful families.

13

Pöllau

🅰F5 🆆 naturpark-poellauertal.at

Pöllau lies at the centre of the Naturpark Pöllauer Tal national park, surrounded by woodland, vineyards and walking trails. This 12th-century market town's main attractions are the former Augustinian abbey and the awe-inspiring St Vitus's Church. Built between 1701

← Fishing in a lake near Turracher Höhe in the Nockbergen

STAY

Gästehaus am Dorfbrunnen
Family-friendly guesthouse in the centre of Bad Blumau.

G5 Hauptstrasse 11, Bad Blumau
W dorfbrunnen.at

€€€

Hotel Birkenhof
A cottage-style hotel just a few minutes' walk from the centre of Bad Radkersburg.

G5 Thermenstr. 8, Bad Radkersburg
W birkenhof-radkersburg.at

€€€

Naturparkhotel Lambrechterhof
Offers peace and tranquillity as well as a little luxury.

E5 Hauptstrasse 38-40, St Lambrecht
W lambrechterhof.at

€€€

↑ The weird and wonderful architecture of the Rogner Bad Blumau resort

and 1712 by Joachim Carlone of the famous family of architects from Graz, this is a splendid example of Styrian Baroque. The vaults and the inside of the dome are decorated with trompe l'oeil frescoes by Mathias von Görz, depicting the four fathers of the church, two Augustinian saints and the 12 apostles. The main altarpiece has a monumental painting by Josef Adam von Mölk showing the martyrdom of the church's patron saint, St Veit (Vitus).

About 6 km (4 miles) northeast of Pöllau, high up on Pöllauberg, stands the 14th-century Gothic pilgrimage church of Maria-Lebing, with vault frescoes by Mölk and two statues of the Virgin Mary from the 15th and 17th centuries.

Rogner Bad Blumau

G5 W blumau.com

In eastern Styria, in an area that has long been famed for its crystal-clear mineral waters, is a spa resort that is certainly worth a detour. The entire resort of Bad Blumau was designed by the painter and architect Friedensreich Hundertwasser, who strove to achieve harmony with nature. The apartment style is somewhat reminiscent of his building in Vienna (p140). The rounded façades, rippling green roofs, colourful walls and irregularly shaped terraces and balconies will transport you into a strange and surreal fairyland. As you stroll along an avenue lined with trees and shrubs that represent the Chinese horoscope, you might find yourself walking on the roof of a building. The resort is ostensibly made up of healing springs, sauna, hotel and garden, but it really sees itself as a work of art.

The outside of the complex can be seen with a guided tour, but the main reason for a visit here is, of course, taking to the waters. Admission to the complex is available for half and full days, and will prove both an artistic experience and a pleasant way to while away some time.

An alpine road winding through the snow-dusted peaks of Ramsau ↑

15

Ramsau

🅐D4 🚌 **🛈 Ramsauerstrasse 756; www.ramsau.com**

At an altitude of 1,000 m (3,280 ft) lies the small town of Ramsau am Dachstein, renowned for its superb cross-country ski runs. Snow is almost guaranteed from November until March and the efficient interconnecting system of lifts, cable cars, trains and buses also puts more difficult runs within easy reach. The peaks opposite the famous Dachstein massif have slopes that are perfectly suited to moderately skilled downhill skiers. In the summer, the *Loipen*, or cross-country ski runs, turn into excellent long-distance walking routes.

From the Ramsau side, you can ascend the south face of Dachstein by cable car. Cable cars also travel up Hunerkogel,

from where a lovely panoramic view of the area unfolds. The descent takes you to Filzmoos, a resort with views of the spectacular Bischofsmütze (Bishop's Mitre).

There are countless ways to spend time in Ramsau. The **Alpinmuseum Austriahütte** illustrates the history of mountaineering in the region. The **Wassermühle Rössing**, meanwhile, is one of several waterwheels built in the area since the 17th century. It lies at the foot of Sattelberg (Saddle Mountain). The waterwheel creaks into motion in summer on Friday afternoons.

Alpinmuseum Austriahütte

♿ Ⓦ 🕐 May–Oct: 10am–5pm daily 🌐 austriahuette.at

Wassermühle Rössing

📞 (03687) 81874 🕐 Mid-Jun–Sep

16

St Lambrecht

🅐E5 🚌🚆 **🛈 Hauptstrasse 12; www.stift-stlambrecht.at**

St Lambrecht, a Benedictine abbey, was founded in the 12th century by Heinrich III, Duke of

Carinthia. The church dates from the 14th century, but it was rebuilt in the 16th century in the Baroque style and today it is a triple-nave basilica with medieval frescoes on the walls and presbytery ceiling, and statues of the church's fathers in the organ enclosure.

North of the church, by the cemetery, stands a 12th-century Romanesque chapel. The abbey also has a magnificent library and the **St Lambrecht Abbey Museum**, with a collection of furnishings including Romanesque sculptures, a 15th-century votive painting, *The Mount of Olives* by Hans von Tübingen, and stained-glass panels. The gem of the museum, however, is its collection of birds. Some 1,500 species were assembled in the 19th century by the amateur collector Blasius Hanf.

St Lambrecht Abbey Museum

♿ Ⓦ 🏠 Hauptstrasse 1–2 📞 (03585) 230529 🕐 Mid-May–mid-Oct: for guided tours only at 10:45am & 2:30pm Mon–Sat, 2:30pm Sun & hols

→

Gazing down the River Mur, in the historic town of Murau

> At an altitude of 1,000 m (3,280 ft) lies the small town of Ramsau am Dachstein, renowned for its superb cross-country ski runs.

> INSIDER TIP
> **Hiking Murau-Kreischberg**
>
> The Murau-Kreischberg mountains are perfect for hiking, and the mountain huts prove enticing places to stop for some Styrian hospitality. Use the gondola at Kreischberg for a leg-up to the lush meadows.

17

Murau

E5 murau-kreischberg.at

Murau sprang up in the 13th century on the left bank of the Mur. The Renaissance houses in its historic town centre are dominated by the Gothic Matthäuskirche (Church of St Matthew), consecrated in the 13th century and later altered in the Baroque style. The church houses the tombs of the Liechtenstein family, but its star attraction is the main altar (1655), a magnificent work by local Baroque masters, incorporating a Gothic painting of the Crucifixion (c 1500). Also worth a look are the medieval frescoes of St Anthony in the transept, and the Entombment of Christ and the Annunciation in the main nave.

The castle behind the church, Schloss Murau, was founded by the Liechtenstein family and later passed into the hands of the Schwarzenbergs. It now offers guided tours, taking in the picture gallery, kitchen, dungeon and chapel. In the vaults of Elisabethkirche, at No 4 Marktgasse, is a diocesan Protestant museum that holds documents relating to the events around the Reformation and the Counter-Reformation in this part of Austria.

18

Oberwölz

E5 Hauptplatz 15; www.oberwoelz-lachtal.at

This small town, which grew rich through its trade in salt and silver, still retains much of its former glory. Excavations in the surrounding area have unearthed a treasure trove of items from the Hallstatt period (from c 1100 BC), revealing a long and rich history.

The town has some well-preserved remains of medieval fortifications, including three turrets and two town gates. Its pride is the Stadtpfarrkirche (parish church) St Martin, a triple-nave basilica with an early- Gothic chapel and a 15th-century Gothic vestibule. In 1777, J A von Mölk painted the ceiling frescoes in the chapel vault. On the external south wall is a relief of the Last Judgement from 1500. Next door stands the 14th-century chapel of St Sigismund, with *The Way of the Cross* by Johann Lederwasch from the turn of the 18th century. In the cultural centre is a regional museum with a collection of archaeological finds from the area.

> **AUSTRIAN WINES**
>
> Austria produces some truly excellent wines. Lower Austria is the largest wine-producing region, particularly the Weinviertel and the Wachau valley. The land around Neusiedler See is famous for its reds: Zweigelt and the full-bodied Blaufränkisch. The light Schilcher rosé comes from Deutschlandsberg in Styria. The dessert wine Eiswein is also produced in Austria.

↑ Springtime at Riegersburg castle, and a regal museum room *(inset)*

19

Schloss Riegersburg

🅰F5 🚌 🕒Apr & Oct: 10am-6pm daily; May-Sep: 9am-6pm daily
🌐dieriegersburg.at

On a steep hill high above the Grazbach stream stands Riegersburg castle, a mighty medieval fortress. It was once Styria's most easterly outpost against raiders from Hungary and Turkey, and, more recently, a German stronghold during World War II. The castle as it stands today dates from the 17th century. The fortress is surrounded by a defensive wall and can only be approached by a long steep climb.

A handful of the castle's rooms now serve as a museum. One section is dedicated to a collection of arms dating from the Middle Ages to the 17th century. Several rooms explore the lives of the Liechtenstein

family, who were pivotal in the turbulent history of Austria and Europe. The Witches' Museum looks at the Styrian witch trials of the 17th century; it features gruesome instruments of torture and grim tales of persecution.

In the castle's first courtyard stands a monument to soldiers killed during World War II. Beyond the second moat, in the inner courtyard, you will find a well surrounded by an elaborate wrought-iron enclosure featuring a horseshoe – it is said that those who succeed in tracing it among the intricate decorations may count on good luck.

20

Bad Gleichenberg

🅰F5 🚌 🌐bad-gleichenberg.at

Once a popular health resort, Bad Gleichenberg was developed in 1834 by the Austrian statesman Matthias Constantin Capello Graf von Wickenburg.

When the potent therapeutic properties of the local spring waters – already known to the Romans – were brought to his attention, he set about developing them. Bad Gleichenberg thus became the go-to place for the health-conscious Austrian aristocracy, who congregated in the park, which now displays statues of its former visitors among the shrubbery. The town has many surviving villas and Secession-style palaces; one of the most beautiful is the old theatre, now housing a cinema.

EAT & DRINK

Weingut Leitgeb
Modern wine bar with a range of the region's fine wines. Food includes meat platters and freshly made bread.

🅰F5 🏠Trautmannsdorf 104, Bad Gleichenberg
🕒Mon 🌐weingut-leitgeb.at

21
Eisenerzer Alpen

🅐E4 🚌 ℹ️ Dr-Theodor-Körner-Pz 1; Eisenerz; (03848) 3700

You can reach the Eisenerzer Alpen (Iron Ore Alps) by following the steep, narrow valley of the Enns river. This gorge, the Gesäuse, begins a short distance from Admont, near Hieflau. The entrance to the gorge enjoys great views of the river and the Hochtor massif. The surrounding area is used as a training ground for advanced mountaineering and as a base for expeditions to the neighbouring peaks. Easily the most famous peak in the region is Erzberg, which has been exploited for its iron ore deposits since ancient times. Resembling a ziggurat, its red pigment contrasts with the surrounding green forests.

In Eisenerz, an old mining town at the foot of Erzberg, you can join an underground tour with **Abenteuer Erzberg**, which includes a ride on a large dump truck.

Abenteuer Erzberg
🎣🎿 🅐Erzberg 1
🕐May-Oct: 11am-3pm daily
🌐abenteuer-erzberg.at

22
Judenburg

🅐E5 🚋🚌 ℹ️ Hauptplatz 20; www.judenburg.com

This old mercantile centre at the fork of a road took its name from the Juden, or Jews, who once lived and traded here. When Emperor Maximilian expelled the Jews in 1496, the town went into decline. Not much remains of the medieval Jewish quarter, but it is worth visiting the Nikolauskirche (Church of St Nicholas). The only original feature is the presbytery – rebuilt in 1673 in the Baroque style. Inside are statues of the 12 apostles by the local artist Balthasar Brandstätter. The town is also home to a museum largely devoted to the region's history and art.

23

Lipizzaner Stud Piber

🅐F5 🚉Köflach 🚌
🕐Apr-Oct: 9:30am-5pm daily; Nov-Mar: for guided tours only 🌐srs.at

Piber is the location of the Lipizzaner Stud Piber, the breeding farm for Vienna's Spanish Riding School *(p82)*. When the town of Lipizza was

PICTURE PERFECT
Lipizzaner Horses

The gleaming white Lipizzaner horses will be familiar to anyone who has visited the Spanish Riding School in Vienna, but in the fields above Piber you can often see herds grazing, which make for a magical shot.

incorporated into Slovenia after World War I, it was in a former castle in Piber, a small Styrian village, that the world-famous Lipizzaner horses found a new home.

The horses are a complex mixture of six different breeds. Born dark chestnut or black, they acquire their famous white colour between the ages of four and ten. In Piber, the initial selection of five out of 40 stallions takes place: they are assessed for their suitability before five years of training at the Spanish Riding School.

Tours of the farm take an inside look at training sessions and give you the chance to see what makes these horses so special. You can also see the farriers at work and explore the farm's collection of ceremonial coaches.

↑ Lipizzaner horses galloping through a lush meadow at Lipizzaner Stud Piber

↑ Bad Aussee, located between the Dachstein massif and the Dead Mountains

2,000 m (6,560 ft). The village was founded by the Celts, and from the 12th century it became an important commercial centre along Hohentauernpass, the mountain pass connecting the Enns and Mur valleys. A drive along Hohentauernpassstrasse, which crosses the range at a height of 1,260 m (4,134 ft), is one of the best ways to enjoy the mountain scenery. From the north, you pass through Rottenmann with its old city walls; Möderbrugg, a former centre of the metal industry; Oberzeiring and its disused salt mine; and Hanfelden, with its large ruined castle. Nearby is Schloss Reifenstein.

EAT

Gasthaus Kamper

Authentic Styrian cuisine with a modern twist. The perfect place to meet fellow travellers.

🅰E4 🏠Hauptstrasse 19, Admont 🕒Mon 🌐gh-kamper.at

€€€

Cafe Passhöhe

Regional dishes served high in the mountains, with wonderful views from every table.

🅰E4 🏠Tauernstrasse 21, Hohentauern 🕒Thu 🌐passhoehe.at

€€€

Hofwirt

Serving warm Styrian hospitality since 1603. The homemade venison stew is a must.

🅰E5 🏠Seckau 3, Seckau 🌐hotel-hofwirt.at

€€€

24 Bad Aussee

🅰D4 🚌🚉 ℹ️Bahnhofstrasse 132; www.ausseerland.salzkammergut.at

Bad Aussee lies at the fork of the Traun river, which cuts a scenic gorge between the Dachstein massif and the Totes Gebirge (Dead Mountains). The town achieved fame when, in 1827, Archduke Johann married Anna Plochl, daughter of the local postmaster. The archduke was grandson to Maria Theresa and the 13th child of Leopold II, and made many important contributions to Styrian life.

The region's wealth was founded on its salt deposits. The former seat of the Salt Office, in Chlumeckyplatz, is a charming 14th-century building which now houses the city's regional museum. The 13th-century Romanesque St Paul's Church boasts a remarkable stone statue of the Madonna.

25 Hohentauern

🅰E4 🚌 🌐hohentauern.at

Hohentauern is the highest village in the Rottenmanner Tauern, surrounded by more than 20 peaks higher than

26 Leoben

🅰F5 🚌🚉 ℹ️Hauptplatz 3; www.tourismus-leoben.at

Beautiful mansion houses line the main square of this large industrial and academic centre, and the adjacent streets bear witness to the town's early iron boom. The delightful old town hall is decorated with coats of arms, and the Hacklhaus has a glittering red façade.

Also worth seeing in the old town is the Pfarrkirche St Xaver (parish church of St Xavier), built in the 17th century by the Jesuits, with its beautiful Baroque main altar and a Romanesque crucifix on the south wall. On the other side of the bridge across the Mur stands the Gothic Church of Maria am Waasen, with original stained-glass windows in the presbytery. On the southern outskirts, in the district of Göss, stands Styria's first Benedictine abbey, built around AD 1000 by Archbishop Aribo, though most of the surviving elements are

→

Priceless volumes in the heavenly ceremonial hall of Admont Abbey library

16th-century. The main nave is a monument to Styria's late Gothic architecture. Other original features include 14th-century frescoes in the presbytery and an 11th-century, early Romanesque crypt.

A short walk from the abbey, Austria's most famous brewery, Gösser, is open to the public. On Kirchgasse in the city centre is the Kunsthalle Leoben, a splendid museum of fine arts.

② Admont

🅐E4 🚉🚌 ⓘ Weng 2; www. admont.at

The village of Admont makes the ideal kicking-off point for the outstanding peaks, forests, and rivers of Gesäuse National Park, a popular spot for hiking, climbing, kayaking and skiing. The information centre to the northeast of town is a good source for tips on trails and tours.

At the centre of the village stands the Benedictine abbey, Stift Admont, whose importance once reached far beyond the region. Built in the 11th

century and often rebuilt, it burned down in 1865, but the fire fortunately spared its most priceless asset: the world's largest monastic library. The library's magnificent Rococo interior, dating from 1773, was designed by the Viennese architect Josef Hueber. The large ceremonial hall's ceiling frescoes show vast allegorical scenes of the arts, the natural sciences and religion. The abbey's south wing has been converted into a museum showcasing both historic treasures and modern art.

Stift Admont

♿🕙 ◯Mid-Mar–Oct: 10am– 5pm daily ⓦstiftadmont.at

② Seckau

🅐E5 🚉🚌 ⓦseckau.at

The small town of Seckau, established in the 13th century, is dotted with attractive houses and boasts the late Gothic chapel of St Lucia in the town square. But its main claim to fame is Seckau Abbey, originally Augustinian and taken

over by the Benedictines in the 19th century. Its present shape, dating from the 17th century, is the work of early Baroque architect Pietro Francesco Carlone, but the abbey's basilica, devoted to the Assumption of the Virgin Mary, has maintained its original late Gothic character.

Among its treasures is the Crucifixion group in the presbytery – highly expressive figures from the 12th and 13th centuries. The lion figures in the portal and the Madonna and Child in the church vestibule are Romanesque and early Gothic, and 13th-century frescoes were discovered on the south wall.

A DRIVING TOUR
STEIRISCHE WEINSTRASSE

Length 65 km (40 miles) **Stopping-off points** Inns and rooms to rent are dotted along the route

Much of southern Styria is given over to vineyards, with vines planted on steep, south-facing slopes. The roads along the foot of the hills run through fields of maize, the region's second crop. The third crop is pumpkins, and pumpkin seeds are used to make *Kürbiskernöl*, a popular salad oil. As you follow the Styrian wine routes you'll find many pleasant places to stop for a meal, but more importantly, a chance to sample the local wine and learn about the grape varieties that cloak the gardens of the restaurants. (A range of soft drinks are available for designated drivers, too.)

At the entrance to the village of **Gundersdorf** is the Klapotetz, a scarecrow that guards the vineyards against birds.

START ▶ Gundersdorf

Stainz owes its former wealth to the wine trade. The abbey houses a museum on farming and hunting.

A health resort with iron-rich mineral waters, **Bad Gams** also produces superb pottery.

Deutschlandsberg is the centre of production for Schilcher rosé wine. It is dominated by a former castle.

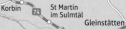

↑ The ruins and remaining 12th-century turret of the castle at Deutschlandsberg

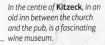

↑ Enjoying a bite to eat and drink in the main square at Leibnitz

Locator Map

STYRIA

Steirische Weinstrasse

Did You Know?

Kitzeck is home to the highest vineyards in Europe, growing on slopes at an altitude of 564 m (1,850 ft).

In the centre of **Kitzeck**, in an old inn between the church and the pub, is a fascinating wine museum.

Several traces reveal earlier Roman settlements in the town of **Leibnitz**. The finds are displayed in Seggau Castle.

Vineyards form the pristine landscape surrounding **Ehrenhausen**. The town is home to the mausoleum of Rupert von Eggenberg, a hero of the Turkish wars.

Pöls an der Wieserbahn

Preding

Grötsch

Spiegelkogel 452 m (1,483 ft)

Lebring

Waldschacher Teich

Unterjahring

Lassnitz

Mur

Demmerkogel 571 m (2,201 ft)

Kitzreck

Leibnitz

Sulm

Grossklein

Gamlitz

Ehrenhausen

FINISH

St Johann im Saggautal

Urlkogel 524 m (1,719 ft)

Spielfeld

0 kilometres 5
0 miles 5

N
↑

Hochschwab mountain ↑
reflected in the crystal-
clear waters of Brunnsee

A DRIVING TOUR
SALZATAL TOUR

Length 100 km (60 miles) **Stopping-off points** The only overnight accommodation is available at Weichselboden.

The small Salza river, a tributary of the upper Enns, cuts its way across the eastern end of the Northern Limestone Alps. A journey along the Salza valley is an expedition through a thinly populated area of entrancing beauty. The trail leads along the foothills of the Hochschwab massif, beside wild mountain streams, small barrier lakes and through dense woodlands. The river flows through virgin mountain terrains and its waters are so crystal clear that you can see every detail reflected in it. For something truly spectacular, hike to the top of the Hochschwab mountain: though challenging, taking 7–8 hours, it is worth it for the stunning views along the way and from the peak.

Locator Map

It is worth stopping off in the small village of **Weichselboden** *to visit its pretty, scenic limetree-shaded church.*

Beyond a rock gate is **Prescenyklause,** *an old dam that once held back the waters of the Salza river so rafts could carry timber to the valleys.*

FINISH
Gusswerk

Mendling

Palfau

Hohckar
△ 1,805 m (5,922 ft)

Dürradmer

Gams bei Hieflau

Fachwerk

Hochstadl
1,919 m (6,295 ft) △

Wegscheid

Landl

Mooslandl

Wildalpen

Salza

Weichselboden

Hinterwildalpen

Brunnsee

Prescenyklause

Gollrad

Buchberg
1,563 m (5,127 ft) △

Griesstein
2,023 m (6,637 ft) △

Ringkamp
2,153 m (7,063 ft) △

START
Hieflau

Enns

Brandstein
2,003 m (6,571 ft) △

Hochschwab
2,277 m (7,470 ft) △

Seewiesen

Grosser Beilstein
2,015 m (6,610 ft) △

Hieflau, *the former centre of the metal industry, is hidden amid dense forests. The local village museum displays historical objects.*

Beyond the village of Wildalpen, a great view opens onto **Brunnsee,** *the lake at the heart of the Hochschwab massif.*

The highest summit in this vast mountain range is the 2,277-m-(7,470-ft-) high **Hochschwab,** *great for summer and winter excursions.*

0 kilometres   8
0 miles   8

N

UPPER AUSTRIA

Upper Austria, or Oberösterreich, is, after Vienna, the most industrialized Austrian province and has remained the richest area of the country since the time when Austria was part of the Roman province of Noricum. For a time, Upper Austria joined Bavaria. Then, under Babenberg rule in the 13th century, it became the cradle of the great future empire, together with neighbouring Lower Austria.

Historically, the province is divided into four regions – Mühlviertel, Innviertel, Hausruckviertel, and Traunviertel, which includes the Salzkammergut, plus the Danube valley, which is generally considered to be a separate region. Linz became the province's fourth capital in 1490, and acted as a local government and provincial city of the Holy Roman Empire. It was an important centre for trade, positioned as it is by the river, and to this day remains a key industrial centre – containing the largest Austrian Danube port – as well as a major transport hub.

Following the introduction of the horse-drawn railway line in 1832, which took passengers between Linz and Budwei, the Salzkammergut region experienced a boom in visitors – mainly to its spa areas. Upper Austria also saw a large increase in its population after World War II, particularly thanks to refugees, and a resurgence in industrial development that has helped it become the modern area it is today.

UPPER AUSTRIA

Must Sees

1. Linz
2. Salzkammergut Lakes
3. The Danube Valley

Experience More

4. Perg
5. Stift St Florian
6. Obernberg am Inn
7. Freistadt
8. Kremsmünster
9. Schärding
10. Braunau am Inn
11. Lambach
12. Steyr
13. Schwanenstadt
14. Wels
15. Dachsteinhöhlen
16. Vöcklabruck
17. Bad Hall
18. Stadl-Paura
19. Kefermarkt
20. Traunkirchen
21. Gosauseen
22. Schafberg
23. Bad Ischl
24. Gmunden
25. Hallstatt

❶
LINZ

🅰E3 🅽N1, exit 47, R45 ✈13 km (8 miles) SW of city centre
🚆🚌🚊 ℹHauptplatz 1; www.linztourismus.at

Straddling the Danube and surrounded by forested hills, Linz owes its former importance and wealth to its location at an intersection of waterways. This strategic position led the Romans to found a substantial settlement called Lentia on the site, and since the 15th century, Linz has been the capital of Upper Austria. A UNESCO City of Media Arts, Linz is a vibrant city with numerous galleries and museums today.

① Hauptplatz

The Hauptplatz, in Linz's old town, is one of Europe's grandest urban squares in scale, and one of the finest to visit. At 220 m (720 ft) long and 60 m (200 ft) wide, it creates a much stronger impression than its component parts would suggest. Many of its buildings are worth a closer look, nevertheless. At No 1, the Gothic Altes Rathaus (old town hall) was built around 1513, and still has its original octagonal tower with an astronomical clock. The fine Feichtingerhaus, a former mail inn (No 21), is also of interest

for its early Baroque façade. The plague column (1723) in the centre of the square was funded jointly by the local council and all citizens, in thanksgiving for sparing Linz from war, fire and the Black Death plague.

② Linzer Schloss

🏰Schlossberg 1 🕙10am–6pm Tue–Sun (to 9pm Thu) 🌐landesmuseum.at

In the 15th century, Emperor Friedrich III built his residence on the Römerberg (Roman Mountain), on the foundations of an earlier structure. The castle acquired its present shape between 1600 and 1607, and its distinctive silhouette has become one of the most famous sights in Linz. Since 1966, this former imperial residence has housed a branch of the Oberösterreichisches Landesmuseum (Upper Austrian Provincial Museum), which has a range of exhibits from paintings to archaeology. Part of the museum is devoted to folk traditions, and there's a reconstructed physics laboratory from Linz's Jesuit school. From the castle, there are superb views over Linz.

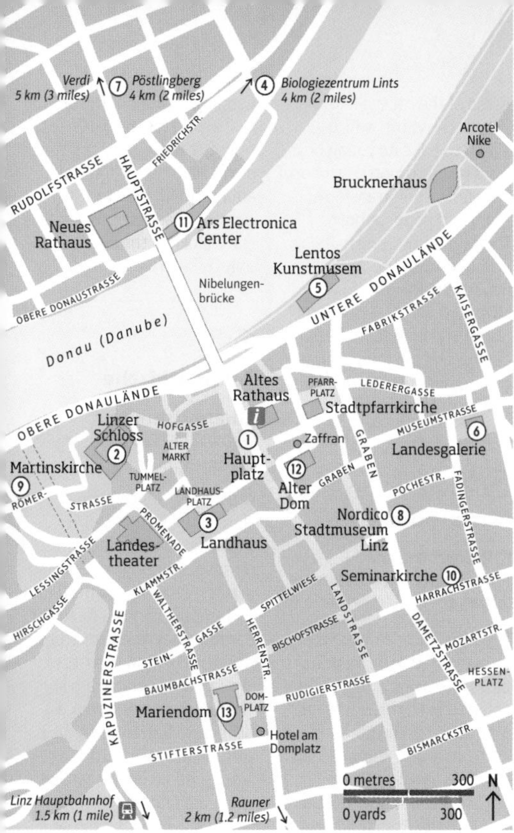
Verdi 5 km (3 miles)
7 Pöstlingberg 4 km (2 miles)
4 Biologiezentrum Lints 4 km (2 miles)
Arcotel Nike
Brucknerhaus
RUDOLFSTRASSE
HAUPTSTRASSE
FRIEDRICHSTR.
Neues Rathaus
11 Ars Electronica Center
Lentos Kunstmusem
5
Nibelungen-brücke
OBERE DONAUSTRASSE
UNTERE DONAULÄNDE
FABRIKSTRASSE
KAISERGASSE
Donau (Danube)
Altes Rathaus
PFARR-PLATZ
LEDERERGASSE
Stadtpfarrkirche
OBERE DONAULÄNDE
Linzer Schloss
2
HOFGASSE
ALTER MARKT
1
Haupt-platz
Zaffran
GRABEN
MUSEUMSTRASSE
6
Landesgalerie
Martinskirche
9
TUMMEL-PLATZ
12
Alter Dom
POCHESTR.
FADINGERSTRASSE
RÖMER-STRASSE
LANDHAUS-PLATZ
3
Landhaus
Nordico 8 Stadtmuseum Linz
PROMENADE
Landes-theater
LESSINGSTRASSE
KLAMMSTR.
Seminarkirche 10
HARRACHSTRASSE
SPITTELWIESE
LANDSTRASSE
HIRSCHGASSE
WALTHERSTRASSE
HERRENSTR.
BISCHOFSTRASSE
DAMETZSTRASSE
MOZARTSTR.
STEIN-GASSE
KAPUZINERSTRASSE
BAUMBACHSTRASSE
HESSEN-PLATZ
DOM-PLATZ
RUDIGIERSTRASSE
Mariendom 13
Hotel am Domplatz
STIFTERSTRASSE
BISMARCKSTR.
0 metres 300
0 yards 300
N
Linz Hauptbahnhof 1.5 km (1 mile)
Rauner 2 km (1.2 miles)

EAT

Rauner

This modern restaurant has tasty options for both carnivores and vegetarians, from burgers to risotto.

Kraussstrasse 16 Thu rauner.restaurant

€€€

Verdi

Slightly off the beaten track, this place is worth seeking out. Beef and lamb dominate the Italian-influenced menu.

Pachmayrstrasse 137 Sun & Mon verdi.at

€€€

Zaffran

The *dal makhani* is a speciality here, one of Austria's best Indian restaurants.

Domgasse 6 (0732) 771083 Thu

€€€

③

Landhaus

Theatergasse 1
(0732) 77200

The regional government is based in a Renaissance palace built on the site of a former Minorite monastery. Its north portal, on Klosterstrasse, is a marble work by Renaissance artists. The Planetenbrunnen (Fountain of the Planets) in the inner courtyard was built to commemorate the astronomer and mathematician Johannes Kepler, who lectured at the college, then based here, for 14 years (1612–26). The seven figures on the fountain's plinth show the planets known at the time.

←

Flowers in bloom beside the plague column in the centre of Hauptplatz

④

Biologiezentrum Lints

Johann-Wilhelm-Klein-Str 73 10am-6pm Tue-Sun (to 9pm Thu) landesmuseum.at

Upper Austria's largest plant and animal research and exhibition centre features special interactive exhibits for children, plus plenty of creepy-crawlies. Outside gardens are devoted to rare flora.

⑤

Lentos Kunstmuseum

Ernst-Koref-Promenade 1 10am-6pm Tue-Sun (to 9pm Thu) lentos.at

The striking glass façade of this modern museum reflects the Danube. Its collection focuses on contemporary pieces, and features Op and Pop Art, Expressionism, Pluralism and plenty of Austrian photography.

⑥

Landesgalerie

Museumstrasse 14 10am-6pm Tue-Sun (to 9pm Thu) landes museum.at

The headquarters of the Oberösterreichisches Landesmuseum, the fine Landesgalerie features a superb collection of 20th-century and contemporary art, and an archive of photographs. Emphasis is placed on artists from Upper Austria.

⑦

Pöstlingberg

A short distance from Linz's centre, on the north bank of the Danube, is the base station of the Pöstlingbergbahn. This 537-m (1,762-ft) electric mountain railway, built in 1898, climbs steeply almost to the top of Pöstlingberg mountain. On the summit stands the Wallfahrtskirche zu den Sieben Schmerzen Mariens, the pilgrimage church of Our Lady of Seven Sorrows, which is regarded as one of the main symbols of Linz.

⑧

Nordico Stadtmuseum Linz

🏠 Dametzstrasse 23
🕙 10am–6pm Tue–Sun (to 9pm Thu) 🌐 nordico.at

In 1675, this 17th-century Baroque complex was the home of the college known as "Nordisches Stift", which aimed to educate young boys from Nordic countries – hence the name – and transform them into good Catholics. Today, this imposing building, now owned by the council, houses the Nordico Town Museum, with its collection of objects relating to the history of Linz. The top floor is given over to temporary exhibitions, mainly of Modern art.

⑨ 📓

Martinskirche

🏠 Römerstrasse/
Martinsgasse 📞 (0732) 777454

A modest façade hides what is considered to be Austria's oldest surviving church. Dedicated to St Martin, it was first mentioned in the 8th century. The Gothic and Romanesque windows and portals are particularly noteworthy. There was an older Roman wall on the same site, and ten Roman tombstones, together with other ancient stones, were used to erect the church. Most of the interior dates from the Carolingian period. The arch that separates the nave from the presbytery and the north wall of the church are adorned with 14th to 15th-century frescoes of the Virgin Mary. Much of the interior can only be seen with a guide.

⑩

Seminarkirche

🏠 Harrachstrasse 7
📞 (0732) 771205
🕙 7am–5pm daily

Artistically, this seminary church, the former church of the Teutonic Order, is the most valuable church building in Linz. It was built in the early 18th century, and its beautiful Baroque façade is topped with the decorative coats of arms of the Harrach family. The tower, crowned with a distinctive flattened dome, is surrounded by sandstone statues depicting the virtues expected of a Knight of the Order. The interior is in the shape of an ellipse and features a ceiling relief showing God the Father reigning among a host of angels on a sky, adorned with filigree leaf ornaments.

STAY

Hotel am Domplatz

This adults-only hotel is perfectly located beside Mariendom. Stylish rooms offer views of Austria's largest cathedral or the centre.

🏠 Stifterstrasse 4
🌐 hotelamdomplatz.at

€€€

Arcotel Nike

High-rise hotel close to the Danube with unbeatable views. The restaurant serves tasty Austrian and international cuisine.

🏠 Untere Donaulände 9
🌐 arcotelhotels.com/nike

€€€

→
The cool Ars Electronica Center, home to Philip Beesley's permanent Hylozoic Grove installation *(inset)*

⑪ ⊘ Ⓜ Ars Electronica Center

⌂ Ars-Electronica-Strasse 1
⏰ 9am–5pm Tue–Fri (to 9pm Thu); 10am–6pm Sat, Sun & hols 🌐 aec.at

At the entrance to the Nibelungenbrücke (Bridge of the Nibelungs), on the north bank of the Danube, stands one of Austria's most unusual museums, or rather exhibition centres. The Ars Electronica Center is a highly original museum of virtual worlds and demonstrates the latest computer wizardry and virtual-reality simulations of space and time travel. You can, for example, journey inside various parts of the universe, visit imaginary Renaissance towns or see a flying saucer disappear into space. There is also a 3D virtual space in the basement where you can explore other worlds with special headsets.

⑫ Alter Dom

⌂ Domgasse 3 ☎ (0732) 7708660 ⏰ 7:30am–6:30pm daily

In 1785, the former Jesuit church was chosen as the cathedral of Linz, which had been made the capital of the archbishopric of Upper Austria two years earlier. Ignatiuskirche, the church of St Ignatius, was built in the second half of the 17th century, and today its green façade and onion-dome-topped twin towers are distinctive features in the town panorama. The modest exterior of the church conceals a beguiling Baroque interior. Particularly fascinating are the beautifully engraved stalls in the presbytery, where local artists carved figures of dwarfs and monsters peeping out from behind the back-rests and armrests. From 1856 until 1868 the composer Anton Bruckner was the cathedral's organist. The present organ was altered according to his desires.

⑬ Mariendom

⌂ Herrenstrasse 26 ☎ (0732) 946100 ⏰ 7:30am–7pm Mon–Sun (from 8am Sun)

This Neo-Gothic cathedral, completed in 1924, is Austria's largest sacred structure, with a capacity of 20,000. It is said that only one condition was stipulated by the local council: the steeple must not be taller than that of the Stephansdom (p76) in Vienna. Complying with the request, the tower is 3 m (10 ft) lower. Don't miss its modern, colourful stained-glass windows.

> 📷 PICTURE PERFECT
> **Ars Electronica in the Evening**
>
> The LED façade of this contemporary building lights up in bright colours at night, making for a cool Instagram shot. Shoot up close and point your camera upwards to get the best angle.

A boat cruising on the warm Lake Mondsee, with scenic views of the mountains ↑

2

SALZKAMMERGUT LAKES

🅰D4 **ⓘ** Salzkammergut Tourism, Salinenplatz 1, Bad Ischl; www.salzkammergut.at

This corner of Austria is one of its most visited regions, with over 70 lakes surrounded by mountains and charming towns. During winter it becomes a hotspot for skiers, while the summer months serve hikers and those keen to take in the views. This is also one of the few areas in Europe to preserve many original folk customs.

① Mondsee

🚌 ⓘ Dr Franz-Müller-Strasse 3; www.mondsee.salzkammergut.at

Mondsee is the warmest of the lakes, set at the foot of craggy mountains. The little town of the same name arose around a Benedictine abbey, founded in 748, now a Gothic structure that dominates the town. The wedding scene in *The Sound of Music* was filmed inside the abbey's church. On the edge of the water are a number of UNESCO-listed Bronze Age stilt-houses, best seen on one of the many boats that offer short cruises around the lake.

② Attersee

🚌 Litzlberg **Ⓦ** attersee-attergau.salzkammergut.at

The largest of the lakes, Attersee is dominated by the Höllengebirge (Mountains of Hell). A great base for boating holidays and water sports, the lake's crystal-clear water is also perfect for bathing, and there are many grassy beaches to relax on.

POLITICIANS AND ARTISTS ON HOLIDAY

The shores of the Salzkammergut lakes have seen many famous visitors. Gustav Klimt had his summer retreat in Attersee, and other visitors included musicians Brahms and Strauss. In the late 20th century, numerous politicians spent their holidays in St Wolfgang, including both the Austrian and German chancellors.

Weisses Rössl hotel, which inspired the operetta *White Horse Inn* by Ralph Benatzky.

④
Seeschloss Ort

🚩 Gmunden 🚌
🕒 9:30am-4:30pm daily
ℹ Toscanapark 1, Gmunden

This pretty castle on the northern edge of the Traunsee has a quadrangular tower topped by an onion dome. Connected to the mainland by a bridge, it is a popular wedding venue and houses a museum dedicated to the lake's mountain rescue teams.

⑤
Ebensee

🚩🚌 ℹ Hauptstrasse 34; www.traunsee-almtal. salzkammergut.at

This town, a centre of the salt industry for more than 1,000 years, is scenically located at the southern end of Traunsee. It is famous for its winter sports and carnival festivities.

③
St Wolfgang

ℹ Au 140; www.stwolf gang.at

The main attraction in this town is the parish church, with its beautiful altarpiece by the South Tyrolean artist Michael Pacher. It is also home to the

Must See

EAT

See Restaurant
It's the wonderful views of the Mondsee from the terrace that bring people here, but the food, including freshly caught trout and zander, helps them stay.

🚩 Robert Baum-Promenade 1, Mondsee
🌐 seerestaurant-mondsee.at

€€€

DRINK

13er haus
Sophisticated gin cocktails are the bar staff's speciality - perfect for sipping on warm evenings out on the terrace.

🚩 Markt 13, St Wolfgang
🌐 13erhaus.at

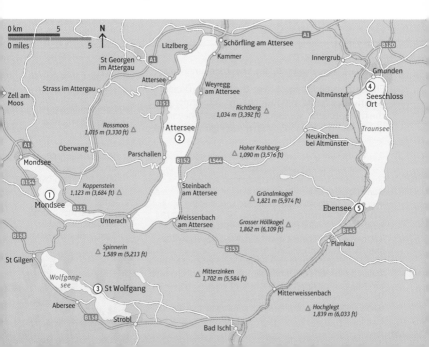

A boat heading towards St Nikola, nestled in dense woodland ↑

③

THE DANUBE VALLEY

🅰 E3-G3 🅰 Lindengasse 9, Linz; www.donauregion.at

Europe's second-longest river, the Danube (Donau) is unrivalled for its romantic charms. A tour along the river provides stunning views of neat vineyards interspersed with looming fortresses along the banks.

Passing through ten countries, the Danube enters Austria as a mountain river just outside of Passau, traverses Upper and Lower Austria for some 360 km (240 miles), and exits after the Hainburg marshes en route to Bratislava in Slovakia. The most impressive section of the Danube, also known as the Wachau, is located between the cities of Krems (p171) and Melk (p160). Now a UNESCO World Heritage Site, this stretch of the river is renowned for its quaint towns and dense woodland. The majestic river is perhaps best experienced by bicycle or foot, if not by boat. Architecture enthusiasts should look out for the romantic silhouette of Clam Castle, rising above a deep ravine, which has remained virtually unchanged since the 12th century. The Danube ends its journey through Upper Austria near St Nikola an der Donau, an area of outstanding natural beauty.

CONCENTRATION CAMPS

Though the valley is a fairy tale delight today, the town of Mauthausen, dotted on the river banks east of Linz, offers a shocking contrast. More than 50 concentration camps were built in Austria during the Third Reich, and the most confronting memorial, the former camp at Mauthausen (p40), has been preserved. Just outside the camp is a visitors' centre and insightful museum. Each year the liberation is celebrated on the Sunday nearest 8 May.

↑ Cycling on the flat paths that run along the scenic Danube

1 Colourful residential houses dot the landscape of St Nikola an der Donau, where the Danube crosses into Lower Austria.

2 The Renaissance municipal tower of Enns stands on the Hauptplatz, on the left bank of the Enns river, just before it joins the Danube.

3 A boat cruise is a scenic way to take in all of the villages along the valley.

STAY

Zum Goldenen Schiff
Located in the centre of Enns, with comfortable rooms and a sauna.

🏠 Hauptplatz 23, Enns
🌐 hotel-brunner.at

€€€

Donauhof
Modern hotel with views of the Danube. The bar serves local beer and wine.

🏠 Promenade 30, Mauthausen 🌐 donau-hof.at

€€€

Goldenes Kreuz
This cosy hotel is one of the oldest houses in Grein, dating from 1491.

🏠 Stadtplatz 8, Grein
🌐 hotel-in-grein.at

€€€

EXPERIENCE MORE

❹ Perg

ⒶE3 🅿🚌 ℹ(07262) 53150

Perg, a small town with a long history situated some 30 km (19 miles) east of Linz, was once owned by the mighty von Perg family, whose last remaining member died in the 12th century, during the Third Crusade. Until the 19th century, Perg was the largest centre of millstone production; now it is the home of Manner, the largest manufacturer of sweet wafers in the world. Worth seeing today are the attractive houses on Herrengasse, a 1683 Baroque pillory in the main square and St James' Church (1416), which has retained its Gothic interior.

Graves and numerous other remains of the Hallstatt civilization have been unearthed in Perg's environs. The excellent Heimathaus, at No 1 Stifterstrasse, exhibits finds from these excavations. It also records the production of millstones and has an interesting collection of 16th- to 17th-century ceramics, decorated using a special local technique.

JAKOB PRANDTAUER (1660-1726)

Austria's most outstanding architect of the Baroque, Prandtauer specialized in sacred buildings and shaped the present look of several medieval abbeys. His greatest masterpiece is the Benedictine abbey in Melk (p160). He also created the church of the Carmelite nuns in St Pölten, and gave a Baroque face to the Augustinian abbey in St Florian and the Benedictine abbey in Kremsmünster (p224). Distinctive features of his work are the variety of forms he used, and the way in which he blended architecture with the surrounding countryside.

---

❺ Stift St Florian

ⒶE3 🚌 🕐May-Oct: guided tours at 11am, 1pm & 3pm daily 🌐stift-st-florian.at

St Florian is an impressive abbey complex, with monks' quarters, reception rooms and a church with an adjoining chapel of the Virgin Mary. Named after Florian, the prefect of the Roman Noricum Province who converted to Christianity and was tortured and thrown into the Enns river in 304, this magnificent complex was built at his burial site by Augustinian monks. They remain the custodians of St Florian to this day. Its present appearance is the work of outstanding Baroque architects Carlo Carlone and Jakob Prandtauer. The main feature in the large courtyard is the Adlerbrunnen (Eagle Fountain), built in 1603. The east wing houses the library, with its vast collection of volumes, incunabula and manuscripts. The ceiling painting shows the marriage of Virtue with Knowledge. Next to the library is the Marble Hall with huge columns. The grand staircase in the west wing leads up to the emperor's

↓ Clouds gathering over St Florian Abbey in the evening

apartments. Adjacent is the room occupied by Austrian composer and organist Anton Bruckner, who was associated with St Florian for many years.

Carlo Carlone remodelled the abbey church – widely considered to be his great masterpiece. Inside, the stained-glass windows, the pulpit and the main altar are all worthy of attention. In particular, the altar is backed with a remarkable painting of the Assumption of the Virgin Mary flanked by columns of pink Salzburg marble. The abbey also has an art gallery.

↑ Statue of St John of Nepomuk by the Linzertor gateway into Freistadt

6
Obernberg am Inn
🅰D3 🚌 🛈 Marktplatz 36; www.obernberg.at

The 1,000-year-old market town of Obernberg has done a grand job of preserving its charming Marktplatz, the central town square, lined with exceptionally beautiful houses with richly ornamented stucco façades. Particularly interesting are Nos 37, 38 and 57, whose decorations are attributed to the prominent Bavarian artist Johann Baptist Modler. The fountain in the centre of the square is surrounded by an assortment of striking sculptures. When visiting the parish church of Obernberg, the Annakapelle, it is worth taking the time to admire the 16th-century wood carving of the Holy Family. A castle, once owned by the bishops of Passau, has

also stood in Obernberg since the 12th century, but little remains of it.

Some 15 km (9 miles) south-east of Obernberg is Ried im Innkreis, the largest town of the Innviertel region, an agri-cultural centre and home of the Schwanthaler family of sculptors. Many members of the family were outstanding artists, active in the region from 1632 to 1838. The local museum, at No 13 Kirchenplatz, exhibits their works.

7
Freistadt
🅰E3 🚃🚌 🛈 Hauptplatz 1; www.freistadt.at

Freistadt, the largest town in the Mühlviertel region, was once the last border fortress on the route leading from the Alpine countries to Bohemia. Much of the medieval town wall has survived to this day, including several bastions and two impressive gateways; one of these, the late Gothic Linzer Tor, is the symbol of the town. The focal point of the old town, the rectangular Hauptplatz, is lined with historic houses. On its east side stands the town hall, with a carved fountain. The 15th-century Katharinen-münster, on the southwest

side of the square, was altered in the Baroque style by Austrian architect Johann Michael Prunner. The castle, not far from the main square, was built in 1397 for the widow of Prince Albert III. It now houses the **Schlossmuseum**, with a large collection of glass paint-ings and 11th-century pottery.

Schlossmuseum
♿ 🏛 Schlosshof 2 🕐 Times vary, check website 🌐 museum-freistadt.at

---

💬 INSIDER TIP
Florian's Finest

Church services at St Florian Abbey often include choral music from the Florianer Sängerknaben, the abbey boys' brilliant choir, one of the most respected choral groups in the country.

8

Kremsmünster

E4 ☐ ☐ For guided tours by appointment
stift-kremsmuenster.at

Perched high above the Krems river, on an impressive terrace formed during the Ice Age, is the 8th-century Benedictine abbey of Kremsmünster, its present appearance dating mostly from the 17th century. The abbey was completed by Jakob Prandtauer (p222); two of its most remarkable features are the 17th-century fish ponds, surrounded by columns and fountains, and the eight-storey Sternwarte, or "Mathematical Tower". Completed in 1756, the 50-m- (165-ft-) high observation tower was probably the tallest secular building of its era. Today it holds collections ranging from palaeontology to physics. The Stiftskirche (abbey church) has rich stucco decorations, and the abbey museum contains works by Austrian and Dutch masters from the Baroque and Renaissance periods. The pride of Kremsmünster are its earliest exhibits, which includes the gilded copper chalice of Tassilo III, Duke of Bavaria (741–796), the founder of the abbey.

→

The Tassilo Chalice in Kremsmünster's Stiftskirche

9

Schärding

D3 ☐ **schaerding.at**

This town on the banks of the Inn river was, until 1779, owned by the Bavarian family of Wittelsbach, whose influence is most conspicuous in the local architecture. Schärding's stand-out feature is without doubt the Stadtplatz, the picture-perfect central square, which is bisected by a cluster of buildings. At the north end of the upper square, Silberzeile (Silver Line) is a row of beautiful colourful houses with gabled roofs, overlooked by the grand steeple of the vast St George's Church. Little of the old castle – apart from the gateway and moat – remains here. The gateway houses a brilliant regional museum with a late Gothic Madonna, a beautiful crucifix and sculptures by the Austrian sculptor Johann Peter Schwanthaler the Elder (1720–95).

10

Braunau am Inn

D3 ☐ ☐ **i** Stadtplatz 2;
www.tourismus-braunau.at

Braunau is a substantial border town on the Inn river and one of the prettiest spots in the entire region. It was built by the dukes of Lower Bavaria, who ruled over the town for several centuries. Originally intended as a bridgehead in their battles with the Turks, it remained one of the best-fortified towns in this part of Europe until the 17th century. The town changed hands several times in the 18th and 19th centuries, eventually being ceded to the Austrian Empire in 1816, when boundaries were redrawn following the Napoleonic Wars. Braunau's Baroque fortifications were dismantled by Napoleon, but the remains of several medieval buildings have survived. The centre of this Gothic town is occupied by the elongated Stadtplatz, surrounded by historic houses. At No 18 Johann-Fischer-Gasse, built in 1385, an old bell foundry has survived virtually intact. Together with the former ducal

Colourful gabled-roof houses on Silberzeile in Schärding

↓

castle at No 10 Altstadt, next door, it is now the home of the Bezirksmuseum Herzogsburg. This good regional museum specializes in the art, handicrafts and traditions of the Inn region.

The town's symbol is the nearly 100-m- (330-ft-) tall tower of the Stephanskirche. Construction of the church began in 1492, but the bulbous Baroque cupola dates from a later period. The interior boasts a fabulous stone pulpit. The only surviving parts of the original altarpiece by Michael Zürn, of the prolific Zürn family of sculptors, are figures of the Madonna with Child and saints Stephen and Laurence. The altar itself is a Neo-Gothic copy of Michael Pacher's altar in St Wolfgang (p219), dating from 1906. Among the tombs outside the church is one of Hans Staininger, mayor of Braunau in the 1600s, who is shown with a curly beard reaching to his toes. Legend has it that his beard may have been the cause of his untimely death – he tripped over his 1.2-m- (4-ft-) long facial hair and broke his neck. The beard was removed after his death and is now on display in the regional museum.

Braunau is also known as the birthplace of Adolf Hitler, who lived at No 15 Salzburger Vorstadt until he was two. In 2016, the Austrian government authorized a plan to demolish the building.

⓫

Lambach

Ⓐ D3 **🚌🚆** **Ⓒ (07245) 283550**

Lambach, on the left bank of the Traun river, grew rich in the Middle Ages thanks to the flourishing salt trade. Around 1040, Count Arnold II von Wels-Lambach and his wife Regilinda transformed the family seat into a monastery. Their son, Bishop Adalbero of Würzburg, invited the Benedictine monks here in 1089. In the same year, the Lambach monks established a second monastery at Melk (p160), which was eventually to surpass the mother abbey in terms of status and beauty. The abbey church was mostly rebuilt in the 17th century; rebuilding of the abbey itself was completed 50 years later.

The Baroque interior of the church is quite beautiful, but Lambach owes its fame primarily to its Romanesque frescoes, dating from around the 11th century. Unique in Austria, they are considered an outstanding example of Romanesque art. At their centre is the Madonna with Child, to the left the Adoration of the Magi, who present gifts to the Holy Infant. The south vault depicts Jerusalem and Herod's palace. The abbey treasury also holds the Romanesque chalice of Bishop Adalbero, as well as other precious religious items. Also on view are ceiling frescos by painters Martino Altomonte

→

Medieval Romanesque fresco in the Benedictine monastery Lambach

EAT

Lukas

Creative, regional cuisine served in an atmospheric former wine cellar with two set menus, crafted to your tastes. Reservations are a must.

Ⓐ D3 **🏠 Unterer Stadtplatz 7, Schärding** **🗓 Sun & Mon** **🌐 lukas-restaurant.at**

€€€

Jack Richard Bögl

Try the smoked mackerel and trout at this well-priced restaurant with views of the Inn. Kids will love the *Curry-wurst* while parents sample local brews.

Ⓐ D3 **🏠 Therese Riggle Str. 27, Obernberg** **🗓 Sun** **🌐 hohlagarten.at**

€€€

and Martin Johann Schmidt. The musical archives hold a copy of Mozart's *Lambacher Symphonie*, which the composer reputedly wrote while staying here. Another highlight in Lambach is a beautifully preserved Rococo theatre.

⑫ Steyr

🏛 E4 🚂🚌 ℹ️ Stadtplatz 27, (07252) 53229

While being one of Austria's largest industrial centres, Steyr has managed to preserve its old town almost intact. Steyr's townscape is punctuated in the north by the turrets of the castle and in the south by the towers of the Stadtpfarrkirche (parish curch), at Brucknerplatz. Stadtplatz (Town Square) lies at the centre of town, and is where most of the historic sights are congregated. Bummerlhaus (1497), at No 32, is a well-preserved Gothic town house with a striking high-pitched roof and three arcaded courtyards; the Rococo Rathaus (town hall), with its slender steeple, was designed by Johann Gotthard Hayberger. The inner court-yards of the houses encircling the square are also worth a look. Built in 1443, the fine Stadtpfarrkirche was re-modelled in the Neo-Gothic style, but it has held on to some of its original 15th-century decor, the work of

> **Steyr's townscape is punctuated in the north by the turrets of the castle and in the south by the towers of the Stadtpfarrkirche (parish church).**

Hans Puchsbaum (builder of Vienna's Stephansdom). The south wall has magnificent 15th-century stained-glass windows; the sculptures in the north portal and the former cemetery chapel of St Margaret (1430), also by Hans Puchsbaum, date from the same period.

The Schloss (castle), first mentioned in 10th-century annals, stands in the oldest part of the town. Today it has a Baroque façade and a mostly Rococo interior. The house at No 26 Grünmarkt, formerly a granary, is now a museum.

Some 3 km (2 miles) west of the town centre, in the suburb of **Christkindl**, is the church of the same name (meaning "Infant Christ"). The name originates from a wax figurine of Jesus, still kept here in a beautifully decorated glass cabinet, which is believed to perform healing miracles. The cabinet itself is arranged as part of a composition symbol-izing the Holy Trinity.

Christkindl Church
🏠 Christkindlweg 69
📞 (07252) 54622

---

⑬ Schwanenstadt

🏛 D4 🚂🚌 ℹ️ Stadtplatz 54, (07673) 2255

Schwanenstadt is a typical small Upper Austrian town, situated between Lambach and Vöcklabruck. In the centre of town stands a Neo-Gothic parish church with a 78-m (256-ft) spire, built in 1900

on the site of an earlier Gothic church. Worth seeing inside are a late-Gothic statue of the Virgin Mary, a 15th-century relief of the Mourning for Christ and 18th-century Baroque statues of the 12 apostles.

In front of the town hall is a 13th-century well, which is set on an attractive square lined with houses with Renaissance and Baroque façades.

---

⑭ Wels

🏛 E3 🚂🚌 ℹ️ Stadtplatz 44; www.wels.at

The history of Wels dates back to the Roman era, as demon-strated by numerous excava-tions in the area. Some of the objects discovered are on display in the former Minorites' abbey, including the famous Wels Venus, a bronze statuette from the 1st–2nd century AD, and the oldest early Christian epitaph in Austria, from the first half of the 4th century.

Today Wels is a centre of agriculture and industry, and once every two years plays host to Agraria, an interna-tionally renowned agricultural fair. Many historic features have also been preserved. The houses in Stadtplatz, the main square in the old town, have attractive façades, such as the Rococo Kremsmünstererhof. Adjacent to it stands a water tower (1577) and the late-Baroque town hall.

Also on Stadtplatz is the Stadtpfarrkirche, with an original Romanesque portal and magnificent 14th-century stained-glass windows. Burg Wels, the imperial palace, first documented in 776, is now a lively cultural and museum centre. As well as collections relating to the city and its

← The high-pitched roof of Bummerlhaus on the Stadtplatz in Steyr

↑ Heading into the ancient Dachsteinhöhlen cave system, home to weird and wonderful ice formations *(inset)*

history, Burg Wels also houses the Österreichisches Gebäckmuseum (Austrian Pastry Museum) and the Museum der Heimatvertriebenen (Museum of the Expellees), dedicated to German-speaking people expelled from Eastern Europe after World War II.

Burg Wels

♿🚫 🏠 Burggasse 13
🕐 10am–5pm Tue–Fri, 2–5pm Sat, 10am–4pm Sun

---

15 ♿ Ⓜ

Dachsteinhöhlen

🅐 D4 🚌🚆 ℹ Winkl 34, Obertraun am Hallstättersee; www.dachsteinsalzkammergut.com

The caves in the slopes of the Dachstein range are among Austria's most beautiful and intriguing natural monuments. The vast Dachsteinhöhlen cave system, one of the largest on Earth and several millions of years old, is covered by a 500-year-old permafrost. After the last Ice Age, underground waters began to create miraculous ice mountains, glaciers and frozen waterfalls, unseen by man. The most spectacular of these is the Rieseneishöhle (Giant Ice Cave). The caverns in this surreal underground ice world are named after King Arthur and the Celtic heroes Parsifal and Tristan. The most arresting cavern formation is the so-called Ice Chapel.

A little further along is the entrance to a second system of caves, known as Mammuthöhle (Mammoth Cave), so named because of the astonishing dimensions of the underground spaces and passageways contained within the cave system. As well as gaining an insight into how the caves developed, you are treated to spectacular light shows, an installation from the Linz University of Art.

Both networks of caves can be reached via paths starting from the first cable-car station. The sightseeing route leads through a labyrinth of tunnels, gorges and chambers that stretch over 44 km (27 miles), with a 1,200 m (4,000 ft) change in altitude. Individual caverns have been given evocative names such as the Realm of Shadows or Midnight Cathedral. Also worth seeing is a third cave, Koppenbrüllerhöhle, which is considered to be the largest water cave in the Dachstein massif.

All caves are open to the public only during the spring and summer seasons. Make sure you take warm clothing.

30,000 m³

The volume of ice in the Mammuthöhle at Dachsteinhöhlen.

↑ Remigiuskirche's carved altar in Gampern, near Vöcklabruck

16
Vöcklabruck

🅐D4 🚃 🆒 ℹ️ Graben 8; (07672) 26644

The name of this town was first documented in 1134 as Pons (bridge) Veckelahe. Soon after, a trading settlement sprang up on the banks of the Vöckla river. The only original structures from this period are two medieval towers.

At the centre of town stands the small, 15th-century, late Gothic St Ulrichkirche (Church of St Ulrich), which has a fine Baroque interior. The site of the former 12th-century hospital and chapel is now occupied by the Baroque St Ägidiuskirche (Church of St Giles), designed by Carlo Carlone, with sculptures by Giovanni Battista Carlone, both Italian painters. Frescoes here depict scenes from the lives of Christ and the Virgin Mary.

The former parish house at No 10 Hinterstadt now houses a regional museum with a room devoted to Austrian composer Anton Bruckner.

The south of the town is dominated by the imposing silhouette of Wallfahrtskirche Maria Schöndorf, first recorded in 824. This pilgrimage church is instantly recognizable thanks to its two unequal towers, a result of the turmoil of the Reformation in the 16th century, which halted building work until the second tower was added much later. It has a Neo-Gothic altarpiece with a beautiful 15th-century statue of the Virgin Mary, and equally pretty stained-glass windows behind the main altar from the same period.

West of Vöcklabruck, about 12 km (7 miles) away, is the small town of Gampern. Its Remigiuskirche (Church of St Remigius) has an attractive late-Gothic polyptych (1507) carved in wood.

17
Bad Hall

🅐E4 🚃 ℹ️ Kurpromenade 1; www.badhall.at

Bad Hall, a market town at the foothills of the Alps between Steyr and Kremsmünster, lies on the so-called "Romantic Route", the 380-km trek from Salzburg and Vienna. But the idyllic scenery is just one of its attractions: it also features the richest iodine springs in Central Europe, around which a spa resort was first built in the 19th century. The Kurpark (spa park), with its excellent sports facilities, makes conva-lescence a real treat. There is also a Rococo church, which belongs to the abbey at Kremsmünster. Another sight worth visiting is the **Forum Hall Museum**, which holds a superb collection devoted to the development of traditional folk handicrafts in Upper Austria, and the history of the local springs.

Forum Hall Museum

⊛ 🅐 Eduard-Bach-Strasse 4 🕒 Apr-Oct: 2–6pm Thu–Sun 🌐 forumhall.at

💬 INSIDER TIP
On Your Bike

Bad Hall is the starting point for 12 cycling routes through the surrounding country-side. Bikes can be rented from the tourism office, and maps are available to ensure you don't get lost en route.

18
Stadl-Paura

🅐D4 🚃 ℹ️ Marktplatz 1; www.traun-ager-alm.at

The history of Stadl-Paura, a small town on the right bank of the Traun river 2 km (1 mile) south of Lambach, has been closely tied to salt shipping on the Traun since the early 1300s. Salt would be trans-ported down the river in long *Trauner* boats and offloaded at the Danube, at which point the boats were sold off as fuel or lumber. To save resources, the boat owners opted to drag the boats back up the

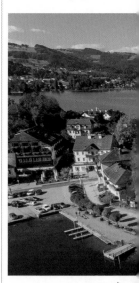

→

The Johannesbergkapelle chapel above Traunkirchen on Traunsee lake river using harnessed horses. Local tour operators allow you to relive this experience with fully costumed boatmen.

Horse breeding has also played a big part in the town's history. Tours can be arranged at the 200-year-old Pferde- zentrum (Horse Centre), where world-class race horses are bred and trained.

The Dreifaltigkeitskirche (Church of the Holy Trinity) dominates the town centre. Construction began in 1714 in thanksgiving for the sparing of the town from the plague.

The house at No 13 Fabrik- strasse is now the Schiffleut- museum (Shipping Museum), which is open on Sundays and holidays in the summer.

> ## Did You Know?
>
> Every June, Stadl-Paura celebrates "Traun in Flammen" by sailing a flaming 24-m (78-ft) boat down the river.

⑲ Kefermarkt

🅰E3 🚌 ℹ️ Oberer Markt 15; www.kefermarkt.at

The main attraction in this little town is its 15th-century Wallfahrtskirche (pilgrimage church), built by Christoph von Zelking, the master of Kefermarkt's castle, Schloss Weinberg. He also commis- sioned its altar, dedicated to his favourite saint, St Wolfgang, bishop of Regensburg and Heinrich II's tutor. The creator of the altar is unknown, but the result is a masterpiece of medieval art. Carved from limewood, it was probably once painted, but the original texture and colour of the wood have since come to the surface. On the wings of the altar, the artist has placed scenes of the Annunciation, the Birth of Christ, the Adoration of the Magi and the Death of Mary. The altar was once riddled with woodworm and only narrowly escaped total destruction. It was restored in 1852–5, under the careful supervision of

Adalbert Stifter, a writer and school inspector for Upper Austria. There is also an inter- esting permanent exhibition in the church called "Jesus on the Road".

⑳ Traunkirchen

🅰D4 🚌 ℹ️ Toscanapark 1; (07612) 74451

Precariously perched on a rocky promontory, the small, pretty village of Traunkirchen clings to the west shore of Traunsee, Austria's deepest lake, with views of the lake's wild southern shore and the Traunstein peak on the eastern shore. Way above the village towers the cheerful Johannesbergkapelle, while on the northern end of the headland stands the Jesuit Pfarrkirche, rebuilt after a fire in 1632. It has an unusual pulpit shaped like a fishing boat, with the apostles drawing nets filled with fish. Since 1632, the town has also hosted an annual Corpus Christi boat procession.

Cycling around the unspoilt Gosauseen mountain lakes as the sun beams down ↑

21
Gosauseen

🅐D4 🚌 ℹ️ Gosausee-strasse 5; www.dachstein-salzkammergut.at

For pure, natural, unspoilt beauty, this area has few rivals. The Gosauseen are three small mountain lakes – Vorderer Gosausee, Gosaulacke and Hinterer Gosausee. They lie one after the other, surrounded by forest and limestone rocks, and intercut with deep gorges. An undemanding walk around Vorderer Gosausee will reward you with superb views of the surrounding mountains and over the Dachstein range,

---

📷 **PICTURE PERFECT**
Go See Vorderer Gosausee

In sunny weather, it is usually impossible not to get a great shot of the view from Vorderer Gosausee looking towards the snow-capped Hoher Dachstein mountains.

---

with its many glaciers. The most picturesque mountain, with zigzag peaks and a sheer drop, is Gosaukamm. This is the easternmost part of the Alps where the snow stays on the ground all year round. The ski area above the lake, with modern lifts providing entry from Mittertal, Russbach and Gosau, is one of the most extensive and snow-sure in the region.

The steep road leading to Hinterer Gosausee climbs through thick forest, and the lake is a good starting point for climbing the adjacent peaks.

22
Schafberg

🅐D4 🅰️ Scharfbergbahn 🌐 scharfbergbahn.at

One of the most picturesque peaks in the Salzkammergut, Schafberg (Sheep Mountain) rises to 1,783 m (5,850 ft) between Wolfgangsee and Attersee. Austria's steepest cog railway runs old steam trains up to a station 50 m (164 ft) from the summit for

unforgettable views of the most beautiful surrounding lakes: Mondsee, Attersee and Wolfgangsee (p218). Looming in the background are the mountain ranges running to the Dachstein massif in the south, and, beyond Salzburg, the Bavarian Alps on the German–Austrian border.

23
Bad Ischl

🅐D4 🚉🚌 ℹ️ Auböckplatz 5; www.badischl.salz kammergut.at

Therapeutic saltwater springs were discovered in this region as early as the 16th century, but Bad Ischl did not become a popular health resort until the early 1800s, when the court doctor ordered saline treatments for Archduchess Sophie after a period of infertility. Soon after, she gave birth to future emperor Franz Joseph and his two brothers after taking the waters at the spa's brine baths. Locals came to refer to the trio as the "Salt Princes". Franz Joseph spent

is known for its fine ceramics. Gmunden's old town centre is situated between the lake and the western bank of the Traun river. Its Hauptplatz boasts a Renaissance town hall with a small, arcaded tower and a carillon that plays regularly. The Stadtpfarrkirche (parish church) has a two-fold dedication: the Virgin Mary and the Three Kings. The Magi are also depicted in the main altarpiece. Each year on Epiphany Eve (5 Jan), a barge travels along the Traun river bringing the "Three Kings" into town; they then solemnly proceed to the church. A ceramic fountain decorated with a figure of a salt miner stands beside the church.

Based in the Renaissance building of the former Salt Mines Authorities is the **Gmunden K-Hof Museum**, which has exhibits on the history of the town and its salt production, a room on the influential astronomer and mathematician Johannes von Gmunden, and a section dedicated to the history of sanitation, which includes displays of locally made toilet bowls and chamber pots.

In Traunsee stands the water fortress of Schloss Ort, a castle built on the lake in the 15th and 16th centuries and rebuilt in 1634. It has an enchanting triangular, arcaded courtyard and remnants of Renaissance frescoes. A popular Austrian TV drama series, *Schlosshotel Orth*, is set in the castle.

Gmunden K-Hof Museum

♨ ☷ 🏠 Kammerhofgasse 8 🕐 10am–4pm Wed–Sun (Jun–Sep: also Tue) 🖥 museum. gmunden.at

his summers with his wife Elisabeth at the **Kaiservilla**, now a museum. It was also here that he declared war with Serbia, on 1 August 1914, signalling the beginning of World War I.

Many aristocrats and artists have been attracted to the spa over the years, among them the composer Franz Lehár, who lived at No 8 Franz-Lehár-Kai, which is now a museum devoted to his life.

Kaiservilla

♨ ☷ 🖕 🏠 Jainzen 38 🕐 For tours only: times vary, check website 🚫 Nov, 24 Dec 🖥 kaiservilla.at

---

24

Gmunden

🄰D4 🚉🚌 🅸 Kammerhof gasse 8; www.traunsee-almtal.at/gmunden

This lakeside town, at the northern end of Traunsee, first established itself as a trading post in the salt trade. Today, it is a popular and well-respected health resort, and

↑ The clock tower of Schloss Ort, Gmunden, towering over the inner courtyard

㉕

Hallstatt

⚑D4 🚗🚌⛴ ℹSeestrasse 99; www.hallstatt.net

The village of Hallstatt is one of the most picturesque tourist destinations in the Salzkammergut. The steep drop of the Dachstein massif provides a scenic backdrop for the town and the adjacent Hallstätter See. The houses are clustered together so tightly that many are accessible only from the lakeside, while the old street runs above the rooftops. Even the local Corpus Christi procession is held on the lake, in festive, decorated boats.

A salt-mining outpost since prehistoric times, Hallstatt is also the starting point of the world's oldest active industrial pipeline, which has been pumping brine to Ebensee since the 16th century. You can now hike the route of the old brine pipeline (Soleweg) for 20 km (12 miles) from Hallstatt to Bad Ischl.

Rising above the village on a rocky headland is the pagoda-like roof of the Pfarrkirche. Its stepped dome dates from a later period, but the church was built in the 15th century and to this day contains many original features, including a carved wooden altarpiece of the Virgin Mary. The figure of the Madonna at its centre is flanked by St Barbara, patron of miners, and St Catherine, revered by woodcutters. The

THE SALZKAMMERGUT

Salt has been excavated here since prehistoric times, and in the second half of the 19th century the area became famous for its therapeutic springs. The "land of salt" includes the eastern part of the Salzburg Alps, with the picturesque mountain ranges of Dachstein, Totes Gebirge (Dead Mountains) and Höllengebirge (Mountains of Hell). Between the mountains lie 76 lakes, including Traunsee, Mondsee, Attersee, Hallstätter See and Wolfgangsee. The largest part is in Upper Austria, a small area in the south belongs to Styria, whilst almost all of Wolfgangsee and the St Gilgen resort are part of Salzburgerland.

altar is guarded by the statues of two knightly saints, George and Florian.

In the cemetery outside the church stands the Beinhaus, a chapel that serves as a store-house for some rather bizarre objects. This former mortuary holds some 1,200 human skulls, painted with floral designs and in many cases inscribed with the name, date and cause of death of the deceased. Shortage of space in the graveyard meant that some ten years after a funeral the remains were moved to

the chapel to make room for the next coffin to be buried, resulting in this unusual depository.

A short distance below the Catholic Pfarrkirche stands the Neo-Gothic Evangelical church, which is distinguished by it's unusually slender steeple.

Directly above the town is **Salzwelten Hallstatt**, one of the oldest known salt mines in the world, which can be reached by cable car. Salt has been mined here from as early as 3000 BC and then transported to the Baltic Sea and the Mediterranean.

In 1846, a large cemetery yielding some 2,000 graves was uncovered in Hallstatt. The burial objects found here date mainly from the Iron Age, but some date even further

back, to the Bronze Age. The Hallstatt finds proved so archaeologically significant that the Celtic culture of that period (800–400 BC) was named the Hallstatt civiliza-tion. Its influence reached far into France, the Slavic countries and Hungary.

Today, Hallstatt treasures can be seen in several Austrian museums, though the bulk of them are held at Schloss Eggenberg, near Graz (p184). A few are still kept in Hallstatt's **World Heritage Museum**.

Salzwelten Hallstatt

♿ 🚻 🅿 🏠 Lahnstrasse 21 🕐 Late Apr–mid-Sep: 9:30am–4:30pm daily; mid-Sep–Oct: 9:30am–2:30pm daily 🌐 salzwelten.at

World Heritage Museum

♿ 🅿 🏠 Seestrasse 56 🕐 Apr & Oct: 10am–4pm daily; May–Sep: 10am–6pm daily; Nov–Mar: 11am–3pm Wed–Sun 🌐 museum-hallstatt.at

---

STAY

Bräugasthof

There are just eight rooms at this family-run guest house, but each is packed with traditional furniture and all offer wonderful views of the lake and mountains, gorgeous both in summer and winter. Bräugasthof also has a lakeside restaurant with a large terrace.

🅰D4 🏠Seestrasse 120, Hallstatt 🌐brauhaus-lobisser.com

€€€

← The peaceful lakeside village of Hallstatt, by the Dachstein massif

The green hills and craggy peaks of Pinzgau

SALZBURGER LAND

Neighbouring Germany, Salzburger Land is divided into five regions: Flachgau, Tennengebirge, Pongau, Pinzgau and Lungau. Colonization of the Salzach valley goes back to prehistoric times. The mineral deposits – copper, precious metals and, above all, salt (*Salz* in German) from which both the town and province take their names – were being exploited as early as 1000 BC. It was salt that created the basis for the development of the so-called Hallstatt civilization that spread from here. The Celtic town of Noricum established in the Alpine region ultimately became a Roman province of the same name.

Christianity arrived here early, and its turbulent progress was halted only by the great Migration of Nations in 5th-century Europe. It was not until the 7th century that monks settled in Mönchsburg, the future Salzburg, which became first a bishopric and then an archbishopric. The entire province was an independent principality for many centuries, governed by an ecclesiastical ruler acting as sovereign prince and, depending on political circumstance and personal preference, associating himself with the Holy Roman Empire, the Austrian Habsburgs or Rome. Following the Congress of Vienna in 1815, Salzburg became part of Austria. Today, the beauty of Salzburg, inextricably linked with Mozart, makes this province a visitor magnet.

SALZBURGER LAND

Must Sees

1 Salzburg
2 Gasteinertal

Experience More

3 Wasserschloss Anif
4 Schloss Hellbrunn
5 St Gilgen
6 Golling
7 Kaprun
8 Mauterndorf
9 Schloss Moosham
10 Hallein
11 Tamsweg
12 Bischofshofen
13 Abtenau
14 St Johann im Pongau
15 Radstadt
16 Wagrain
17 Werfen
18 Zell am See
19 Saalbach
20 Lofer
21 Mittersill
22 Krimmler Wasserfälle

TYROL AND
VORARLBERG
p258

OBER-
ÖSTERREICH

UPPER AUSTRIA
p210

SALZBURGER
LAND

Mattighofen

Strasswalchen

Mattsee

Wallersee

Neumarkt
am Wallersee

Seekirchen

Vöcklamarkt

Schörfling

Attersee

Traunsee

Grünau im
Almtal

Mondsee

Mondsee

Attersee

Weissenbach am
Attersee

Ebensee

Thalgau

1 SALZBURG
Salzburg Airport

Fuschl

4 SCHLOSS HELLBRUNN

5 ST GILGEN

Wolfgangsee St Wolfgang

**3 WASSERSCHLOSS
ANIF**

Oberalm

Salzkammergut Berge

Strobl

Bad Ischl

10 HALLEIN

Bad
Dürrnberg

Kuchl

Postalm

Bad Aussee

6 GOLLING

Scheffau

13 ABTENAU

Lueg Pass

Annaberg

Hallstatt

Pürgg

Annaberg

Tennengebirge

Lammer

Dachstein

△ Torstein
2,948 m (9,672 ft)

Gröbming

WERFEN 17

BISCHOFSHOFEN 12

Eben im Pongau

**ST JOHAN
IM PONGAU**

*Filzen
Pass*

Altenmarkt

15 RADSTADT

Schladming

STEIERMARK

14

Flachau

Schieferalpen

Lend

16 WAGRAIN

Untertauern

STYRIA
p178

Schwarzach im
Pongau

Flachauwinkl

Zauchensee

Dorfgastein

Grossarl

△ Fulseck
2,033 m (6,670 ft)

Obertauern
Radstädter Tauern Pass

Lessach

2 GASTEINERTAL

Bad
Hofgastein

Hüttschlag

Radstädter Tauern

△ Lungkogel
2,327 m (7,635 ft)

Bad Gastein

Kreuzkogel
2,620 m (8,596 ft)

MAUTERNDORF 8

11 TAMSWEG

**9 SCHLOSS
MOOSHAM**

St Michael im
Lungau

Stadl an
der Mur

Bockstein

Katschberg Pass

Predlitz

**CARINTHIA AND
EAST TYROL**
p288

Saraberg

Kremsbrücke

Königstuhl
2,336 m (7,664 ft)

KÄRNTEN

Gmünd

Obervellach

0 kilometres   20

0 miles   20

N

↑ Salzburg's fairytale steeples and iconic fortress on the hill

❶ SALZBURG

Ⓐ D4 ✈ Salzburg Airport W A Mozart, 4 km (2.5 miles) SW of town centre 🚃 Hauptbahnhof, Südtirolerplatz 🛈 Mozartplatz 5; www.salzburg.info

Steeped in legend and unrivalled for its Baroque architecture, Salzburg is most famous as the home of Mozart, who was born here in 1756. Music remains the city's main attraction: the annual Salzburg Festival is the largest of its kind in Europe, while some 300,000 visitors a year enjoy tours of the original locations used in the 1965 film *The Sound of Music*. It is also famous for its monumental fortress, Hohensalzburg.

① Kapuzinerberg

This hill on the right bank of the Salzach river is reached via 250 steep steps, known as the Imbergstiege, that climb up from Linzer Gasse. A small castle once stood on top of the hill and formed part of the medieval fortifications; later it was partly incorporated into the Capuchin monastery complex whose church was completed in 1602. Below the church, from the top of an old tower, the Hettwer Bastei, you can enjoy picture-perfect views over the many domes and spires that dot the Salzburg landscape.

② Stift Nonnberg

Ⓐ Nonnberggasse 2
Ⓒ (0662) 841607
🕐 7am-7pm daily (winter: to 5pm)

The Benedictine nunnery on the slope of Mönchsberg (Monks' Hill), now known as Nonnberg (Nuns' Hill), was founded in 714 by St Rupert, who established his niece, St Erentrude, as Mother Superior. Her tomb lies in the crypt of the church. The church was extended in the 11th and 15th centuries, and a true jewel of Nonnberg is its late-Gothic main altarpiece, brought from Scheffau and reputedly produced to sketches by Albrecht Dürer. Behind the main altar, in the central window of the apsis, is an interesting stained-glass panel by Peter Hemmel von Andlau, one of the most renowned stained glass artists in the late Gothic style.

③ Haus der Natur

Ⓐ Museumsplatz 5
🕐 9am-5pm daily
🌐 hausdernatur.at

Salzburg's Natural History Museum has a huge collection of fauna across 90 rooms and five floors. As well as exhibitions describing the animals, it has a space centre, an aquarium and a reptile zoo.

> 💬 INSIDER TIP
> **Start at the Very Beginning**
>
> Though many *Sound of Music* tours run in Salzburg, Panorama Tours (*www.panorama tours.com/salzburg*) offer unique experiences, from private tours to breakfast.

The museum's galleries are arranged thematically. In "Sea World", a gigantic aquarium re-creates conditions that closely resemble the natural habitat of various water creatures. There are also huge rooms simulating the natural habitat of Mississippi alligators and the lost worlds of Jurassic creatures, including firm favourites, the dinosaurs.

④
Sebastiansfriedhof

🏠 Linzer Gasse 41 ☎ (0662) 875208 🕒 9am–6:30pm daily (winter: to 4pm)

The St Sebastian cemetery lies just below the church of the same name. All that remains of the old church is a portal and a wrought-iron grille; the present modest building is from the early 19th century. The cemetery is older, dating from the 15th century, and was designed along the lines of the Italian *campo santo*,

with burial sites surrounded by columns. Beside the church is the tomb of the father of pharmacology, Paracelsus, who died in Salzburg in 1541.

⑤
Schloss Mirabell

🏠 Mirabellplatz ☎ (0662) 80720 🕒 8am–4pm Mon, Wed & Thu (from 1pm Tue & Fri)

The site of the present Mirabell Palace was originally used by Archbishop Wolf Dietrich von Raitenau in 1606; in 1727, Johann Lukas von Hildebrandt rebuilt it for Archbishop Franz Anton Fürst von Harrach as a royal Baroque home. A fire in 1818 destroyed part of the building, but fortunately the superb Angels Staircase and the gilt-stuccoed Marble Hall, where a young Wolfgang Mozart performed, were spared. The palace is now a civic administration building.

EAT

Bärenwirt
Popular with the locals, this spot offers huge portions of inexpensive staples such as goulasch and schnitzel.

🏠 Müllner Hauptstrasse 8 🌐 baerenwirt-salzburg.at

€€€

Esszimmer
Exquisite modern-European cuisine in a Michelin-starred restaurant. Three set menus include one for vegetarians.

🏠 Müllner Hauptstrasse 33 🕒 Sun & Mon 🌐 esszimmer.com

€€€

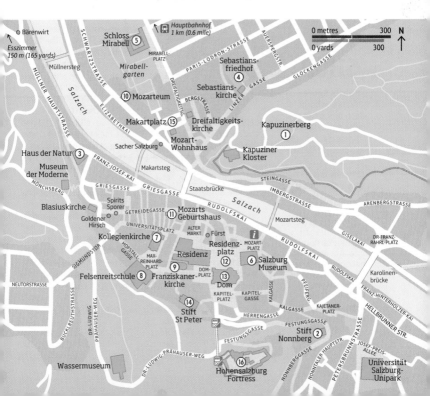

⑥

Salzburg Museum

⌂ Neue Residenz Mozartplatz 1 🕘 9am–5pm Tue–Sun (Jul & Aug: also Mon) 🌐 salzburgmuseum.at

This excellent history museum was founded in 1834 by the amateur collector and treasury official, Vinzenz Maria Süss, who donated his collections to the town. The most exciting items on display date back to Celtic times and include a Celtic pitcher from the Dürnberg area and a Bronze Age helmet from the Lueg Pass. The exhibits from Roman Salzburg, or Juvavum, are also interesting; there are fragments of mosaics and numerous architectural features and statues. Also worth seeing are paintings by the Baroque masters Paul Troger and Johann Michael Rottmayr, as well as those by Hans Makart, who was born in Salzburg. Other departments are devoted to handicrafts, musical instruments and coins.

SHOP

Spirits Sporer

Taste and buy a selection of schnapps and liqueurs made by the Sporer family, who have been producing spirits since 1903.

⌂ Freiheitsplatz 2
🕘 Sun 🌐 sporer.at

Fürst

The founder of this store, Paul Fürst, created Mozartkugeln – chocolates made with marzipan, hazelnut nougat presented in boxes carrying the portrait of Mozart.

⌂ Brodgasse 13
🌐 original-mozart kugel.com

---

⑦

Kollegienkirche

⌂ Universitätsplatz
📞 (0662) 841327
🕘 9am–dusk daily

The university church, consecrated in 1707, is one of Salzburg's finest Baroque structures. It was designed by Johann Bernhard Fischer von Erlach, who achieved fantastic and unusual effects by letting natural light shine through windows of various shapes. Italian artisans produced the beautiful stuccowork on the church walls to a design by von Erlach. The ornate main altarpiece shows the university as a temple of art and science and features winged figures symbolizing music, poetry, painting, architecture, philosophy, law and medicine.

---

⑧

Felsenreitschule

⌂ Hofstallgasse 1 📞 (0662) 80450 🕘 For guided tours at 2pm daily

Archbishop Wolf Dietrich von Raitenau started building the palace stables on the site of the former barracks in 1606. The marble fountain in the stable yard was built in 1695.

In 1917, it was decided that Salzburg should host a theatre and opera festival, and the stables were converted into the Small and Grand Festival Theatres. One of Austria's most outstanding architects, Clemens Holzmeister, designed the Small Festival Theatre during the 1920s, and then from 1956 until 1960 supervised the rebuilding of the Grand Festival Theatre. The building incorporates the original façade of the former stables and is one of the largest opera houses in the world. Its vast stage is 100 m (328 ft) wide and is carved deep into the rockface of Mönchsberg. It can accommodate up to 2,180 spectators.

↑ The impressive interior of the light-filled Franziskanerkirche

⑨

Franziskanerkirche

⌂ Franziskanergasse 5
📞 (0662) 843629
🕘 6:30am–8:30pm daily

The Franciscan Church with its Romanesque origins mixed with a Gothic style seems somewhat out of place in Baroque Salzburg. The 13th-century Romanesque portal leading to the presbytery is particularly fine, with a figure of Christ on the throne.

In the 16th century, when the Franciscan Church was used as a cathedral, it gained an additional Baroque portal, a ring of chapels and many rich interior furnishings. The architect of the new altar, Johann Bernhard Fischer von Erlach, preserved the central statue of the Madonna from the earlier Gothic altar made by Michael Pacher, the famed artist of the late Gothic. On the opposite side of the street are the monastery buildings, which are connected with the church by a bridge.

→

Neue Residenz with its iconic carillon opposite the Residenzplatz

Did You Know?

Part of the collection at the Mozarteum is Mozart's skull: it can be viewed on request.

⑩ 🅜

Mozarteum

🏠 Schwarzstrasse 26
🆆 mozarteum.at

In 1870, the International Foundation of Mozarteum was established here to celebrate Salzburg's favourite composer. Today, the Mozarteum stages concerts, is home to a music school and helps manage Salzburg's Mozart museums. In its grounds stands the cottage in which Mozart wrote *The Magic Flute*, brought here from Vienna.

⑪ 🄯 🅜

Mozarts Geburtshaus

🏠 Getreidegasse 9
☎ (0662) 844313
🕑 Jul & Aug: 8:30am-7pm daily; Sep-Jun: 9am-5:30pm daily

Music lovers should not miss Hagenauerhaus, at No 9 on the narrow Getreidegasse: the house where Wolfgang Amadeus Mozart was born on 27 January 1756. In 1880, a museum was established here, featuring a collection of Mozart memorabilia, including family portraits, documents and his first instruments. On the second floor is a delightful exhibition on the theatrical staging of Mozart's operas.

⑫

Residenzplatz

This popular square in the old town is home to a number of important buildings. The **Residenz**, built for Archbishop Wolf Dietrich von Raitenau, houses central government agencies and university offices, while the upper storeys are occupied by the Residenz-galerie, which displays art from the 16th to 19th centuries.

On the opposite side of the square stands the Neue Residenz (New Residence), used as a temporary abode while the bishop's seat was being rebuilt. It has a carillon and the bells can be heard at 7am, 11am and 6pm from Mozartplatz, where a statue of the great composer stands.

Residenz

🏠 Residenzplatz 1 ☎ (0662) 80422690 🕑 10am-5pm daily (Sep-Jun: Wed-Mon)

TOP
3

UNIQUE MUSEUMS

Weihnachtsmuseum

🏠 Mozartplatz 2 🕑 10am-6pm Wed-Sun 🆆 salzburger-weihnachtsmuseum.at
Advent and nativity displays bring together German and Austrian Christmas traditions.

Museum der Moderne

🏠 Wiener-Philharmoniker-Gasse 9 🕑 10am-6pm Tue-Sun (to 8pm Wed) 🆆 museumdermoderne.at
Art from the 1940s to the present day is housed in two modern buildings, both works of art in their own right.

Spielzeugmuseum

🏠 Bürgerspitalgasse 2 🕑 9am-5pm Tue-Sun 🆆 spielzeugmuseum.at
Toy museum with hundreds of hands-on exhibits and a large indoor playground.

Did You Know?

The Dom was designed to hold 10,000 worshippers, more than Salzburg's population at the time.

⑬

Dom

🏠 Domplatz 1a
📞 (0662) 80477950

Built in the 8th century, the Dom was the first cathedral church in Salzburg. After several remodellings and a fire in 1598, the archbishops set out to build an almost entirely new church, designed by the Italian architect, Santino Solari, on the site of the earlier one. The new Dom, consecrated in 1628, became a model of Baroque church architecture north of the Alps. The façade is particularly impressive, decorated with vast sculpted figures of the cathedral's patron saints, Rupert and Virgil, and saints Peter and Paul. You can admire the church's treasures in the **Cathedral Museum**. The Dom is also renowned as a spot where Mozart played

the Baroque organ, and the great Mozarteum choir continue his legacy today with concerts of his music in the cathedral.

Cathedral Museum

♿ 📞 (0662) 80471860
🕙 10am–5pm Mon, Wed–Sun (Jul, Aug & Dec: to 6pm daily)

⑭

Stift St Peter

🏠 St Peter Bezirk 1/2
📞 (0662) 8445760 🕙 8am–noon, 2:30–6:30pm daily

Salzburg's Benedictine Abbey was founded in the 7th century by St Rupert, who is said to have resurrected the town after the Great Migration of Nations *(p52)*. It is the only abbey in this part of Europe that has survived intact since then. Though built in the 12th and 13th centuries and remodelled during the Baroque era, some of the old sculptures have survived, including the early 15th-century *Beautiful Madonna*. The abbey interior is an impressive display of Baroque opulence.

In the cemetery, Salzburg's oldest, are the final resting places of Mozart's sister Nannerl and of Johann Michael Haydn, brother of Joseph.

⑮

Makartplatz

This square was given its current name in memory of the Salzburg-born painter Hans Makart, whose work influenced fashion, architecture and interior design in the mid-19th century.

The Tanzmeisterhaus at No 8 was Mozart's home from 1773 to 1787. The original house, destroyed in World War II, was rebuilt, and is a museum, **Mozart-Wohnhaus**, dedicated to the composer.

The Dreifaltigkeitskirche (Church of the Holy Trinity), in the northeast corner of the square, dates from 1694. It is one of the earliest works of architect Johann Bernhard Fischer von Erlach, and shows signs of Roman influence.

Mozart-Wohnhaus

♿ 🏠 Makartplatz 8 📞 (0662) 87422740 🕙 9am–5:30pm daily (Jul & Aug: to 7pm)

↑ Rehearsing for a concert inside the sumptuous Stift St Peter

The Fire Dance lighting up Salzburg, and enjoying a beer *(inset)*

THE SALZBURG FESTIVAL

The Salzburger Festspiele, the largest and most important opera and theatre festival in Europe, was first held in 1920. Now held over five weeks every July and August, the festival programme has become increasingly rich and varied, with tickets selling out months in advance.

FESTIVAL ORIGINS

The eminent writer Hugo von Hofmannsthal, the composer Richard Strauss, and the greatest theatrical innovator of the 20th century, Max Reinhardt, decided to honour the memory of Mozart by organizing a festival devoted to his work. It was to be held in his home town and be a celebration of theatre and opera.

FINE VENUES

The Grosses Festspielhaus was inaugurated in 1960 and designed by Clemens Holzmeister especially for the festival. The former court stables were converted to create two festival theatres and performances are also held in the Makartplatz theatre, in Schloss Mirabell and in many open-air venues around town.

FESTSPIELE PERFORMANCES

Since 1920, the festival has opened with a performance of Hugo von Hofmannsthal's morality play *Jedermann* (*Everyman*). Today, theatre troupes come from all over the world with original performances prepared specifically for the festival. The Fire Dance is one of the most beautiful spectacles staged regularly; as soon as night falls, the whole town comes alive with lights.

HERBERT VON KARAJAN (1908-89)

Herbert von Karajan, born in Salzburg and one of the most outstanding 20th-century conductors of symphonies and operas, was the musical director of the Salzburg Festival for almost 30 years. He continued to shape the direction of the festival until his death.

(16) ⚡ 🏔 🍴 🛍

HOHENSALZBURG FORTRESS

🏠 Mönchsberg 34 🕐 Jan-Apr & Oct-Dec: 9:30am-5pm daily; May-Sep: 9am-7pm daily; Easter & Advent weekend: 9:30am-6pm daily 🌐 salzburg-burgen.at

Early cannons can be found among the bastions and bulwarks of the castle.

Perched on the rocky peak of Festungsberg, Salzburg's monumental fortress is the city's very own emblem and holds the title as the largest and best-preserved medieval fortress in Europe.

The imposing fortress was built in the 11th century during the wars between the Holy Roman Empire and the Papacy, and served as a refuge for Salzburg's archbishops whenever they felt threatened. Many museums are housed inside the castle and provide fascinating insights into its architectural history and the lifestyles of those who lived here. The main attraction, though, is the decoration in the Golden Hall, which simulates the night sky with gold stars on a blue background. A modern funicular provides easy access up the steep hill, but the fortress can also be reached on foot.

1 Aimed at the town, many cannons can be seen among the numerous walkways.

2 Archbishop Leonhard von Keutschach gave the castle its present look in the 16th century.

3 The richly ornamented Golden Stube (Golden Chamber) is one of the castle's loveliest rooms.

The vast ↑ Hohensalzburg Fortress complex

The well, dating back to 1539, is an interesting feature in the fortress courtyard.

Salzburg's coat of arms is placed above the wicket leading to the inner courtyard, in front of the old castle.

The Schoolhouse and Kitchen Tower are the remains of fortifications built outside the castle in the 16th century during a revolt against the archbishops.

GREAT VIEW
Choose a Terrace
The fortress has two terraces: the southern terrace affords wonderful views of the hills and forests to the south of the city, while the northern terrace offers a bird's-eye view of the city and the Salzach.

Archbishop Johann Jakob Khuen von Belasi (1560–86) carried out the final remodelling of the old fortress. His portrait hangs in one of the rooms of the old castle.

The lavish Golden Chamber has a large tiled stove in Gothic style.

In a small square on the castle ramparts stand an old salt warehouse and two towers, Hasenturm (Hares' Tower) and Schwefelturm (Sulphur Tower).

The Glockenturm (bell tower), through which the castle's residential quarters can be reached, has a bell case created in 1505.

Reckturm, the corner tower, was once a prison and torture chamber. Prisoners were still being tortured at Hohensalzburg until 1893.

A SHORT WALK
OLD TOWN

Distance 2 km (1 mile) **Time** 20 minutes
Nearest bus stop Salzburg Rathaus

Founded by Benedictine monks, Salzburg has one of the most evocative old town centres in Europe, which occupies the area between Mönchsberg (Monks' Hill) and the Salzach river. The town that grew up on the left bank of the Salzach was built almost entirely in the Baroque style and is unusually uniform in appearance. As you stroll around the beautiful old town, look out for ubiquitous Baroque-period designs that have been faultlessly and seamlessly blended with both earlier and modern architecture.

One of the longest and busiest streets in Salzburg's old town, **Getreidegasse** *accommodates modern-day commerce in medieval settings. No 9 is the house where Mozart was born and lived until he was 17; it is now Mozarts Geburtshaus (p241) – a museum of the composer's life.*

The university church, **Kollegienkirche** *(p240), is one of the earliest works of the renowned Austrian architect Johann Bernhard Fischer von Erlach.*

GRIESGASSE

GETREIDEGASSE

REINHARD PLATZ

S. HAFFNER-GASSE

Franziskanerkirche *(p240) has a Baroque altarpiece by Johann Bernhard Fischer von Erlach, which has as its centre an exquisite figure of the Madonna and Child.*

↑ Walking through the charming snow-covered Getreidegasse in winter

The most opulent building in town, **Residenz** (p241) is the former home of the archbishop and clearly reveals his wealth and power.

The angular tower of the 15th-century **Altes Rathaus** (old town hall) comes into view at the end of a narrow medieval alleyway.

START

Locator Map
For more detail see p239

RUDOLFSKAI

0 metres 100
0 yards 100

N

MOZART PLATZ

1996
—
The year the old town was designated a World Cultural Heritage Site by UNESCO.

RESIDENZ PLATZ

The **Dom** (p242), known as the cathedral church of St Rupert and St Virgil, was first built in 774, but has been frequently altered.

KAPITEL PLATZ

Kapitelplatz is Salzburg's bustling market square and has one of the city's most attractive fountains. It also offers outdoor games, including a huge chessboard.

HERRENGASSE

Stift St Peter (p242), the 12th-century Benedictine church, is dedicated to St Peter, whose statue adorns the fountain (1673) in front of the church.

FINISH

The mighty **Hohensalzburg Fortress** (p244), on top of the rocky Mönchsberg, is best reached by the funicular from Festungsgasse.

2

GASTEINERTAL

◭D5 🚉🚌 ℹ Tauernplatz 1, Bad Hofgastein; www.gastein.com

Surrounded by mountains, the Gasteiner valley is the ultimate skiing, snowboarding and summer walking area. The valley flourished in late medieval times and more recently it has become a popular spa, with a long list of clients including royalty and artists.

Dotting Gasteinertal are the charming villages of Bad Gastein, Dorfgastein, and Bad Hofgastein, of which the ancient resort of Bad Gastein is still the most popular. The therapeutic properties of the radon-rich mineral springs in and around Bad Gastein were known to the Celts and Romans, and this was when the first settlements grew in the valley of the Gasteiner Ache stream. The best, and largest, of the thermal bath complexes today is the Alpentherme Gastein *(alpentherme.com)* in Bad Hofgastein, which has a wide selection of indoor and outdoor thermal lakes, filled daily with fresh water from the natural springs.

Hit the Slopes

At the same time, the valley has developed into a fabulous winter sports centre, with a number of different skiing areas for all levels. The best can be found south of the valley on the Kreuzkogel above Sportgastein, which reaches over 2,600 m (8,530 ft) and offers a range of steep red and black runs for experienced skiers. The most extensive ski area, however, and more suited to beginners and intermediates, is on the Fulseck above Dorfgastein, which links up with the town of Grossarl on the other side of the mountain.

Did You Know?

The "Bad" in Bad Gastein means "spa", indicating the town's history as a popular health resort.

Bad Hofgastein's town centre and attractive church in the snow ↑

Must See

1 The Gasteiner Ache flows through the valley, but is at its most beautiful running right through the centre of Bad Gastein in a series of attractive waterfalls.

2 A ride on the Gastein lifts in the winter is a highlight of any trip to the valley, taking you from the traditional village of Dorfgastein up into the snow-clad mountains.

3 The hot springs in Bad Gastein are renowned for promoting well-being, and are considered very beneficial for those suffering from cardiac and gastric ailments, rheumatism and allergies.

STAY

Haus Hirt
Spectacular mountain views and a small spa ensure relaxation.

⌂ Kaiserhofstrasse 14, Bad Gastein � haus-hirt.com

€€€

Der Salzburgerhof
Comfortable rooms and a restaurant serving both modern and traditional dishes.

⌂ Kaiser-Franz-Platz 1, Bad Hofgastein � hotel-salzburgerhof.com

€€€

Landhotel Römerhof
The main draw of this ski and wellness hotel is its tranquil location.

⌂ Römerplatz 2, Dorfgastein � roemerhof.com

€€€

EXPERIENCE MORE

❸
Wasserschloss Anif

🅐D4 🚌🚉 **(** (06246) 72365

Some 2 km (1 mile) beyond Hellbrunn stands the small Neo-Gothic castle of Anif. Once a suburban residence, it now lies virtually within the limits of the town of Anif. Its earliest historic records date from the 15th century, but it bears signs of an earlier, late Gothic structure. Once the summer estate of the rulers of Salzburg, it belonged to the Chiemsee bishops from 1693 to 1803 and later passed to Count Aloys Arco-Stepperg. The new owner had it converted into a romantic English-style Neo-Gothic castle that has survived unchanged to this day. Its rectangular turret is proudly mirrored in the lake; the interior is furnished in the English fashion of the day. At the end of World War I, on 13 November 1918, the last king of Bavaria, Ludwig III, signed his abdication in Anif. The castle is privately owned, though, and there is no access.

PICTURE PERFECT
The Water Castle

Wasserschloss Anif, snapped from across the lake with the castle reflecting in the water, is as quintessentially Austrian a shot as you could wish for. You will need good weather, but luckily you're in the right place.

---

❹
Schloss Hellbrunn

🅐D4 🚌🚉 **◷** Apr & Oct: 9am–4:30pm daily; May–Sep: 9am–5:30pm daily (Jul–Aug: to 6pm)
ⓦ hellbrunn.at

Schloss Hellbrunn, once the summer residence of Salzburg's Archbishop Markus Sittikus, stands about 4 km (2 miles) south of Salzburg. Sitticus was a nephew of then-archbishop Wolf Dietrich von Raitenau, whom he later had captured and imprisoned for life upon succeeding him. He spent most of his life in Italy, and so his small, suburban castle resembles a Venetian villa. It has an interesting state room with architectural paintings and a tall, octagonal music room. However, the most popular feature is its garden, which contains ornamental fountains and scenic grottoes, including a mechanical theatre and trick fountains.

---

❺
St Gilgen

🅐D4 🚌 **ℹ** Mondsee, Bundesstrasse 1A; www.wolfgangsee. salzkammergut.at

Set on the western shores of the warm Wolfgangsee amid mountain scenery, St Gilgen is one of the most picturesque

↑ Admiring the majestic Gollinger Wasserfall near the town of Golling

health resorts in the region. St Gilgen was the birthplace of Mozart's mother, Anna-Maria Pertl. Later, the composer's sister, Nannerl, lived here with her husband, a local office worker. In 1927, the Mozart Fountain was erected in the town square.

The local Church of St Giles (St Ägidius) shows hints of an earlier structure. It was extended in the 18th century. St Gilgen is a watersports centre and harbour, with cruises on Wolfgangsee aboard the steamer *Kaiser Franz Josef I*, which has been in continuous service since 1873. Not far from St Gilgen, on the shores of the neighbouring Fuschlsee, stands Schloss Fuschl, a small hunting lodge that's now a luxury hotel.

6
Golling

🅐D4 🚉🚍 🆆golling.info

South of Hallein lies the small town of Golling. At its centre stands the church of St John the Baptist and St John the Evangelist, with a Gothic main nave and remodelled Baroque side naves. A small medieval castle, devoid of ornaments and adjoined by a chapel with a Rococo altar, now houses a regional museum.

There are many natural features of interest near Golling. Head to the Lueg Pass with the spectacular Salzach river gorge, as well as the beautiful Schwarzbacher Wasserfall, better known as Gollinger Wasserfall, which is much beloved by painters of romantic natural scenes.

←

Trick fountains and sculptures in the ornamental garden of Schloss Hellbrunn

EAT

Seegasthaus Fischer-Wirt
Fresh fish from the Wolfgangsee dominates the menu here.

🅐D4 🏠Ischlerstr. 21, St Gilgen 🕐Mon
🆆fischer-wirt.at

€€€

Gasthaus Adler
Smart but affordable restaurant and guest house with great schnitzel as well as veggie options.

🅐D4 🏠Markt 58, Golling 🕐Sun & Mon
🆆adler-golling.com

€€€

Lechenauers
This modern Italian-influenced gastropub opens early and is the perfect breakfast spot.

🅐D4 🏠Molnarplatz 16, Hallein 🕐Mon
🆆lechenauers.at

€€€

Mesnerhaus
Inventive interpreta-tions of traditional dishes. There is a luxury apartment to rent too.

🅐D5 🏠Markt 56, Mauterndorf 🕐Sun & Mon 🆆mesnerhaus.at

€€€

Die Schneiderei
Large restaurant and bar set over two levels with tables and chairs made from local timber.

🅐D5 🏠Sigmund-Thun-Strasse 12, Kaprun
🕐Wed 🆆schneiderei-kaprun.at

€€€

Skiing over fresh snow on the Kitzsteinhorn glacier above Kaprun

7

Kaprun

🅐D5 🌐 Ⓦzellamsee-kaprun.com

Together with its neighbour, Zell am See (p256), Kaprun makes up one of the largest ski regions in Austria. The 140 km (87 miles) of interconnected ski slopes offer superb modern facilities and spectacular views of the two reservoirs below. The slopes are dominated by the Kitzsteinhorn glacier, which is open for skiing ten months of the year. The region is renowned for its tough runs but there are family and beginner areas. For the adventurous, there are nighttime ski runs on the floodlit Schmitten slopes and a number of snowboard parks with fun jumps, rails and pipes.

Aside from its renowned ski slopes, Kaprun is famous for its sophisticated hydroelectric power station, Kapruner Ache, after whose construction the town became one of Austria's foremost sports resorts. As well as being an engineering marvel, the power station offers great views over the towns of Kaprun and Zell am See. The reservoirs, weirs and dams, set amid the rocky limestone peaks of the Hohe Tauern mountain range, create a unique environment, with numerous trails among attractive scenery. The highest artificial lake is Mooserboden, situated at 2,036 m (6,680 ft) and fed by the melting ice of the Pasterze glacier.

> **HIDDEN GEM**
> **Maiskogel**
>
> The year-round alpine coaster at Maiskogel (www.kitzsteinhorn.at) amusement park in Kaprun offers thrills for all ages. Guided safely on rails, you race 1,300 m (4,265 ft) downhill in two-seater coasters at speeds of up to 40 km/h (25 mph).

8

Mauterndorf

🅐D5 🌐 Ⓦmauterndorf.at

Strategically positioned on the road connecting Salzburg with the Hohe Tauern passes, this little town owed most of its former wealth to road tolls. Mauterndorf's greatest attraction is its scenically located and well-proportioned castle, built in the 13th century and extended three centuries later under Archbishop Leonhard von Keutschach. The rooms are richly decorated with stucco-work and furnished to appear as they would have in the Middle Ages. Arguably the castle's best feature is its chapel, devoted to St Henry (Emperor Heinrich II), which features superb 14th-century frescoes of the Coronation of the Virgin Mary on the rainbow arch, and a carved altarpiece from the 1400s. Mauterndorf also offers excellent summer and winter activities, including an open-air pool, rafting tours and the Outdoorparc Lungau adventure park.

9

Schloss Moosham

🅐D5 🅐Moosham 13 🌐 ⓞFor guided tours only; check website Ⓦschloss moosham.at

Moosham Castle, near the southern end of Radstädter Tauernstrasse, high above the Mur river, is famous for its ghosts and witch trials, as popularized on American TV. The structure probably dates from around the 13th century and consists of an upper and a lower castle. Among its original features are the Baroque roadway, Gothic stained-glass windows in the presbytery of the chapel and a collection of local works of art, which are kept in the castle museum. The coach house and the armoury are also worth a closer look. Some rooms are open to the public, such as a torture chamber and a Gothic bedchamber. Below the castle is the popular resort of St Michael, with an interesting Gothic church.

10
Hallein

🅐D4 🚆🚌 🅘 Mauttor-promenade 6; www.hallein.com

The town of Hallein was founded in the 13th century, but salt was mined here way back in prehistoric times. The long association with the salt trade is most apparent in the town's name: *hall* is the Celtic word for salt. The "white gold", as it was called, brought great wealth to the entire region for many centuries, until the 18th-century Counter-Reformation led to the emigration of the predominantly Protestant salt miners.

Hallein's old town, on the left bank of the Salzach river, is mainly 18th-century in appearance, following much remodelling. The Church of St Antonius has a Gothic presbytery, but the rest is much newer. The painting of the Birth of Christ in the main altarpiece is by the last court painter of the Salzburg rulers, Andreas Nesselthaler, who was known for his Neo-Classical style. Hallein was the home of composer and organist Franz

> The largest town in the Lungau region, Tamsweg is famous for its curious Samson Procession, when an effigy of Samson and other figures are paraded around town.

Xaver Gruber, who wrote the music for popular Christmas carol "Silent Night". His house at No. 1 Gruberplatz is now a small museum. The most interesting sight in Hallein, however, is the impressive **Keltenmuseum**, with its collection of Celtic objects from the La Tene period of the Iron Age.

From the southern end of Hallein you can drive to the top of Dürrnberg, one of the most important prehistoric sites in Central Europe. The remains of the settlements that grew up around the rich local salt deposits can be seen to this day.

The spa of Bad Dürrnberg has a show mine, and you can even take a ride on an underground salt lake. In the village stands a 14th-century Marian church, now a Baroque structure. The altarpiece contains a picture of the Madonna that was believed to be miraculous, and which became an important pilgrimage site.

Keltenmuseum
♿🚻 🅐 Pflegerplatz 5
🕘 9am–5pm daily
🌐 keltenmuseum.at

11
Tamsweg

🅐E5 🚆🚌 🅒 (06474) 2145

The largest town in the Lungau region, Tamsweg is famous for its curious Samson Procession, when an effigy of Samson and other figures are paraded around town. Tamsweg owes its past wealth to the iron and salt trades. Fine town houses, such as the 15th-century Mesnerhaus and the 16th-century turreted town hall, line the market square. The 18th-century Post House has frescoes by Gregor Lederwasch, who also painted the fine Pfarrkirche zum heiligen Jakobus (St James's Church), built in 1741. The original Rococo interior has been well preserved. Towering above the town is the 15th-century St Leonard's Church. Originally built in the early part of the century, it was fortified in the late 15th century in anticipation of Turkish attacks. Of its many stained-glass windows, the famous "Golden Window" (1430–50) is exceptional. The interior furnishings are almost entirely late medieval.

→ The Samson Procession marching through the town square in Tamsweg

STAY

Post
Idyllic mountain guest house complete with huge timber balconies, a great restaurant and indoor pool.

🅐D4 🏠Markt 39, Abtenau 🅦hotel-post-abtenau.at

€€€

Alpenland
A good mix of traditional and modern design and close to the Alpendorf ski area.

🅐D5 🏠H Kappacher-strass 7, St Johann im Pongau 🅦alpenland-sporthotels.com

€€€

Schattauer
Simply furnished but comfortable rooms in a splendid location with mountain views.

🅐D5 🏠Markt 91, Wagrain 🅦schattauer.at

€€€

Bischofshofen

🅐D4 🏠💬
🅦bischofshofen.at

The Celtic settlement that once stood on this site was a centre of the copper mining trade; the area was also rich in salt mines. Colonization of the region began well before recorded history and traces of ancient cultures can be found all over.

The town is dominated by the spire of St Maximilian's Church, reputedly built on the site of an older church established by St Rupert, founder of Salzburg. Its most valuable historic relic is St Rupert's crucifix, a simple gilded cross, encrusted with precious stones.

Bischofshofen is renowned for its excellent ski-jumping hills. Every year, on 6 January, the town hosts the final event of the world-famous Four Hills Ski-Jumping Tournament.

Abtenau

🅐D4 🏠💬 ℹMarkt 165; www.abtenau-info.at

Abtenau, a summer resort situated in the Salzburg Dolomites, is surrounded by the mighty peaks of the Tennengebirge. Pfarrkirche zum heiligen Blasius (St Basil's Church) was built around 1500. Its main nave is guarded by figures of St George and St Florian. An original late Gothic fresco can be seen on the north wall, but the new main altar and side altars are built in the Baroque style. It is worth taking a walk upstream along the Lammer river, which cuts a scenic valley between the Tennengebirge and the craggy wall of the Dachstein massif.

St Johann im Pongau

🅐D5 💬 📞(06412) 6036

The largest town in the region, St Johann im Pongau is popular for its excellent skiing conditions in winter and is great for swimming and walking in summer.

Little remains of its original buildings due to a series of fires in the 19th century; the town was almost entirely rebuilt. The Neo-Gothic Domkirche, the Cathedral of St John the Baptist (1861), is one of the most outstanding works of

Snow blanketing the rooftops in the town of Abtenau ↓

Neo-Classicism in the Salzburg area. Some 5 km (3 miles) south of the town run the torrential waters of Grossarler Ache, a rapid mountain stream that winds through the scenic Liechtensteinklamm ravine.

15

Radstadt

A D5 🚌🚆 **w** radstadt.com

The small town of Radstadt grew up around a 13th-century fortress on the banks of the Enns. Its wealth hailed from its propitious location on the road to Venice, and its monopoly position in the wine trade. Its medieval fortifications have remained intact.

The surrounding area has many small, beguiling castles, including the Renaissance Schloss Tandalier, southwest of the town. Schloss Lerchen, in the centre of town, shows some traces of original 13th-century architecture; today it houses a regional museum.

East of Bischofshofen runs Radstädter Tauernstrasse, one of the most scenic roads in the Alps. The Rossbrand, rising north of Radstadt and accessible by car via Rossbrand Panoramastrasse, offers astonishing views of Alpine summits on a clear day.

16

Wagrain

A D5 🚌🚆 **w** skiamade.com

Wagrain is part of the family-oriented Ski Amadé resort group. This vast terrain extends between the Tennengebirge and Radstädter Tauern ranges, and includes several villages connected by good public transport links, funiculars and buses. The area is further linked to the overall Salzburger Sportwelt skipass area of eight resorts and 270 ski installations, mostly for intermediate skiers.

Year-round fun in the water is guaranteed at the Amadé Water World's all-weather pool. However, the most interesting spot is Zauchensee, the highest village in the region (1,361 m/ 4,465 ft). Also worth a closer look is the Gothic church in Altenmarkt im Pongau. Wagrain itself has a museum devoted to Joseph Mohr, who wrote the words for the carol "Silent Night", and to the 20th-century Austrian writer Karl Heinrich Waggerl.

If you're in need of a detour, check out the stunning views from the tops of Schwarzkopf, Rosskopf and Mooskopf.

↑ Exploring stalagmites in the Eisriesenwelt ice cave, near Werfen

---

17

Werfen

A D4 🚌🚆 **w** werfen.at

The little town of Werfen has several interesting sights. The present style of St James's church dates from a 17th-century Baroque conversion, while the Marian Church was built in the early 18th century. Hohenwerfen fortress, on an outcrop over Werfen, dates back to the 11th century. Today, it is an interactive museum.

A major attraction nearby is **Eisriesenwelt** (Ice World), the largest ice cave in the world. Accessed by cable car, there are some 42 km (26 miles) of stalagmites and ice galleries to be explored.

Eisriesenwelt

♿🚭♨ **A** Eishöhlenstr. 30 **O** May–Oct: 8am–3pm daily (Jul & Aug: to 4pm) **w** eisriesenwelt.at

18

Zell am See

D5 🚗🚌 **w** zellamsee-kaprun.com

This picture-postcard town on the western shores of Zeller See is connected to the slopes of Kaprun (*p252*) to form one of the best sports resorts in Austria. First recorded as the Roman settlement of Bisontio, in medieval times Zell was a mining centre. Among its more interesting historic sights are the 13th-century Vogtturm, and the Church of St Hippolytus, which once belonged to the Augustinian order. The 16th-century frescos of St George and St Florian in the western gallery are by an artist from the Danube School.

South of town is the Hohe Tauern mountain range and national park; to the north is the rugged scenery of the Steinernes Meer (Stone Sea); and to the west is the Schmittenhöhe, divided into the Sonnkogel and Hirschkogel regions, with the highest peak rising to over 2,000 m (6,562 ft).

The Pinzgauer Spaziergang is one of the most beautiful walking trails in the Austrian Alps, running high above the valley floor, from Zell am See to Saalbach via Schmittenhöhe (a seven-hour walk).

19

Saalbach

C5 🚗🚌 **𝑖** Glemmtaler Landesstrasse 550; www.saalbach.com

At the heart of the Glemmtal lies this small town marking the border between Salzburger Land and Tyrol. A charming winter resort, it provides access to 200 km (120 miles) of pistes, with beginner and more challenging runs, and facilities for tobogganing and tubing. Exciting as the winter sports are, the resort claims to be the home of *lässig*, an Austrian concept perhaps best translated as "contentment".

To the north of Saalbach the Spielberghorn comes into view, while to the south the Schattberg marks the end of the Pinzgauer Spaziergang, which affords breathtaking views over the neighbouring mountain range.

> 💬 **INSIDER TIP**
> ### Saalbach for Kids
>
> Children will love the Kids Hiking Challenge at Saalbach. The gentle, themed walks – all clearly marked on a map – are perfect for introducing young children to hiking.

20

Lofer

C4 🚗🚌 **𝑖** Lofer 310; www.lofer.com

The town of Lofer, in the green Salzach valley, has retained much of the charm of an old mountain village. It is surrounded by the snow-covered rocky summits of the Loferer Steinberge (Stone Mountains). These limestone mountains hide many caves still waiting to be explored. The Lamprechtsofenloch is said to be the deepest water-bearing cave in the world.

A short distance south of Lofer, outside the village of St Martin, is the pilgrimage church Maria Kirchenthal, built between 1693 and 1701. It is one of the greatest works by architect Johann Bernhard Fischer von Erlach, in which he employed some of the ideas that he had developed earlier in Salzburg.

The building is blended into the rocky mountain scenery of the Saalach valley, and two white towers are prominent against the distant snowy mountains. The Neo-Baroque altarpiece includes the 15th-century picture of the Madonna that was once the destination for pilgrims. One of the two altars depicts Mary's parents, St Jacob and St Anne.

↑ Mountains looming over Zell am See at dusk, and cable cars above Lake Zell *(inset)*

㉑
Mittersill

Ⓐ C5 🚌🚆 **ⓘ** Stadtplatz 1; www.mittersill-tourismus.at

This summer resort in the upper Salzach valley sprang up around a castle. The castle was built in the 12th century and rebuilt many times. Today it is the seat of the International Protestant Youth Community, a cultural centre and a hotel.

The chapel (1533) features an interesting late Gothic polyptych attributed to an Aussee master. St-Leonhard-Kirche was originally Gothic, but was remodelled in the 18th century. It contains a heavily ornamented Rococo pulpit and remains of the old decorations, including an early 15th-century statue of St Leonard.

Mittersill lies at the Salzburg end of a beautiful mountain trail leading from East Tyrol, among the wild scenery of the Hohe Tauern National Park. The road known as Felbertauernstrasse affords lovely views of the rugged slopes of Grossvenediger.

㉒ ⏍
Krimmler Wasserfälle

Ⓐ C5 🚌 **Ⓞ** Apr–Oct: daily **ⓦ** wasserfaelle-krimml.at

In the northwestern part of Hohe Tauern National Park are the famous Krimmler Wasserfälle. These waterfalls of the Krimmler Ache are a stream flowing from the glacier of the same name at an altitude of around 3,000 m (9,850 ft). The water falls in three steps – each of which can be appreciated individually at the 11 viewpoints along the way to the top – with a total drop of 380 m (1,247 ft). Allow a few hours to do the round trip.

The journey to the falls can be made by car, but hiking the Wasserfallweg (waterfall path) will prove to be a truly unforgettable experience. The best starting points are the Gerlos Pass or Krimmel village. In winter, the falls freeze solid.

$\longrightarrow$

Young couple watching the famous Krimmler Wasserfälle in summer

DRINK

Gin House
With 450 varieties of gin, this pub is one of main the reasons Zell am See has become a party town for skiers.

Ⓐ D5 **Ⓓ** Dreifaltigkeits-gasse 1, Zell am See **Ⓒ** Sun **ⓦ** ginhouse.at

Grand Hotel
Sip cocktails on leather armchairs, listen to live music and enjoy amazing views of the lake.

Ⓐ D5 **Ⓓ** Esplanade 4–6, Zell am See **ⓦ** grandhotel-zellamsee.at

Schwips
Dancing in full ski gear and drinking flaming shots of schnapps is the norm at this riotous bar, where the party starts as soon as the slopes have closed.

Ⓐ C5 **Ⓓ** Schulstrasse 739, Saalbach **ⓦ** schwips-bar.at

TYROL AND VORARLBERG

Tyrol was first inhabited by Rhaetian and Illyrian tribes before it came under Roman rule in the 1st century BC, and later fell to the Bavarians and the Lombards. In the 12th century, it became an independent principality within the Holy Roman Empire, which it remained until 1363, when, having been a bone of contention between the Habsburgs and the Bavarians, it was bequeathed to the Habsburgs. Tyrol was a domain of the family's junior line and as such enjoyed a degree of independence. To this day it has maintained its unique character, music, dialect and fashion, which has influenced cultural life in the rest of Austria.

Vorarlberg, in contrast, has for many years been culturally fairly separate, largely orientating itself towards its neighbours Germany, Liechtenstein and Switzerland. Its original Celtic tribes were conquered by the Romans in 15 BC, and it became part of the province of Rhaetia. It was later vanquished by Allemanic tribes around AD 450 before becoming part of Bavaria. From the 15th century, the area of present-day Vorarlberg passed gradually into the hands of the Habsburgs, and in 1919 it finally became a province of independent Austria.

TYROL AND VORARLBERG

↑ Innsbruck's charming colourful houses at dawn

❶
INNSBRUCK

🅰 B5 ✈ 4.5 km (2.5 miles) SW of city centre
🛈 Burggraben 3; www.innsbruck.info

The capital of the province of Tyrol, and one of Austria's most important tourist regions, Innsbruck is an Alpine delight. In 1964, and again in 1976, Innsbruck was the host city for the Winter Olympics, and it continues to be a top choice for winter sports holidays as well as a haven for enthusiasts of Baroque architecture.

①
Dom St Jakob

🅰 Domplatz 📞 (0512) 58390

Originally built in the Gothic style, St James's Cathedral was converted to Baroque in the early 18th century. Regarded as the most magnificent Baroque church building in North Tyrol, it was severely damaged during World War II and rebuilt in the 1950s, when the church acquired the equestrian statue of St James on top of the building. The splendid Baroque interior is the work of Munich artists, the Asam brothers.

The old town houses with their rich stucco ornaments, reliefs and frescoes provide an enchanting backdrop to the cathedral.

②
Goldenes Dachl

🅰 Herzog-Friedrich-Strasse 15 📞 (0512) 581111

The Golden Roof is one of Innsbruck's most popular attractions. In about 1500, the tall oriel window, with its 2,657 gilded copper tiles, was added to the former residence of the Tyrolean rulers, creating a viewing box from which Emperor Maximilian I could observe street life on Innsbruck's main square. Highlights include the six coats of arms under the first-floor windows and the second-floor balustrade, decorated with reliefs. The building behind houses the small **Maximilianeum**, a museum of the emperor's life.

Maximilianeum
⊘ 🕐 8am–5:30pm Mon–Fri (to noon Fri)

③
Altes Landhaus

🅰 Maria-Theresien-Strasse 43 📞 (0512) 5900
🚫 To the public

This house, built in 1725–8 and today the seat of Tyrol's provincial government, is one of Austria's most beautiful

> **TOP 3** **HIKES AROUND INNSBRUCK**
>
> **Kellerjoch Loop**
> A relatively easy 4-hour hike which starts and ends at the top of the Arzberg chairlift.
>
> **Schaflegerkogel Loop**
> A long (6- to 7-hour) but amazing hike taking in four peaks from Grinzens, a 20-minute drive from Innsbruck.
>
> **Goetheweg**
> This 5-hour hike offers great city views. Take the Hafelekar cable car to the top station and begin your descent.

secular structures. It has an attractive inner courtyard and colourful elevations. Though closed to the public, the most opulent room is the Rococo conference hall. Along the same street, the Annasäule (St Anne's Column) rises in front of the Neues Rathaus (new town hall).

④ Hofburg

🏛 Rennweg 1 **🕘 9am–5pm daily (Mar–Aug: to 7pm Wed)** **🌐 hofburg-innsbruck.at**

In the 1460s, Archduke Sigismund embarked on a project to build a princely residence in Innsbruck. His Gothic castle, extended by Maximilian I, survived for several centuries, and to this day the castle dungeons feature the original late Gothic vaults. A major remodelling took place in 1755, under Maria Theresa, when plans for a Rococo south wing were prepared.

The interior of the Hofburg is furnished in Rococo style. The most beautiful of the state rooms on the second floor is the Riesenhalle (the Giants' Hall), embellished with white and gold stucco and a ceiling painting depicting the triumph of the House of Habsburg-Lothringen.

⑤ Herzog-Friedrich-Strasse

Herzog-Friedrich-Strasse is one of Innsbruck's loveliest streets. Its main historic sights include the Rococo Helblinghaus (No 10), the Gothic old town hall (No 21) and its adjacent Stadtturm (city tower), with a brilliant viewing terrace.

Many of the other houses along the street also warrant a close look. The four-storey Ottoburg at No 1 has four oriels stacked on top of each

other and late Gothic interior vaults. The Baroque façade of the Altes Regierungsgebäude (old government building) at No 3 hides some beautiful rooms including the Claudia-Saal, the Hall of Claudia de Medici, with a late Renaissance coffered ceiling. The best of Innsbruck's Christmas markets is also held on this street.

⑥ Tiroler Landesmuseum Ferdinandeum

🏛 Museumstrasse 15 **🕘 9am–5pm Tue–Sun** **🌐 tiroler-landesmuseum.at**

Together with the former armoury of Maximilian I at No 1 Zeughausgasse, this 19th-century building houses the collection of the Tiroler Landesmuseum (the Tyrol Provincial Museum). The museum has galleries devoted to the natural environment, history, art and handicrafts, and it is also home to a library. Among its most precious

SHOP

Markthall
Large market in the city centre selling fresh produce from local farmers, as well as fine delicacies from around the world and a range of local crafts. Cafés, bars and street food vendors are on hand, too.

🏛 Herzog-Siegmund-Ufer 1–3 **🕘 Sun** **🌐 markthalle-innsbruck.at**

exhibits are Gothic panel paintings, sculptures by Michael Pacher, and works by old German and Dutch masters – Lucas Cranach the Elder, Rembrandt, Pieter Bruegel the Younger and others. The museum also exhibits more recent Austrian art, including works by Klimt, Schiele and Kokoschka.

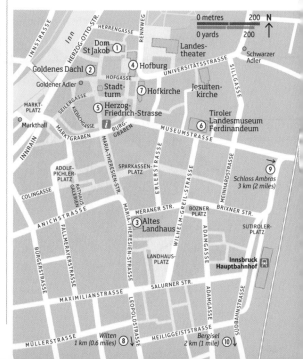

EAT

Goldener Adler

Located in the Golden Eagle, one of the oldest inns in Europe, the beautiful serves Austrian dishes.

🏠 Herzog-Friedrich-Strasse 6 🌐 goldeneradler.com

€€€

Schwarzer Adler

Locally sourced meat and fish are served at this roof top eatery at the Black Eagle hotel.

🏠 Kaiserjägerstrasse 2 🌐 schwarzeradler-innsbruck.com

€€€

---

⑦

Hofkirche

🏠 Universitätsstrasse 2
🕐 9am–5pm daily (from 12:30pm Sun & hols)
🌐 tiroler-landesmuseen.at

The court church was built by Ferdinand I to house the cenotaph of his grandfather, Emperor Maximilian I. The cenotaph was designed by Maximilian himself and, although his plans were never fully realized, the ensuing structure, completed in 1584, is very impressive and ranks as a masterpiece of Renaissance sculpture. It stands in the centre of the church, alongside a kneeling figure of the emperor, and is guarded by 28 larger-than-life bronze statues. Reliefs on the side panels depict scenes from the emperor's life. Maximilian's body was laid to rest in the castle of Wiener Neustadt, in Lower Austria.

---

⑧

Wilten

In the southeastern suburb of the district of Wilten stands a lovely Baroque basilica, built in 1751–6 on the foundations of a former chapel. The church was intended to provide a worthy setting for the picture of *Our Lady at Four Columns*, which miracles were attributed to. It was designed by the architect Franz de Paula Penz and the interior has been kept in the Rococo style. The altarpiece has a splendid gold, pink and yellow colour scheme.

The Romanesque abbey of Wilten has a church built in the 12th century, devoted to St Lawrence. According to legend, the abbey was built by the giant Haymon, in atonement for the murder of another giant, Thyrsus; both are commemorated by statues. The abbey was rebuilt in Baroque style in the 17th–18th centuries.

The various rooms and hidden gems inside ↓ the Hofkirche

The vaults acquired their present form in the early 17th century, when the church was rebuilt in the Baroque style.

An onion dome crowns the octagonal tower of the church.

The Renaissance portal leading into the church was built in 1554 as a tribute to the House of Maximilian I.

Kneeling figure of Emperor Maximilian I

The cenotaph of Maximilian I, at the centre of the church, is guarded by 28 giant figures representing members of his family.

The Silberne Kapelle (Silver Chapel) holds the tombs of Archduke Ferdinand II and his beloved wife, Philippine Welser.

Main entrance

⑨

Schloss Ambras

🏠 Schlossstrasse 20
🕐 10am–5pm daily
🚫 Nov 🌐 schlossambras-innsbruck.at

On the southeastern city limits, this castle was once the symbol of Tyrol's power and glory. In the 12th century it was the seat of local rulers.

The present 16th-century building consists of a lower castle with entrance gate and spacious courtyard, and an upper castle built on the site of an earlier structure. The two parts are connected by the early Renaissance Spanish Hall, built in 1569–72.

Archduke Ferdinand II established his own museum at Ambras, but the exhibits

↑ The attractive grounds and façade of Schloss Ambras, with equally lavish rooms inside *(inset)*

ended up being dispersed in various Viennese museums. Nonetheless, there is still plenty to see, including the Rüstkammer (Arsenal), the Kunst- und Wunderkammer (Chamber of Arts and Marvels), and the gallery with portraits of members of the Habsburg family by artists such as Lucas Cranach and Diego Velázquez.

⑩

Bergisel

The hill of Bergisel, in the south of the city, is a popular place for weekend walks.

Historically, this hill was the site of a battle fought by Andreas Hofer and his army of insurgent highlanders, who defeated the combined occupying forces of Bavaria and France in 1809. A monument to Hofer and the **Kaiserjägermuseum** serve as reminders.

Das Tirol Panorama, a museum on top of Bergisel, holds the *Riesenrundgemälde*, a panoramic painting of the Battle of Bergisel. It also hosts temporary exhibitions alongside its permanent collection of Tyrolean artifacts.

One of the competitions in the world-famous Vierschanzentournee (Four Hills' Ski-Jumping Tournament) is held at Bergiselschanze every year on 4 January.

Kaiserjägermuseum and Das Tirol Panorama
🏠 Bergisel 1–2 ☎ (0512) 59489611 🕐 9am–5pm Wed–Mon (Jul & Aug: to 7pm Thu)

ANDREAS HOFER (1767–1810)

Andreas Hofer is regarded as Austria's national hero, widely extolled in its literature and poetry. In 1809, he led the Tyrolean uprising against the Bavarian rulers, who were allied with Napoleon's forces. He succeeded in beating the Bavarians, and forced the French army, led by Marshal Lefebvre, to retreat from Tyrol after their defeat on Bergisel, a hill just outside Innsbruck. Hofer assumed civilian power in Tyrol, but was soon betrayed and captured, and subsequently executed by the French in the town square of Mantua.

A SHORT WALK
INNSBRUCK

Distance 1 km (0.5 miles) **Time** 15 minutes
Nearest bus stop Innsbruck Museumstrasse

Built at the confluence of the Sill and Inn rivers, Innsbruck became an important trading post in the Middle Ages. Its lovely old town is situated on the right bank, close to the river. The most impressive historic buildings are found on Herzog-Friedrich-Strasse, Stadtplatz, Hofgasse and Rennweg. A stroll around Innsbruck's centre is not the urban city experience you may expect, with the mountains providing an Alpine background to the imperial elegance of the city's Baroque and Gothic architectural gems.

↑ Admiring the distinctive and lavishly decorated Goldenes Dachl landmark

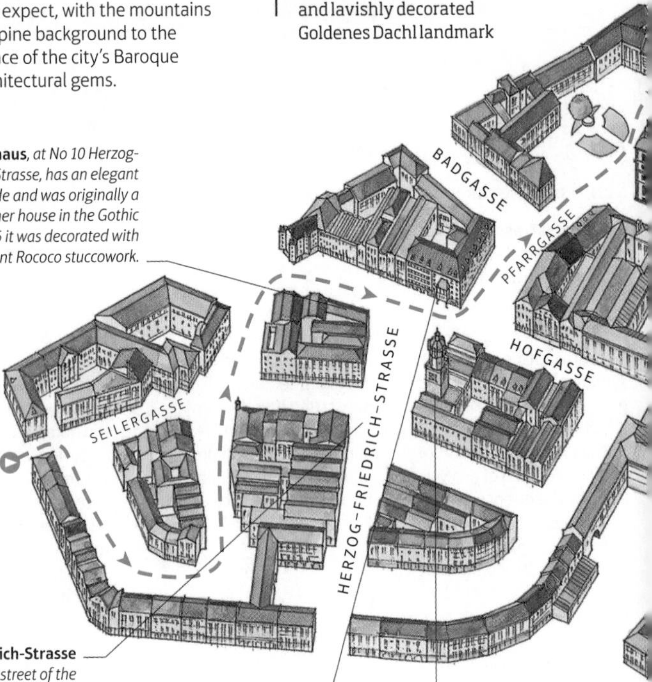

Helblinghaus, *at No 10 Herzog-Friedrich-Strasse, has an elegant Baroque façade and was originally a medieval corner house in the Gothic style. In 1725 it was decorated with opulent Rococo stuccowork.*

START ○

Herzog-Friedrich-Strasse *(p263), the main street of the old town, is lined with the attractive façades of numerous Baroque buildings.*

The symbol of Innsbruck, the **Goldenes Dachl** *(p262) is an oriel window added in 1500 by Maximilian I to Friedrich IV's former residence.*

Stadtturm *(p263), the 15th-century city tower next to the old town hall, acquired its present Renaissance look in 1560. The observation deck affords great views.*

BADGASSE

PFARRGASSE

HOFGASSE

SEILERGASSE

HERZOG–FRIEDRICH–STRASSE

0 metres   75
0 yards   75   N ↗

INNSBRUCK

Locator Map
For more detail see p263

The interior of the imperial **Hofburg** (p263) *was extensively rebuilt in Rococo style during the reign of Maria Theresa, to designs by Johann Martin Gumpp the Younger.*

Dom St Jakob (p262) *has enchanting vault frescoes by the German painter Cosmas Damian Asam and a picture of the* Madonna and Child *by Lucas Cranach the Elder.*

2,657

fire-gilded copper shingles decorated the Goldenes Dachl when it was completed.

RENGASSE

RENNWEG

UNIVERSITÄTS-STRASSE

ANGERZELLGASSE

PROF. F. MAIR-GASSE

Jesuitenkirche

○ **FINISH**

Hofkirche (p264), *built in 1553–63 as a mausoleum for Maximilian I, is guarded by 28 large bronze statues.*

Landesmuseum

→ One of the massive statues inside the Hofkirche

❷

BREGENZ

🅰A4 🚉🚌 ℹ Rathausstrasse 35a; www.bregenz.travel

The capital of Vorarlberg since 1923, Bregenz is attractively situated on the eastern shore of Bodensee (Lake Constance), at the edge of the Rhine valley and the foot of the Austrian and Swiss Alps. It is a meeting point of four countries: Austria, Germany, Switzerland and Liechtenstein. The promenades along the lake, always shrouded in a gentle mist, are worth exploring, as are the grounds of the popular summer festivals.

Bregenz and Lake Constance, reaching towards the Swiss Alps ↑

① 🎨
Vorarlberg Museum

🏛 Kornmarktplatz 1
🕐 10am–6pm Tue–Sun (Jul & Aug to 7pm; to 8pm Thu year round)
🌐 vorarlbergmuseum.at

Through superb collections of prehistoric relics, Roman artifacts and objects from the days of the Alemanni settlers, all found in Bregenz and its vicinity, this museum illustrates Vorarlberg's history. A separate department houses regional handicrafts and costumes, old weaponry, coins and medals. The jewels of the museum, though, are a 9th-century stone tablet from Lauterach and an early 16th-century crucifix from the collegiate church in Mehrerau.

②
Martinsturm

🏛 Martingsgasse 3b
📞 (0557) 44101560 🕐 May–Oct: 10am–6pm Tue–Sun

The square St Martin's Tower, the symbol of Bregenz, was probably built in the 14th century on earlier Romanesque foundations. Its present look and its staircase date from 1599, while the Baroque cupola was added at a later date. With its Venetian windows and overall muted colour scheme, the tower is reminiscent of Moorish architecture. It houses a city archive which presents changing exhibitions. In the adjacent St Martin's Chapel, you can see beautiful frescoes that date back to 1362 and depict Christ in Mandorla.

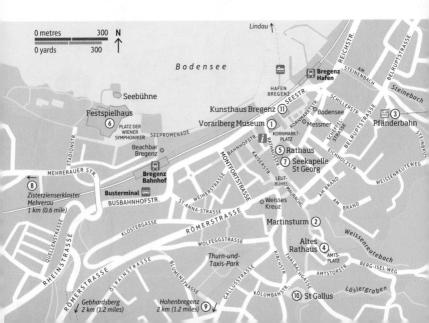

③

Pfänderbahn

📍 Steinbruchgasse 4, Bregenz ⏰ 8am–7pm daily 🌐 pfaenderbahn.at

The glass-sided, panoramic Pfänderbahn cable car climbs from Bregenz to the top of the Pfänderspitze at 1,022 m (3,353 ft), offering amazing views all the way. At the top, more than 240 peaks across Austria, Germany, Liechtenstein and Switzerland are visible, making Pfänderspitze one of the best lookout points in the region. The 94-m- (308-ft-) high tower at the summit provides TV and radio signals to the Lake Constance region. Open in summer, the restaurant next to the cable car station has a terrace that offers a great view of the lake.

The area at the foot of the Pfänder is a favourite destination for walkers. Nature trails have information signs on the area's flora and fauna.

---

④

Altes Rathaus

📍 Oberstadt

The old town hall, built in 1662, was the seat of the Bregenz municipal authorities until the 19th century. This solid, half-timbered structure stands in the centre of Oberstadt (upper town), close to the former town gate. A relief depicts Epona, the Celtic goddess of agriculture, on horseback.

---

⑤

Rathaus

📍 Rathausstrasse 4

The former granary, built in 1686, became the town's chancellery in 1720 and, in 1810, the seat of the town's authorities. It remains the town hall to this day.

> 💬 INSIDER TIP
> **All Aboard!**
>
> The fully restored Art Nouveau paddle steamer *Hohentwiel (www. hohentwiel.com)* operates trips around Lake Constance, as well as cruises complete with live jazz and food.

EAT

Gebhardsberg
Dine in a 900-year-old castle high in the hills with fantastic views over Bregenz. Try the Vorarlberg beef, local fish and suckling pig, and choose from a selection of wines.

📍 Gebhardsberg 1
🚫 Mon 🌐 greber.cc

€€€

DRINK

Beachbar Bregenz
Creative cocktails are the order of the day at the hippest and liveliest bar on the shore of Lake Constance. There's live music and a range of themed party nights in the summer.

📍 Seepromenade 2
🌐 beachbar-bregenz.com

↑ A show at the wacky Seebühne, connected to the Festspielhaus

⑥ Festspielhaus

🏛 Platz der Wiener Symphoniker 1
🌐 bregenzerfestspiele.com

This conference and convention centre, situated next to Lake Constance, was created for the Bregenz arts festival that has been held every year since 1946, from late July until late August. The festival events feature theatre and opera performances, as well as symphony concerts and art exhibitions. Since 1955, the shows have been staged at the Theater am Kornmarkt, one of the other festival venues in the city centre.

In 1980, the modern festival complex Festspielhaus was opened, with show and concert halls, exhibition rooms and a convention centre. The most spectacular of the festival venues is the famous Seebühne, a floating stage extending far onto the lake. Shows and concerts are staged here and watched by the public on the shore. The centre also hosts all kinds of events throughout the year.

⑦ Seekapelle St Georg

🏛 Rathausstrasse

The small chapel of St George, known as the Lakeside Chapel, was built in 1445 and was once lapped by the waters of Lake Constance. Today it is separated from the lake by roads and a railway line. In 1690–98 it was moved and rebuilt in the Baroque style by the bricklayer Kaspar Held.

⑧ Zisterzienserkloster Mehrerau

🏛 Mehrerauerstrasse 66
📞 (0557) 471461 🕐 For guided tours for groups only

To the west of the city centre stands this Cistercian monastery, which has been a

> INSIDER TIP
> **Say Cheese**
>
> There's plenty to smile about on the Bregenzerwald cheese trail. Work your way along a network of dairies and Alpine farmsteads, where you can sample the local mountain and forest cheeses and try your hand at making your own.

centre of spiritual and intellectual life since the 11th century. The church and monastery complex, originally built for the Benedictines and subsequently taken over by the Cistercians, was remodelled in 1740 in the Baroque style; the new tower was built using material from the previous Romanesque basilica. It was destroyed in the Napoleonic wars, rebuilt in 1855 and renovated in the 20th century. Inside, two pictures survive with the Stations of the Cross and late-Gothic statues of the Madonna.

Today, adjacent to the reconstructed church and the Romanesque crypt there is a secondary school, a monastery and a sanatorium.

Did You Know?

Festspielhaus's Seebühne is the largest floating stage in the world.

⑨

Hohenbregenz

The Hohenbregenz fortress, whose ruins stand to this day on Gebhardsberg, was built in the 10th century. In 1338, the recorded owner of the castle was Hugo de Montfort. Following the death of the last ruler of that line in 1451, the castle, together with the town and Bregenz province, were bought by Sigismund of Tyrol.

Though the castle was blown up during the Thirty Years' War, the original gateway, walls, barbican and a single turret are still standing today.

In 1723, a chapel devoted to the saints Gebhard – a 10th-century bishop of Constance – and George was built on top of Gebhardsberg and it became a popular pilgrimage site.

⑩

St Gallus

🏠 **Kirchplatz 3**

Opposite the city centre, on the banks of the Thalbach stream, stands the Stadt-pfarrkirche St Gallus (the parish church of St Gallus). According to legend, a previous church on this site had been consecrated by Gallus, an Irish missionary who arrived here in the 7th century. The present church was consecrated in 1318, and in 1738 the church was altered in the Baroque style. At that time, the nave was raised and a chapel was added in the transept.

The rather modest interior of the church is typical of Vorarlberg's ecclesiastical style and contrasts sharply with the styles of Tyrol and Bavaria, where Baroque opulence is much more in evidence. The main altarpiece includes statues of the saints

Gallus, Peter, Paul and Ulrich, while the side chapel has figures of saints Magnus and Nicholas. St Magnus, an 8th-century Benedictine monk, is the patron saint of the Allgäu, the German region between Tyrol and Vorarlberg. St Nicholas is said to keep a careful watch over the navigation on Lake Constance.

⑪

Kunsthaus Bregenz

🏠 **Karl-Tizian-Platz, Postfach 45, Bregenz**
🕐 **10am-6pm Tue-Sun (to 8pm Thu)** 🌐 **kunsthaus-bregenz.at**

A contemporary art gallery made of glass and steel and a cast concrete stone, the Kunsthaus was constructed to the designs of Swiss architect Peter Zumthor between 1990 and 1997. Much of the work that features in the regularly changing exhibitions is created on site in order to allow artists to respond to the building's unique architecture, particularly the façade, which consists of 712 finely etched glass panels. Rachel Whiteread and Anthony Gormley are just two of the world-famous artists who have exhibited here. Great coffee and a unique bar made from local wood make the gallery's KUB café as attractive as any of the gallery's exhibits.

STAY

Weisses Kreuz

Centrally located hotel with large, bright rooms. Many rooms have views of the mountains, and there is a good restaurant with terrace on site.

🏠 **Römerstrasse 5**
🌐 **hotelweisseskreuz.at**

€€€

Bodensee

This traditional guest house, much of which architecturally dates back to 1870, is located close to the lake. A lavish breakfast buffet features locally sourced produce.

🏠 **Kornmarktstrasse 22**
🌐 **hotel-bodensee.at**

€€€

Messmer

The oldest inn in Bregenz, with a history dating back 400 years, is today a modern place whose rooms offer contemporary comforts and design.

🏠 **Kornmarktstrasse 16**
🌐 **hotel-messmer.at**

€€€

→

The Kunsthaus Bregenz's cool interior complementing the interesting art on display

❸

ZILLERTAL

🅐C5 🚆🚌 **ℹ** Bundesstrasse 27d, Schlitters; www.zillertal.at

Extending from Innau to the border with Italy, the Zillertal, the valley of the Ziller river, is an enchanting setting. The well-marked trails in breathtakingly beautiful countryside lure ramblers here in the summer, and there are many attractive cycling routes.

Initially a wide upland, beyond Mayrhofen the Zillertal splits into four narrower valleys that cut into the mountain ranges. Artificial lakes and large dams were built into most of the local rivers to provide a power supply for the entire region.

Mayrhofen is the most popular destination in the Zillertal. During the summer, the lush green pastures are perfect for climbing, cycling and hiking. In the winter, the town comes alive with its legendary Harakiri piste and the best après-ski in the region. Mayrhofen

isn't the only attraction, though. The valley of the Tuxerbach (Tux stream) is particularly picturesque, with many attractive resorts. Tuxer Ferner, also known as the Hintertux Glacier, is the local glacier and offers great year-round skiing conditions.

For a picture-perfect spot, check out the splendid Stilluppspeicher lake, southeast of Tuxerbach. The best views of the lake in its pristine natural environment are gained from the top of the dam at 1,130 m (3,707 ft). Nearby are two gorgeous waterfalls.

ZILLERTAL'S GAUDER FEST

Held annually in the first week of May in the municipality of Zell am Ziller, at the top of the Zillertal valley, Gauder Fest is Austria's biggest and most renowned traditional costume and spring festival in the Alpine region. With a parade of decorated carriages and folk costumes, musical concerts, the strongest beer in the country and even wrestling competitions, this festival entertains the whole family.

1 River Ziller provides the perfect conditions for whitewater rafting.

2 Dairy cows graze in the flower meadows on the mountain slopes.

3 Schlegeispeicher is the largest artificial lake in the area and a picturesque backdrop for hiking.

Did You Know?

Hintertux is now the only year-round ski resort in Austria.

STAY

Strass
Next to the Penkenbahn gondola lift, this is one of the best hotels in the Zillertal. Rooms are big and have balconies, and there is an indoor swimming pool.

◫ Hauptstrasse 470, Mayrhofen ⓦ hotel strass.com

€€€

Gletscherhotel Hintertuxerhof
In winter, you can ski to the door of this luxury hotel at the foot of the Hintertux glacier, while in summer there are tennis courts to enjoy. Children are well-catered for with play areas and a crèche.

◫ Hintertux 780, Tux ⓦ hintertuxerhof.at

€€€

DRINK

Harakiri
One of the liveliest après-ski bars and nightclubs in the Alps. The huge dance floor fills up early with party people of all ages dancing to timeless europop classics. Serves excellent local beers.

◫ Hauptstrasse 454, Mayrhofen ⓦ harakiri.cc

←
Skiing on the pristine white slopes above the Zillertal

EXPERIENCE MORE

4

Achensee

🄰C4 🚌 🚠 �w achensee.at

Situated between the Inn and the Isar basins is Achensee, the largest lake in Tyrol, about 9 km (6 miles) long. Surrounding ski slopes provide great views of the lake. The town also promotes a range of alternative winter sports, including snowshoeing, cross-country trails and tobogganing.

Achensee can be reached by cog-wheel train from Jenbach. Worth seeing here is the

> 💬 INSIDER TIP
> **On the Water**
>
> Achensee is a major watersports centre. You can rent sailing boats, wind- and kite-surfing equipment from several places, most of which offer lessons. Alternatively, take a cruise around the lake.

Church of St Wolfgang, a late Gothic structure built in 1487–1500; its Baroque tower was added later. Although rebuilt many times, it still has many of its late Gothic features. One of the side altars has a late-Gothic statue of the Madonna.

5

Hall in Tirol

🄰B5 🚌 🚠 𝒊 Wallpachgasse 5; www.hall-wattens.at

Hall ranks mostly as a holiday resort, but the old town, with much of its original architecture intact, bears testimony to the town's former glory. The symbol of Hall is the 12-sided tower known as Burg Hasegg or the Mint Tower. This castle, with its beautiful inner courtyard, once formed a corner section of the town's fortifications. It was the seat of the Tyrolean rulers and, in the 16th century, it became the mint. Today it houses a museum. In the old town, the town hall

consists of two parts: the 1406 Königshaus (Royal House), with a beautiful debating hall with an exposed-beam ceiling; and a large building on the south side of Oberer Stadtplatz, with a Renaissance portal and a balcony from which the town fathers used to make their proclamations. The nearby 14th-century Nikolauskirche (Church of St Nicholas), has a delightful portal featuring the Sorrowful Christ, the Virgin Mary and St Nicholas, and an attractive Baroque interior. Particularly worth seeing is the Waldaufkapelle, which houses a collection of rare reliquaries.

6

Igls

🄰B5 🚌 𝒊 Hilberstrasse 15; (05123) 77101

This small town south of Innsbruck has long been popular as a holiday centre and winter-sports resort, and

Admiring the natural beauty of Achensee from above →

The Crystal Dome, and the Chambers of Wonder (inset), at Swarovski Crystal Worlds

hosted a number of events at the 1976 Winter Olympics. The resort is not the most extensive in the region, but the skiing is challenging and the mountain is served by a modern lift system. An old salt track, Römerstrasse, runs above the Sill valley, providing views of the Europabrücke (Europe Bridge; p279), which spans the Alpine gorges.

The Aegidiuskirche (Church of St Giles) probably dates to around the 13th century but was remodelled in the Baroque period. The vault is decorated with beautiful frescoes by Josef Michael Schmitzer.

Near Igls is the pilgrimage chapel Heiligwasser (1662), with attractive stuccowork from 1720 as well as a wooden statue of the Virgin Mary dating back to the early 15th century.

7
Schwaz

🅰 C5 🚉🚌 🛈 Münchner-strasse 11; www.silber region-karwendel.com

This busy commercial town in the Inn valley suffered extensive damage during the battle of 1809 (p265), but it has preserved several valuable historic sights. The most

impressive of these is the 15th-century Pfarrkirche, with its high copper-shingled tower and crenellated gables. The most striking elements inside are the stone balustrade of the gallery with intricate lacework (c 1520) and a superb Baroque organ enclosure.

The Franziskanerkirche, the Franciscan church and monastery, has retained its original late Gothic interior, clearly visible despite Baroque additions made in the 18th century. The cloister along the south wall of the church was built in 1509–12 and features a series of 16th-century paintings with Passion scenes.

Schwaz was once a major centre for the production of silver, and one of the mines, the **Silberbergwerk**, is now open to the public and can be explored by train and on foot, on a guided tour.

Silberbergwerk

🔞🔞 🏠 Alte Landstrasse 3a ⏰ May-Sep: 9am-5pm daily, Oct-Apr: 10am-4pm daily 🌐 silberbergwerk.at

8
Wattens

🅰 B5 🚉🚌 🌐 hall-wattens.at

The biggest attraction in Wattens is Swarovski Kristallwelten (**Swarovski Crystal Worlds**) – part factory, part gallery, part jewellery shop. In the Chambers of Wonder – accessed through a giant grass and crystal head that spouts water – you can see the world's largest cut crystal (300,000 carats), and a crystal wall 11 m (36 ft) high, with several tons of glittering semiprecious stones.

Nearby Volders has an unusual church devoted to St Charles Borromeo, considered a Rococo masterpiece.

Swarovski Crystal Worlds

🔞🔞🔞🔞 🏠 Kristallwelten-strasse 1 ⏰ 8:30am-7:30pm daily (Jul & Aug: to 10pm) 🌐 kristallwelten.swarovski. com

9

Söll

⚑ C4 🌐 soell.at

Söll, a pleasant small town in the foothills of the Hohe Salve mountain, part of the Wilder Kaiser (Wild Emperor) massif, grew around the Church of St Peter and St Paul. Built in 1361 but altered in the Baroque style in 1768 by Franz Bock of Kufstein, it contains beautiful vault paintings and a picture of the Madonna in the main altarpiece by Austrian artist Christoph Anton Mayr.

Söll is dotted with attractive houses with superb façades. The greatest attraction, however, is the Hohe Salve mountain, visible from every point in town. Two gondolas are on hand to provide transport to the summit. There is a small chapel here, and the view over Brixental, the Kitzbühel Alps and the Hohe Tauern Mountains in the distance is truly majestic.

Söll lies at the centre of a large skiing region, SkiWelt Wilder Kaiser-Brixental, in the southern part of Kaisergebirge. SkiWelt is one of the most extensive resorts in Europe, and incorporates a total of nine villages, 90 cable cars and lifts, and 81 alpine huts.

Did You Know?

The SkiWelt resort around Söll has over 280 km (174 miles) of ski runs.

10

Wörgl

⚑ C4 ℹ Bahnhofstrasse 4a; www.tirol-erleben.at/woergl

The industrial town of Wörgl lies at the fork of the Inn river and the Brixentaler Ache stream. The earliest settlement on the site, revealed by archaeological finds on the northeastern outskirts of town, date from the Bronze Age. In later years this was the site of a Roman settlement, and in the 4th century a Christian community was founded in the area. In the 13th century, Wörgl belonged to Bavaria; during the reign of Maximilian I, it finally became incorporated into Tyrol. Wörgl was also the scene of fighting during the Napoleonic Wars, when the Tyrolean highlanders fought for their independence from the Bavarians and the French. A monument commemorating the battle now stands in front of the Church of St Lawrence. Built in the Baroque style in 1748, it has some tasteful stuccowork, vault paintings and a medieval statue of the Madonna.

Wörgl's convenient location between the popular tourist regions of Kaisergebirge and the Kitzbühel Alps makes it a convenient base for winter and summer expeditions.

11 ⚡ Ⓜ ▢

Schloss Tratzberg

⚑ C5 🏠🏠 ⏰ Apr–Oct: 10am–4pm daily (Jul & Aug: to 5pm) 🌐 schloss-tratzberg.at

A short way from Schwaz, in the Inn river valley, stands the impressive Renaissance Schloss Tratzberg. This castle was once a frontier fortress that guarded Andechs county against the Bavarians. It now operates as a small museum.

The castle is entered from the west side through a Renaissance portal. The inner courtyard, with its heavily decorated low arcades, was built in two stages: the first around 1500 and the second in the late 16th century. The most interesting parts of the castle are the armoury, with its tremendous collection of early arms; the Royal Room, with its exposed-beam ceiling; and the Habsburg Hall, with the family tree of Emperor Maximilian I and 148 portraits. The room has a red marble column at its centre and is covered by a coffered ceiling. The emperor's room on the second floor has retained its intricately carved wooden ceiling, and the bedroom is decorated with a series of 16th-century paintings of a knightly tournament. The Fugger family room still has its original Renaissance decor. Its best feature is the richly inlaid door dating from 1515.

↑ Crossing Hohe Salve mountain near Wörgl overlooking the Kitzbühel Alps

↑ A mountain road winding through the handsome alpine houses of Alpbach

⑫ Alpbach

🅐 C5 🅦 alpbachtal.at

Set in a high mountain valley and often proclaimed the most beautiful village in Austria, Alpbach's charm is undeniable: traditional wooden chalets and houses are surrounded by lush pastures, unspoilt woodlands and beautiful mountain scenery.

It is also one of Austria's most popular ski resorts, with a range of cross-country skiing trails and ski slopes. The terrain is gentle and undulating, ideal for beginners and families. During the summer months, cycling, hiking and even para-gliding are major attractions.

The beautiful, typically Tyrolean Church of St Oswald sits in the centre of town. Its earliest records date from 1369, although it was altered in 1500 and the Baroque interior dates from 1724.

⑬ Lustenau

🅐 A4 🚊🚌 🅘 Rathaus-strasse 1; www.lustenau.at

Lustenau lies 5 km (3 miles) north of the mouth of the Rhine, and is famous for its embroidery and lace-making. Until 1806, it was a free terri-tory within the Habsburg Empire, but in 1814, after the Congress of Vienna, Lustenau came under Austrian rule.

Museum Rhein-Schauen documents the history of the local people and the Rhine. It is also the terminus of the Rheinbähnle, a narrow-gauge train line that takes passen-gers along the shores of the Rhine to the outmost point of the delta in Lake Constance.

Museum Rhein-Schauen

🏠 Höchsterstrasse 4
🕐 1–5:30pm Thu–Sun (Rheinbähnle: to 3pm Fri–Sun) 🅦 rheinschauen.at

Alpbach's charm is undeniable: traditional wooden chalets and houses are surrounded by lush pastures, unspoilt woodlands and beautiful mountain scenery.

STAY

Eggerwirt
Cosy rooms and home-cooked food, just a short walk from the gondola.

🅐 C4 🏠 Dorf 14, Söll
🅦 eggerwirt.cc

€€€

Gästehaus Weiherhof
Country living in a leafy setting with an exten-sive buffet breakfast.

🅐 C5 🏠 Alpbach 445, Alpbach 🅦 weiherhof.at

€€€

Residenz Alexado
Elegant villa with richly decorated rooms and a host of health and beauty treatments.

🅐 C4 🏠 Sepp Gangl-Strasse 4, Wörgl
🅦 alexado.at

€€€

14
Kitzbühel

🅰C4 🚌 🚆 ℹHinterstadt 18;
www.kitzbuehel.com

One of the most charming and
upmarket of the Tyrolean ski
resorts, the town of Kitzbühel
has quaint cobbled streets
leading out into gentle summer
pastures filled with cows. Every
January, however, the town is
filled by daredevils arriving for
the Hahnenkammrennen, the
most dangerous downhill ski
race in the world.

But Kitzbühel is more than
a sporting resort; untouched
by wartime ravages, many of
its historic sights have survived
to this day. The Andreaskirche
(Church of St Andrew) was
built in 1435 on the site of a
Romanesque church; in 1785 it
was rebuilt in the Baroque
style. Inside are late-Gothic
columns and 15th-century
traceries and frescoes. The
altar was created in 1663 by
the sculptor Simon Benedikt
Faistenberger and his brother-
in-law, Veit Rabl.

Adjacent to the parish church
is Liebfrauenkirche (Church of
Our Lady), distinguished by its
prominent square tower, which
houses a large church bell. The
14th-century Katharinenkirche
(St Catherine's Church) is now
a monument to those killed in
the two world wars.

15
Kufstein

🅰C4 🚌 🚆 🌐kufstein.com

This charming town on the
banks of the Inn is filled with
cobbled streets, boutiques and
historic sights, earning it the
nickname the "Pearl of Tyrol".
On a rocky hill to the north
of the town stands the gleaming white Festung Kufstein
(Kufstein Fortress). Today it
houses a regional museum
and the Heldenorgel (Heroes'
Organ), built to commemorate
those who lost their lives in
World War I. The magnificent
sound of the organ fills the
streets every day at noon. The
late-Gothic Church of St Vitus
was rebuilt in the 17th century
in the Baroque style, but in
the late 20th century it was
partly returned to its original
Gothic appearance.

Hechtsee and Stimmersee,
two small, scenic lakes west
of Kufstein, are excellent for
watersports enthusiasts.
About 30 km (22 miles) northeast of Kufstein, beyond the
Kaisergebirge ridge known as
Zahmer Kaiser (Tame Emperor),
is Walchsee, a beguiling town
centred on a lake of the same
name, with many fine houses
with picturesque façades and
a superb water sports centre.
The road from Kufstein along
the Sparchenbach river leads
to Stripsenkopf, the highest
peak in the Zahmer Kaiser
range, with great views of
the Kaisergebirge.

⑯ St Johann in Tirol

AC4 **C**(05352) 633350 **🚉 🚌**

St Johann in Tirol is a bustling market town that has also made its name as a popular winter-sports resort, with good downhill runs on the northern slopes of the Kitzbüheler Horn and splendid conditions for cross-country skiing. The town has several Baroque buildings, and the first large Baroque church in the area was built in 1728, on the site of an earlier Gothic structure. Inside Mariä Himmelfahrtskirche (Church of the Assumption of the Virgin Mary) the vault is daubed with some magnificent paintings by one of the great masters of Baroque art, Simon Benedikt Faistenberger. Another major landmark in town is the 30-m-(98-ft-) tall tower of the Huber Bräu brewery, where you can enjoy some excellent Alpine beer and food with unparalleled views of the area.

⑰ Stubaital

AB5 **🚌 ℹ**Bahnstrasse 17, Fulpmes; www.stubai.at

Travelling on the Brenner motorway from Innsbruck towards Italy you will pass the Stubai Alps to your right, a high ridge massif with few valleys. The lowest route to the centre of the massif runs along the Stubaital, with the busy resorts of Fulpmes and Neustift. Zuckerhütl (Little Sugar Loaf), the highest peak, rises to 3,507 m (11,506 ft). Stubaital is notably quiet, particularly compared with neighbouring Zillertal (p272). The Stubai glacier, the largest glacier ski resort in Austria, provides excellent conditions for skiing.

←

Alfresco dining in the colourful, bustling town centre of Kitzbühel

↑ Driving on the high Europabrücke, heading towards the Brenner Pass

⑱ Brenner Pass

AB5

The Brenner Pass is the lowest passage across the Eastern Alps, and as such one of the most easily accessible routes connecting northern Europe with Italy. Lying between the Stubai Alps and the Zillertal Alps, the pass was originally used by the Romans as a trade and military route. Today the motorway across the Brenner also boasts the highest and most impressive road bridge in Europe, the Europabrücke, 815 m (2,674 ft) long.

⑲ Seefeld

AB5 **🚉 ℹ**Klosterstrasse 43; www.seefeld.com

This small town, occupying a large sunny plateau, is one of Austria's best resorts for family-oriented skiing, with its gentle, welcoming runs. Its cross-country skiing trails are the longest in the Alps, measuring some 250 km (155 miles).

At the centre of Seefeld stands the huge 15th-century Church of St Oswald, while at the western end of the town is a chapel built on the orders of Archduke Leopold V to house a supposedly miraculous 16th-century crucifix. The crucifix stands in the altarpiece today.

EAT

Huberbräu-Stüberl
Lively restaurant in the heart of old Kitzbühel. Serves a fantastic goulash and a great range of local beer.

AC4 **🏠**Vorderstadt 18, Kitzbühel **C**(05356) 65677

€€€

Hahnenkammstüberl
At the top of the Hahnenkamm ski lift, this place serves great Tyrolean food and has superb views of the mountains.

AC4 **🏠**Hahnenkamm 17, Kitzbühel **C**(05356) 62521

€€€

Südtiroler Stube
Picturesque restaurant in an old farmhouse with beautifully restored stone floors and timber cladding. Offers good-value local dishes.

AB5 **🏠**Reitherspitz-strasse 17, Seefeld **🚫**Wed **🌐**suedtiroler-stube.com

€€€

20

Ötztal

A B5 🚆 🚌 **i** Gemeinde-
strasse 4, Sölden; www.
oetztal.com

Following the course of the
Ötztaler Ache, a tributary of the
Inn river, is the long valley of
Ötztal. At its southern end, near
the border with Italy, rise the
Ötztal Alps, with many peaks
above 3,500 m (11,500 ft).

Nestling within the Ötztal
Alps is also the highest parish
in Austria, the ski resort of
Obergurgl. The largest settlement in the lower part of Ötztal
is Oetz, a village with colourful
houses. The paintings on the
Gasthof zum Stern (Star Inn)
date from 1573 and 1615.

The largest town at the
upper end of the Ötztal valley
is Längenfeld. Ötztal's administrative centre is the classically
Tyrolean village of Sölden. The
Tiefenbach glacier attracts
early- and late-season skiers.

In 1991, a frozen human
body was discovered on the
Italian side of the Ötztal Alps.
Although over 5,000 years old,
Ötzi, as he was named, was
perfectly preserved by the ice.

21

Ehrwald

A B5 🚆 🚌 **i** Schmiede 15;
www.zugspitzarena.com

Nestling below the western
side of Zugspitze, the highest
peak of the Bavarian Alps, is
the resort village of Ehrwald.
On the German side of the
mountain is the resort of
Garmisch-Partenkirchen, the
most popular winter-sports
centre in that area. Several
resorts, including Garmisch-
Partenkirchen and Ehrwald,
have joined up to form one
vast skiing area.

The summit of Zugspitze
can be reached from both
the German and the Austrian
sides. From Ehrwald, you take
the cable car from the lower
station of Ehrwald/Obermoos.
There are magnificent views
to be enjoyed from the upper
station. To the south, beyond
the Kaisergebirge, Karwen-
delgebirge and Dachstein
mountain ranges, you can
see the snow-covered peaks
of the Hohe Tauern. To the
west is the vast Piz Bernina in
Switzerland, while to the east
are the Arlberg mountains

HIDDEN GEM
**Zugspitze
Cable Car**

At the summit of the
Zugspitze is a fascina-
ting museum telling the
story of the Tyrol's first
cable car. This has a
glass floor, over which
you can walk some
200 m (656 ft) above
the Zugspitze massif
(*www.zugspitze.de*).

and the Allgäu mountains
in the distance. To the north
is Bavaria.

Clemens Krauss, the founder
of the Vienna New Year's Day
concerts *(p128)*, lived in
Ehrwald and lies buried here.

22

Lech am Arlberg

A A5 🚆 🚌 **W** lechzuers.at

This small resort is situated on
a large plateau at an altitude
of 1,450 m (4,800 ft), not far
from the source of the Lech
river. Lech is regarded as one
of Austria's most beautiful and

luxurious mountain resorts and regularly attracts celebrities and royals, who come to spend their winter holidays here. Today, Lech, Oberlech and neighbouring Zürs are linked by ski lifts to form the formidable Ski Arlberg skipass region, with 305 km (190 miles) of runs. Lech is never crowded; once a certain number of ski passes are sold, the authorities simply close the roads.

Summers, too, can be a pleasant experience here, and there is a wide selection of beautiful trails for walking or mountain biking. Sights to see include the 15th-century Gothic Church of St Nicholas, and the Huber-Hus, a 16th-century house that forms the architectural heart of the town museum. In addition,

---

Did You Know?

100 life-sized human sculptures by artist Anthony Gormley are in the mountains above Lech.

←
Sky walking over the Tiefenbach glacier in the Ötztal mountains

---

there are swanky hotels, chic shops, smart cafés and outstanding restaurants.

23
Elbigenalp

Ⓐ A5 **Ⓒ (05645) 315** 🚃

The Lech river valley, which is parallel to the Inn river valley and snakes between mountain passes, cuts a deep ravine between the Allgäuer Alps and the Lechtal Alps. About halfway between the towns of Reutte and Warth (a popular ski area) lies Elbigenalp, a small village worth visiting for the local Nikolauskirche (Church of St Nicholas). Built in the 14th century, the church's oldest surviving parts include the Gothic tower, presbytery and font. It was altered in the Baroque style, and the vault and wall paintings as well as the Stations of the Cross are the work of the artistic Zeiller family, who lived in Reutte. St Martin's cemetery chapel has some sumptuous Gothic frescoes depicting scenes from the life of St Magdalene and the Dance of Death by Austrian painter Anton Falger.

24
Reutte

Ⓐ B4 **ℹ Untermarkt 34; www.reutte.com**

Reutte is the largest town in the Ausserfern district, a remote area that was cut off from the world for some time: reportedly, the first car arrived here only in 1947. Reutte can be reached from Innsbruck via the Fern Pass, a route first used in Roman times. In the valley of the Lech river, it is today the main town and trade centre of the region. In medieval times it grew rich on the salt trade, and to this day it has some lovely town houses with oriel windows, open staircases and painted façades. Many of the paintings are by Johann Jakob

---

↑ The oriel window and painted façade of Zeiller Haus in Reutte

---

Zeiller, the most famous member of an artistic family that settled in Reutte in the 17th and 18th centuries – they once lived at No 1 Zeiller Platz.

The 15th-century convent church of St Anna features several works of art. In the main altarpiece are a picture of the Madonna with Child and St Anna (c 1515) and two vast figures of St Magnus and St Afra from the 18th century.

The **Heimatmuseum** (local museum) has a fine collection of paintings by outstanding masters of the Baroque, mainly of the Zeiller family members, as well as exhibits associated with transport and salt mining.

Specimens representative of the local flora can be seen in the Alpenblumengarten, an Alpine flower garden on top of the Hahnenkamm, at a height of about 1,700 m (5,577 ft) above sea level.

Heimatmuseum

⊗ ⊗ 🕐 🅰 **Grünes Haus, Untermarkt 26** 🕐 8am–noon & 1–5pm Mon–Fri 🌐 museum-reutte.at

㉕ Bludenz

A5 🚍 ℹ️ Werden-
bergerstrasse 42; www.
bludenz.at

Beautifully situated at the confluence of three mountain ranges and five Alpine valleys, the town of Bludenz will leave you spoilt for choice with the skiing areas in its environs.

Between the 15th and the 19th centuries, Bludenz served as the seat of the Habsburg governors, and despite several devastating fires, this historic old town with Mediterranean arcades has much to offer beyond its slopes. The oldest building is Oberes Tor (Upper Gate), which houses the local history museum (open in summer). Inside the Church of St Lawrence (1514) are two original altars made from black marble and paintings (1510) showing the Marriage of the Virgin Mary and the Visitation. The seat of the regional authorities is Gayenhofen Castle, a medieval building remodelled in Baroque style in 1643.

Today, the town is often permeated by the aroma of chocolate drifting down from the Suchard factory, home to the famous purple Milka cows. Stop by the Milka Lädele, just across from the train station, to stock up on chocolatey treats. Younger visitors will enjoy the small museum on site and the annual Chocolate Festival, held in mid-July.

> 💬 **INSIDER TIP**
> ### Brandnertal
>
> Besides great skiing, the Brandnertal region above Bludenz has the most extensive network of marked and prepared winter walks in Austria. It's perfect for families and groups, including non-skiers who may want to meet up at one of the mountain restaurants for lunch.

↑ Snowboarding on the slopes above the famous resort of St Anton am Arlberg

㉖ St Anton am Arlberg

B5 🚍 🌐 stantonam
arlberg.com

St Anton is something of a skiing mecca. Consistently ranked as one of the top five skiing resorts in the world, it is without doubt number one in Austria. Runs range from those for beginners to the challenging Valluga peak, restricted to expert skiers accompanied by a guide. The après-ski is very enthusiastic, with the nightlife going into the early hours.

The resort is often heralded as the "birthplace of skiing"; it was here that Johann "Hannes" Schneider conceived the "Arlberg method", a step-by-step transition from the snow-plough to the Christie. The method is still in use today.

St Anton also features a charming village with a 17th-century church, an Alpine museum and a plethora of traditional houses. It has a number of luxurious spas, too.

㉗ Lünersee

A5 🚍

Lünersee lies at the foot of the Schesaplana peak, and is the starting point for many hikes. Once, this was the largest lake in the Eastern Alps, surrounded by rugged mountains crisscrossed with ravines. The dam built here in 1958 raised the water level by 27 m (89 ft), creating an artificial reservoir.

㉘ Bodensee

A4 🚍 ℹ️ Römerstr. 2,
Bregenz; www.bodensee-
vorarlberg.com

Bodensee, or Lake Constance in English, is one of the largest and best-known European lakes, and divides its waters between Austria, Germany and Switzerland. At 74 km (44 miles) long, it is the largest lake in

A number of attractive towns line Bodensee's shores, including Konstanz, whose island of Mainau is known for its flower-filled gardens.

the Alps. The Rhine flows into the lake in a broad delta and, having passed through the entire length of Bodensee, it emerges as a turbulent mountain river near Schaffhausen, in Switzerland. The countryside around the lake benefits from a pleasant, moderate climate.

Today, Bodensee forms not so much a border as a link between the countries that lie on its shores. For Austria it is a highly convenient transport route to western Europe, while for the surrounding towns and villages it provides excellent water sports and relaxation.

The mountains around the town of Bregenz extend right up to the water, creating a picturesque setting for the countless artistic events that take place here, such as the Bregenz Spring dance festival (March) and the acclaimed Bregenz Festival (p270).

A number of attractive towns line Bodensee's shores, including Konstanz, whose island of Mainau is known for its flower-filled gardens, arboretum and butterfly house, and Friedrichshafen on the German side, which can be reached by ferry or pleasure craft from Bregenz.

29
Ischgl

🅰A5 🚉 🌐ischgl.at

Ischgl, on the Trisanna river at the eastern end of the Silvrettastrasse, may retain the charm of a small farming village, but it is in fact the venue for a distinctly young, affluent and often raucous clientele of skiers and snowboarders. An international ski centre, it provides access to 200 km (120 miles) of ski runs and 40 lifts within the Silvretta range on the Austrian–Swiss border. The town is also an ideal starting point for a drive along the Silvrettahochalpenstrasse, a hairpin mountain road (closed Nov–May), which connects the Montafon valley and the Ill river with the Trisanna valley. The road drops by 1,000 m (3,280 ft) over just 15 km (9 miles).

The area around Silvretta-Stausee, a reservoir on the Bielerhöhe Pass at 2,036 m

EAT

Fliana Gourmet
Gastronomic treats and world-class wines await, but booking is a must.

🅰A5 🏠Fimbabahnweg 8, Ischgl 🚫Wed
🌐fliana.com

€€€

Salnerhof
Enjoy fresh game and fish at this bright and breezy restaurant with great mountain views.

🅰C4 🏠Hahnenkamm 17, Kitzbühel
🌐salnerhof.at

€€€

(6,680 ft), has been made a national park; the ski runs in the Silvretta massif start here. The most beautiful views are to be had from Hohes Rad, at 2,934 m (9,626 ft). The high mountain section of Silvrettastrasse ends in Galtür, a village on the Ballunspitze.

↑ Enjoying the glorious sunset at a pavilion on Lake Constance

A DRIVING TOUR
ARLBERG

Length 45 km (30 miles) **Stopping-off points** The hotel by the hospice in St Christoph offers accommodation. There are many restaurants and shops in St Anton am Arlberg.

The Arlberg Pass in the Eastern Alps is part of the European watershed between the catchment areas of the North Sea, the Black Sea, the tributaries of the Rhine and the Danube. Arlberg used to be completely cut off from the rest of the country, oriented more towards Germany and Switzerland, until the railway tunnel was built in 1880–84, connecting Vorarlberg with the rest of Austria. The tunnel, at an altitude of 1,310 m (4,298 ft), measures 10 km (6 miles) in length, and was for many years the longest in Austria. Today, the Arlberg region has some of the country's most exclusive ski resorts, many of which you'll pass through on this delightful driving tour.

*The breathtaking view extending from the **Valluga** summit at 2,809 m (9,216 ft) embraces the Montafon valley, the Brenner Pass, the Ötztal and the Stubai Alps.*

Flexenpass
is surrounded by the Rätikon mountain peaks.

Lechtaler

Griesskopf
△ 2,581 m (8,468 f

Zürsbach

Zürs

198

Gloggerspitze
△ 2,523 m (8,277 ft)

Roggspitze △
2,747 m (9,012 ft)

Bacher
△ 2,391 m (7,844 ft)

Flexenpass

Rosskopf △
2,200m (7,218 ft)

Trittkopf △
2,720 m (8,924 ft)

Valluga △
2,809 m (9,216 ft)

Pettneu
am Arlberg

S16

FINISH
Stuben

Alpe Rauz

St Jakob
am Arlberg

Alfenz

ARLBERGTUNNEL

Arlbergpass

St Christoph

St Anton
am Arlberg

197

ARLBERG STRASSENTUNNEL

Zwölferkopf
△ 2,558 m (8,392 ft)

Rosanna

Hochkarkopf
△ 2,772 m (9,094 ft)

Albonakopf △
2,654 m (8,707 ft)

Sattelkopf
△ 1,985 m (6,512 ft)

Verwall

Wildebene
△ 2,570 m (8,432 ft)

Moosbach

*The quiet village of **Stuben** at the foot of the Albonagrat has ski runs leading to St Anton.*

*The **Arlbergtunnel** underneath the Arlberg Pass and 10 km (6 miles) long was the longest in the world when it opened in 1978.*

*The ski resort of **St Christoph** is one of the best in Austria and one of the highest in the Alps. This tiny village makes for a peaceful retreat and is popular with families*

*The largest tourist resort in Arlberg, **St Anton** is surrounded by numerous ski trails, and good snow conditions are guaranteed.*

1901

The year Austria's first regular ski school was founded in St Christoph.

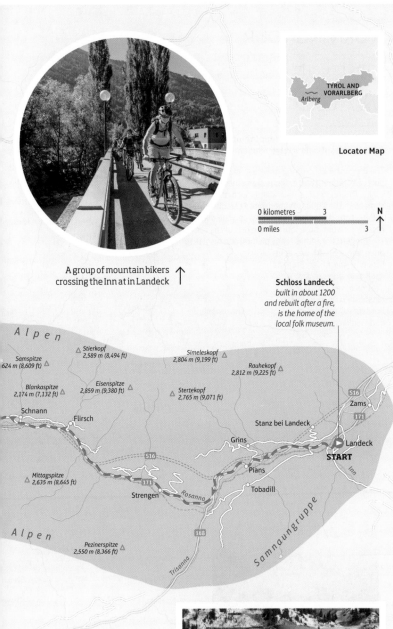

Locator Map

0 kilometres 3
0 miles 3

N ↑

A group of mountain bikers ↑
crossing the Inn at in Landeck

Schloss Landeck,
*built in about 1200
and rebuilt after a fire,
is the home of the
local folk museum.*

A l p e n

Samspitze
624 m (8,609 ft) △

Stierkopf
2,589 m (8,494 ft) △

Simeleskopf
2,804 m (9,199 ft) △

Rauhekopf
2,812 m (9,225 ft) △

Blankaspitze
2,174 m (7,132 ft) △

Eisenspitze
2,859 m (9,380 ft) △

Stertekopf
2,765 m (9,071 ft) △

Schnann

Flirsch

Stanz bei Landeck

Zams

S16

171

Grins

Mittagspitze
2,635 m (8,645 ft) △

S16

Pians

Landeck
START

Strengen

Rosanna

Tobadill

Inn

A l p e n

188

S a m n a u n g r u p p e

Pezinerspitze
2,550 m (8,366 ft) △

Trisanna

→
A bus driving past snow-
covered houses in the
pretty village of Stuben

285

A DRIVING TOUR
BREGENZER WALD

Length 65 km (40 miles) **Stopping-off points** There are good restaurants and accommodation in Dornbirn

The Bregenzer Wald (Bregenz Forest) occupies the northern part of Vorarlberg and extends along the Bregenzer Ache valley. This region has maintained much of its individual character: its inhabitants cherish their traditions, and the architecture, the national costumes and the dialect spoken here differ from those found in the rest of the country. The Bregenz Forest has many picturesque resorts to drive through, with excellent facilities. Apart from Bregenz itself, two larger urban centres have become established on its borders – Dornbirn and Feldkirch.

*At **Schwarzenberg** you'll find paintings by former resident Angelika Kauffman, a prominent artist of the Neo-Classical period, in the local Holy Trinity church.*

*You can enjoy lovely views from the forecourt of the Sonnblick Inn in **Ammenegg**.*

Müselbach

Alberschwende

Ammenegg

Haselstauden

Egg

Dornbirn

Schwarzenberg

Bersbuch

*The largest town in Vorarlberg, **Dornbirn** is a centre for the textile industry.*

Hochälpelekopf 1,464 m (4,803 ft)

Bezau

Rappenlochschlucht ■ **FINISH**

Reuthe

*The road to the impressive **Rappenlochschlucht** gorge runs steeply uphill along the Dornbirner Ache stream and ends at a reservoir*

Ebnit

Guntenkopf 1,811 m (5,941 ft)

Mellau

Mörzelspitze 1,830 m (6,003 ft)

Salzbödenkopf 1,765 m (5,790 ft)

Hochblanken 2,068 m (6,784 ft)

Damüls

*A quiet village on the Bregenzer Ache, **Mellau** is famous for its wooden houses.*

*The picturesque village of **Bezau** has a lovely church and a small museum devoted to the region's folk art.*

↑ Wooden houses with shingle-clad roofs in the scenic town of Mellau

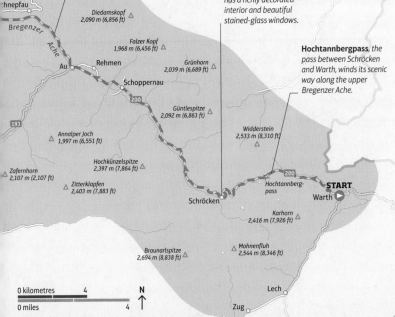

Driving past monumental peaks along the Hochtannbergpass

Did You Know?

The Hochtannberg-pass reaches its highest point near Schröcken at 1,679 m (5,508 ft).

The valley of the **Bregenzer Ache** is the main axis of the Bregenzer Forest. The river flows between steep rock faces and gentle hills on its way to the Bodensee (Lake Constance).

The church in **Schröcken**, at the foot of the Widderstein, has a richly decorated interior and beautiful stained-glass windows.

Hochtannbergpass, the pass between Schröcken and Warth, winds its scenic way along the upper Bregenzer Ache.

Baumgarten
△ 1,649 m (5,410 ft)

Diedamskopf △
2,090 m (6,856 ft)

hnepfau

Bregenzer Ache

Falzer Kopf △
1,968 m (6,456 ft)

Grünhorn
2,039 m (6,689 ft) △

Au

Rehmen

Schoppernau

200

Güntlespitze △
2,092 m (6,863 ft)

Widderstein △
2,533 m (8,310 ft)

193

Annalper Joch △
1,997 m (6,551 ft)

Hochkünzelspitze
2,397 m (7,864 ft) △

200

Hochtannberg-pass

START

Warth

Zafernhorn △
2,107 m (2,107 ft)

Zitterklapfen
△ 2,403 m (7,883 ft)

Schröcken

Karhorn △
2,416 m (7,926 ft)

Braunarlspitze △
2,694 m (8,838 ft)

△ Mohnenfluh
2,544 m (8,346 ft)

0 kilometres   4

0 miles   4

N
↑

Lech

Zug

CARINTHIA AND EAST TYROL

The earliest inhabitants of what is now Kärnten (Carinthia) were the Celtic Carnuni. In the 1st century AD the area was part of the Roman province of Noricum, and by the 6th century Carinthia was overrun by the Slav Carantani tribe, from whom it probably took its name. Although Carinthia belonged to the Habsburgs from 1335, a Slav national minority has survived in the area to this day.

After World War I, the newly formed state of Yugoslavia tried to annex part of Carinthia from the defeated Austro-Hungarian Empire, but a plebiscite kept the region with Austria. At the same time, the southern part of Tyrol (Südtirol) became an autonomous province of Italy. Thus, geographically isolated from other parts of Tyrol, East Tyrol (Osttirol, now known administratively as Bezirk Lienz) grew closer to its Carinthian neighbour than it was to the Tyrolean administration in Innsbruck. For a brief period during World War II, these two areas together became *Reichsgau* (imperial province) Kärnten following the annexation of Austria by Nazi Germany, but by the end of the war they were each *Bundeslands* (states) in their own right once again.

CARINTHIA AND EAST TYROL

Must Sees

1. Klagenfurt
2. Hohe Tauern National Park

Experience More

3. Burg Hochosterwit
4. Völkermarkt
5. Maria Saal
6. St Paul im Lavanttal
7. Magdalensberg
8. St Veit an der Glan
9. Villach
10. Gurk
11. Spittal an der Drau
12. Friesach
13. Lienz
14. Gmünd
15. Millstatt
16. Mölltal

❶

KLAGENFURT

🅐E6 ✈Annabichl 🚍🚌 🛈Rathaus, Neuer Platz 5; www.
visitklagenfurt.at

Situated at the eastern end of Wörthersee, the
warmest lake in Austria, Klagenfurt is the attractive
provincial capital of Carinthia. An important trade
centre and transport hub founded in the 12th century,
Klagenfurt today is a thriving university town and a
great base for visiting the surrounding mountains and
waters. With attractions ranging from classical
concerts and theatre shows to nearby bathing
beaches, Klagenfurt offers something for everyone.

①

Dom St Peter und Paul

🅐Domplatz 📞(0463)
54950 🕐7am-7pm daily

The town's cathedral was
built in 1578 as a Protestant
church by Klagenfurt's mayor,
Christoph Windisch. In 1604,
the church was taken over by
the Jesuits, and was elevated
to the rank of cathedral in
1787. Following a fire in 1723,
the late Gothic interior was
rebuilt in the Baroque style.

Though badly damaged in
World War II, it has been restored to its former splendour;
rich stucco decoration on the
walls and ceiling blend various
architectural styles into one
successful composition. The
vestry holds the last work by
renowned Austrian painter
Martin Johann Schmidt.

②

Neuer Platz

Lindwurmbrunnen (Dragon
Fountain), whose winged beast
has become the symbol and
crest of the town, dominates
Klagenfurt's square. The town
hall, formerly the palace of
the Rosenberg family, also
stands on this square and has
been the seat of the municipal
authorities since 1918. Once
outside the town walls, it
became the centre of the new
Renaissance town. The square
is lined by beautiful 16th- and
17th-century mansions.

③ 🔧 Ⓜ 🛍

Landhaus

🅐Alter Platz 📞(0463)
577570 🕐Apr-Oct: 9am-
4pm Mon-Sat (to 2pm Sat);
Nov-Mar: 9am-4pm Thu-
Sat (to 2pm Sat)

The Landhaus, the present
seat of the Carinthian
provincial government, stands
on the western side of Alter
Platz. Commissioned by the
Carinthian estates, it was built
in 1574 on the site of a former
ducal palace. The resulting
structure is Klagenfurt's most
important secular building
and a Renaissance gem, with
two symmetrically spaced
spires, beyond which is an open
two-storey, galleried courtyard.

The most beautiful room,
the Wappensaal (heraldic hall),
is almost entirely the work of
Josef Ferdinand Fromiller, the
foremost Carinthian artist of
the day. The walls of the hall
display numerous Carinthian
coats of arms, while the ceiling
painting shows the Carinthian
nobles paying homage to
Charles VI; the flat ceiling is
made to look vaulted in this

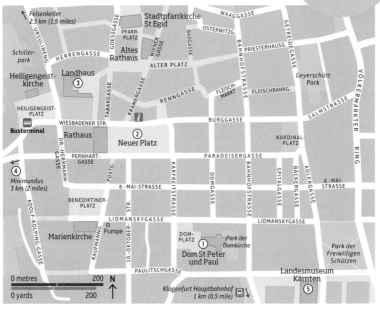

trompe l'oeil. The north wing of the Landhaus houses the remains of the armoury.

---

④ ⊕ Ⓜ ▣ 🛍

Minimundus

🏛 Villacher Strasse 241
🕐 Apr–Nov: times vary, check website
🌐 minimundus.at

Europapark, a large green space west of Klagenfurt, is home to this collection of over 170 miniature models of the world's most famous buildings. They are crafted in minute detail to a scale of 1:25, and have been added to since 1959, when a children's charity, Rettet das Kind (Save the Children), set up the first architectural miniatures near Wörthersee. All the profits go to the foundation.

Among the models from all continents are Paris's Eiffel

←

The intricate courtyard of the Landhaus, one of the key buildings in Klagenfurt

Tower, London's Big Ben, Agra's Taj Mahal and New York's Statue of Liberty, as well as Austria's own historic buildings. There are also inventions such as the earliest steam trains. You can even leave suggestions about which other buildings you would like to see added.

---

⑤ ⊕ Ⓜ 🛍

Landesmuseum Kärnten

🏛 Museumgasse 2
📞 (0505) 3630599 🕐 For refurbishment until 2021

The collections of the Provincial Museum, founded in 1844, illustrate centuries of history in Carinthia as well as its art, rooted in Celtic and Roman cultures. One of the museum's curiosities is a "dragon's skull" (in fact a rhinoceros), found nearby, which served as a model for the fountain dragon in Neuer Platz. Its discovery gave credence to the legend that a dragon once tormented the town, demanding the sacrifice of animals and humans.

EAT & DRINK

Felsenkeller

Wonderful restaurant and beer garden that has been brewing its own ale since 1607. The huge gourmet burgers are a treat.

🏛 Feldkirchner Strasse 141 🕐 Sun 🌐 schleppe-felsenkeller.at

€€€

Pumpe

Simple yet delicious food served in giant portions at bargain prices. The Puntigamer beer, available on draught, is one of the region's best.

🏛 Lidmanskygasse 2
📞 (0463) 5796 🕐 Sun

€€€

A SHORT WALK
KLAGENFURT

Distance 1 km (0.5 miles) **Time** 15 minutes
Nearest bus stop Heuplatz

Klagenfurt's historic centre is the district around Alter Platz (Old Square). In 1544, the city was almost entirely destroyed by fire and had to be rebuilt. Reconstruction was undertaken mainly by Italian architects and the city you see today is highly reminiscent of Italian towns in style. During the Baroque period it was extended and partially rebuilt, although most of its historic buildings date from an earlier era. With bustling farmers' markets, a literary hotspot in summer, and a Mediterranean climate that makes for a sunny forecast all the year, a stroll around Klagenfurt's pretty centre is a delight.

The Baroque **Stadtpfarrkirche St Egid** was built on the site of an earlier church destroyed by an earthquake in 1692. Its spire rises to 91 m (299 ft).

START

HERRENGASSE

URSULINENGASSE

Heiligengeistkirche, the Church of the Holy Spirit, was built in 1355 and altered in 1660. It features a beautiful altarpiece and an interesting Baroque pulpit.

HEILIGEN GEIST PLATZ

WIESBADENER STRASSE

PARADEISERGASSE

Rathaus

The 16th-century **Landhaus** (292) is home to a lovely galleried inner courtyard and a magnificent heraldic hall with stunning ceiling paintings.

←

Klagenfurt's iconic Lindwurmbrunnen fountain standing in Neuer Platz

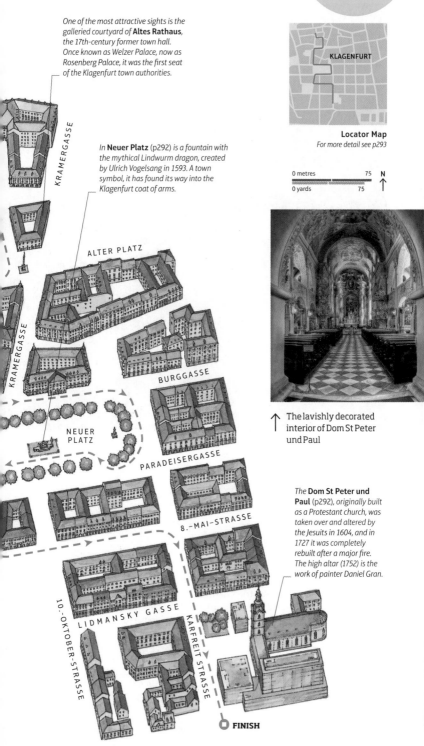

One of the most attractive sights is the galleried courtyard of **Altes Rathaus**, the 17th-century former town hall. Once known as Welzer Palace, now as Rosenberg Palace, it was the first seat of the Klagenfurt town authorities.

KLAGENFURT

Locator Map
For more detail see p293

0 metres   75

0 yards   75

N

In **Neuer Platz** (p292) is a fountain with the mythical Lindwurm dragon, created by Ulrich Vogelsang in 1593. A town symbol, it has found its way into the Klagenfurt coat of arms.

KRAMERGASSE

ALTER PLATZ

KRAMERGASSE

BURGGASSE

↑ The lavishly decorated interior of Dom St Peter und Paul

NEUER PLATZ

PARADEISERGASSE

The **Dom St Peter und Paul** (p292), originally built as a Protestant church, was taken over and altered by the Jesuits in 1604, and in 1727 it was completely rebuilt after a major fire. The high altar (1752) is the work of painter Daniel Gran.

8.-MAI-STRASSE

10.-OKTOBER-STRASSE

LIDMANSKY GASSE

KARFREIT STRASSE

🔵 FINISH

300

The number of peaks rising above 3,000 m (9,850 ft) in the Hohe Tauern.

2

HOHE TAUERN NATIONAL PARK

🗺 C/D5 ℹ Nationalpark Hohe Tauern, Kirchplatz 2, Matrei in Osttirol; www.hohetauern.com

The beautiful area around Austria's highest peak, the Grossglockner, is Austria's largest national park. This pristine land overwhelms with its topography, ranging from glistening glaciers to dense forests.

The unique landscape, flora and fauna of the region, the Hohe Tauern, is jointly protected by the provincial governments of Salzburger Land, Tyrol and Carinthia – the three federal provinces that the national park straddles. Protected as it is by law, it is necessary to keep to the marked trails when exploring the park. You can also join a guided tour with one of the knowledgeable national park rangers. One of the great attractions of the Hohe Tauern is its many tranquil reservoirs, gathering the crystal-clear meltwaters from the glaciers high above each spring. On its edges you'll also be close to many popular tourist resorts, such as Bad Gastein, Kaprun, Zell am See and East Tyrol's capital, Lienz.

↑ Looking out over the unforgettable panorama of peaks and valleys

TOP 4 FLORA AND FAUNA

Black Goats
Far smaller than standard alpine goats, they have distinctive thin horns, curved at the top with black and white marks.

Edelweiss
No trip to Austria is complete without seeing the national flower. It loves sunny, chalky grassy slopes.

Gentian
A beautiful, navy blue flower which blooms between March and August. Trumpet-shaped petals make it easy to spot.

Mountain Eagles
There are believed to be more than 360 pairs of these birds in the Austrian Alps. Their wingspans can reach up to 2.3 m (7.5 ft).

1 Edelweissspitze is the central peak of the Fusch-Rauriser range. There are amazing views from the Edelweisshütte.

2 Grossglockner mountain is a habitat for a range of animals, including cute stoats.

3 The largest glacier in the Eastern Alps is the 8-km- (5-mile-) long Pasterze. Like many glaciers, it is slowly shrinking in size.

STAY

Villa Streintz

Elegant villa with private access to Millstätter See. Rooms are simple but big and bright, and many have lake views. Try a champagne breakfast in the garden.

🅐D5 🅒Überfuhr-gasse 94, Millstatt
🅦villa-streintz.at

€€€

Traube

A romantic spa hotel located in the centre of Lienz town, with wonderful views of the alps and beautifully furnished rooms.

🅐D5 🅒Hauptplatz 14, Lienz 🅦hoteltraube.at

€€€

Moos-Alm Familienhotel

Perched high on a mountain above Lienz, all of the large rooms here have balconies with unbeatable alpine views.

🅐D5 🅒Schlossberg 24, Lienz 🅦moosalm.info

€€€

Today, following alterations, the church is predominantly Baroque in style. The lovely Franziskanerkirche (Franciscan Church), built around 1350, features original 15th-century frescoes and a Gothic Pietà standing by a side altar.

High above the town sits Schloss Bruck, the seat of the Görz counts, built between the 13th and 16th centuries. The castle has a tall Roman-esque turret, and its main body contains a Romanesque chapel with 13th- and 15th-century frescoes. Today it houses a regional museum.

14

Gmünd

🅐D5 🚍 🅸Hauptplatz 20; (04732) 221514

In the 12th century, the arch-bishops of Salzburg, who ruled Gmünd, began to encircle the town with mighty fortifications, many of which survive to this day, including old gate turrets and bastions. Two castles tower over the town: the older of the two, Altes Schloss, was commissioned in 1506. It was largely destroyed by a fire in 1886, but was restored and is now used as a cultural centre. The Neues Schloss (New Castle) was built in 1651–4, and today the former castle keep houses a school and a concert hall.

13

Lienz

🅐D5 🅡🚍 🅸Hauptplatz 7; www.lienz.gv.at

Lienz has been the capital of East Tyrol since 1919, but its origins date back to the Middle Ages. The Stadtpfarrkirche St Andrä (parish church of St Andrew), a triple-nave Gothic basilica, was built in the 15th century; western sections include parts of an earlier Romanesque church.

> The greatest attraction in Millstatt, on the northern shore of Millstätter See, is a Benedictine abbey dating from 1070.

Porsche's Stuttgart office relocated to Gmünd to avoid the bombing raids during World War II, and the Austrian designer Ferdinand Porsche worked here from 1944 to 1950. Fifty-two of the classic 365 models were hand made locally. The most famous models and construction frames are displayed in the **Porsche Automuseum**.

Porsche Automuseum

⊘ 🅒Riesertratte 4a
🕒15 May–15 Oct: 9am–6pm daily; 16 Oct–14 May: 10am–4pm daily 🅦auto-museum.at

15

Millstatt

🅐D5 🚍 🅸Rathaus, Markt-platz 8; www.millstatt.at

The greatest attraction in Millstatt, on the northern shore of Millstätter See, is a Benedictine abbey dating from 1070. From then until 1469 it was run by the Hirsau

↑ Wooden construction frame of a racing car at the Porsche Automuseum in Gmünd

Benedictines; later the church and monastery passed into the hands of the Order of the Knights of St George, and from 1598 until 1773 it was owned by the Jesuits. The construction of a railway in the 19th century accelerated the development of Millstatt into a spa town, and the adjacent former castle belonging to the Grand Master of the Knights of St George was converted into a hotel in 1901.

The most beautiful part of the abbey is its Renaissance arcaded courtyard. The monastery is linked with the church by a 12th-century cloister whose pillars, decorated by medieval carvers, display a grotesque world of animals, plants and faces. Even older, dating back to the Carolingian period, are the magical ornaments on the old buildings, possibly representing some pagan spells. An eye-catching feature inside the church is the Romanesque portal, made by master craftsman Rudger in 1170. In the side chapels are the marble tombs of the order's Grand Masters.

16

Mölltal

AD5 🚌🚆 **W**moelltal.at

The Möll river, a tributary of the Drau and overshadowed by Grosses Reisseck peak, runs along the Mölltal, a valley whose upper reaches form a natural extension of the

---

ALPE ADRIA TRAIL

One of the most spectacular hiking trails in Europe, the Alpe Adria stretches for 750 km (466 miles) and links Austria with Slovenia and Italy. There are 43 stages, each around 20 km (12 miles) long and taking an average of 5–6 hours. The most superb section is S13, the Millstätter Summit Trail, which begins above Millstadt and leads across lush alpine meadows to Döbriach *(www.alpe-adria-trail.com)*.

↑ Hiking along the Raggaschlucht in the Mölltal

magnificent road known as Grossglockner Hochalpenstrasse. The river meanders scenically between the high mountain peaks, while the road along the valley winds its way between old mills, stunning waterfalls and traditional huts, blending in seamlessly with its spectacular natural surroundings.

The parish of Grosskirchheim was once a major mining district, and the 16th-century Schloss Grosskirchheim in Döllach now houses a museum that covers local history and the gold mining industry. Döllach is also known for its 14th-century Church of St Andrew, which has elements of late Gothic and Baroque. Sagritz also features the late Gothic Church of St George.

Also worth a visit is Schloss Falkenstein, on a rocky promontory near Obervellach, which has an unusual tower with a wooden top.

A DRIVING TOUR
AROUND WÖRTHERSEE

Length 45 km (30 miles) **Stopping-off points** There are several resorts around the lake offering restaurants and hotels; Velden is the largest

Wörthersee is the warmest lake in Austria; in summer, the temperature of its waters can reach 25°C (77°F). Numerous resorts line its shores, and the largest of these is the modern, brash town of Velden, with its casino. Krumpendorf and the exclusive resort of Pörtschach lie on the easily accessible northern shore, while quiet Reifnitz is on the southern shore. Nearby are other, smaller lakes, including Ossiacher See, in a scenic mountain setting. To the south, a drive will take you past the Carinthian lake district, which extends along the Slovenian border, surrounded by the snowy peaks of the enchanting Karawanken Alps.

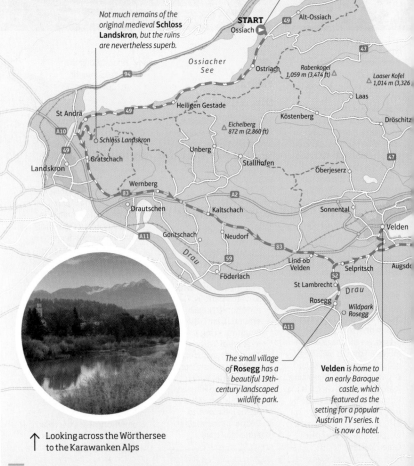

Ossiach is home to the oldest monastery in Carinthia, which is now a hotel.

Not much remains of the original medieval **Schloss Landskron**, but the ruins are nevertheless superb.

START Ossiach

Ossiacher See

Alt-Ossiach

Ostriach

Rabenkogel 1,059 m (3,474 ft)

Laaser Kofel 1,014 m (3,326

Heiligen Gestade

Köstenberg

Laas

Dröschitz

St Andrä

Eichelberg 872 m (2,860 ft)

Schloss Landskron

Unberg

Stallhofen

Oberjeserz

Gratschach

Landskron

Wernberg

Drautschen

Kaltschach

Sonnental

Velden

Goritschach

Neudorf

Lind ob Velden

Selpritsch

Augsd

Drau

Föderlach

St Lambrecht

Drau

Rosegg

Wildpark Rosegg

The small village of **Rosegg** has a beautiful 19th-century landscaped wildlife park.

Velden is home to an early Baroque castle, which featured as the setting for a popular Austrian TV series. It is now a hotel.

↑ Looking across the Wörthersee to the Karawanken Alps

↑ The futuristic wooden observation tower surrounded by forest at Pyramidenkogel

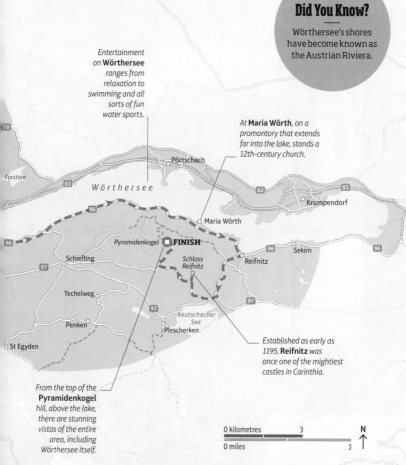

Did You Know?

Wörthersee's shores have become known as the Austrian Riviera.

*Entertainment on **Wörthersee** ranges from relaxation to swimming and all sorts of fun water sports.*

*At **Maria Wörth**, on a promontory that extends far into the lake, stands a 12th-century church.*

Pörtschach

Forstsee

Wörthersee

Krumpendorf

Maria Wörth

Pyramidenkogel ☐ **FINISH**

Schiefling

Schloss Reifnitz

Sekirn

Reifnitz

Techelweg

Keutschacher See

Penken

Plescherken

St Egyden

*Established as early as 1195, **Reifnitz** was once one of the mightiest castles in Carinthia.*

*From the top of the **Pyramidenkogel** hill, above the lake, there are stunning vistas of the entire area, including Wörthersee itself.*

0 kilometres   3

0 miles   3

N ↑

The narrow 15th-century church in scenic Heiligenblut ↑

A DRIVING TOUR
GROSSGLOCKNER HOCHALPENSTRASSE

Length 48 km (30 miles) **Stopping-off points** There are plenty of mountain hostels, and many restaurants offer accommodation

Traversing the Hohe Tauern National Park *(p296)* is the splendid Grossglockner High Alpine Road, regarded as one of the world's most beautiful mountain routes. Completed in 1935, the road was built along the old mountain passes between Bruck in Salzburger Land and Heiligenblut in Carinthia. Measuring 48 km (30 miles) long, it forms part of a north–south route from Bavaria to Italy. The route is a toll road, open to cars only from May to early November.

Grossglockner Hochalpenstrasse

CARINTHIA AND EAST TYROL

Locator Map

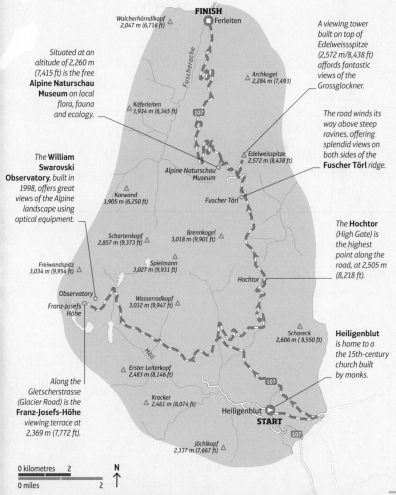

FINISH
Ferleiten

Walcherhörndlkopf △
2,047 m (6,716 ft)

Archkogel △
2,284 m (7,493)

*Situated at an altitude of 2,260 m (7,415 ft) is the free **Alpine Naturschau Museum** on local flora, fauna and ecology.*

Käferleiten △
1,934 m (6,345 ft)

Fuscherache

107

A viewing tower built on top of Edelweissspitze (2,572 m/8,438 ft) affords fantastic views of the Grossglockner.

Edelweissspitze △
2,572 m (8,438 ft)

*The road winds its way above steep ravines, offering splendid views on both sides of the **Fuscher Törl** ridge.*

*The **William Swarovski Observatory**, built in 1998, offers great views of the Alpine landscape using optical equipment.*

Alpine Naturschau Museum

Karwand △
1,905 m (6,250 ft)

Fuscher Törl

Schartenkopf △
2,857 m (9,373 ft)

Brennkogel △
3,018 m (9,901 ft)

*The **Hochtor** (High Gate) is the highest point along the road, at 2,505 m (8,218 ft).*

Freiwandspitz △
3,034 m (9,954 ft)

Spielmann △
3,027 m (9,931 ft)

Hochtor

Observatory

Wasserradkopf △
3,032 m (9,947 ft)

Franz-Josefs-Höhe

Schareck △
2,606 m (8,550 ft)

Heiligenblut *is home to a the 15th-century church built by monks.*

Möll

Erster Leiterkopf △
2,483 m (8,146 ft)

*Along the Gletscherstrasse (Glacier Road) is the **Franz-Josefs-Höhe** viewing terrace at 2,369 m (7,772 ft).*

Kracker △
2,461 m (8,074 ft)

107

Heiligenblut
START

107

Jöchlkopf △
2,337 m (7,667 ft)

0 kilometres   2
0 miles   2

N ↑

NEED TO KNOW

Skiing down powder snow tracks, Tyrol

BEFORE
YOU GO

Forward planning is essential to any successful trip. Be prepared for all eventualities by considering the following points before you travel.

AT A GLANCE

CURRENCY
Euro (EUR)

AVERAGE DAILY SPEND

SAVE	SPEND	SPLURGE
€50	€150	€200+

BOTTLED WATER	COFFEE	BEER	DINNER FOR TWO
€1.50	€2.50	€4.00	€60

ESSENTIAL PHRASES

Hello	Guten Tag
Thank you	Auf Wiedersehen
Please	bitte
Thank you	danke
Do you speak English?	Sprechen Sie Englisch?
I don't understand	Ich verstehe nicht

ELECTRICITY SUPPLY

Power sockets are type F, fitting type C and F plugs. Standard voltage is 230v.

Passports and Visas

EU nationals and citizens of the UK, US, Canada, Australia and New Zealand need a valid passport but do not need visas for stays of up to three months for the purpose of tourism. Consult your nearest Austrian embassy or check online at **Austria Visa Info** if you are travelling from outside these areas.
Austria Visa Info
🆆 austria.org/visa-application

Travel Safety Advice

Visitors can get up-to-date travel safety information from the **US Department of State**, the **UK Foreign and Commonwealth Office** and the **Australian Department of Foreign Affairs and Trade**.
Austrailia
🆆 smartraveller.gov.au
UK
🆆 gov.uk/foreign-travel-advice
US
🆆 travel.state.gov

Customs Information

Limits vary if travelling from outside the EU, so check restrictions before departing. An individual is permitted to carry the following within the EU for personal use:
Tobacco products 800 cigarettes, 400 cigarillos, 200 cigars or 1 kg of smoking tobacco.
Alcohol 10 litres of spirits, 20 litres of alcoholic beverages up to 22 per cent strength, 90 litres of wine (60 litres of which can be sparkling wine) and 110 litres of beer.
Cash If you plan to enter or leave the EU with €10,000 or more in cash (or equivalent in other currencies) you must declare it to the customs authorities.

Insurance

It is wise to take out an insurance policy covering theft, loss of belongings, medical problems, cancellation and delays. Residents of countries

in the European Union can claim free medical treatment in Austria with a valid **EHIC** (European Health Insurance Card). It is also advisable to take out supplementary health insurance as some services, such as winter sporting injuries, or repatriation costs, are not covered. Visitors from outside these areas must arrange their own private medical insurance.
EHIC
W gov.uk/european-health-insurance-card

Vaccinations

No inoculations are required for Austria.

Money

Major credit and debit cards are accepted in most shops and restaurants; prepaid currency cards and American Express are accepted in some. It is always wise to carry cash for smaller items, as some businesses won't accept card payments. Cash machines are frequently found in town and city centres.

Booking Accommodation

Austria offers accommodation to suite all tastes and budgets, from luxury five-star hotels and boutique city hotels to farm stays, family-run B&Bs, mountain refuges and budget hostels. Year round, lodgings are snapped up quickly in major cities and tourist centres, and most notably in mountainous regions during ski season (December–April), when prices are often inflated and advance booking is essential. The website of the **Austrian National Tourist Office** is a good resource for accommodation details.
Austrian National Tourist Office
W austria.info/uk/where-to-stay

Travellers with Specific Needs

Austria offers a high standard of facilities for travellers with specific needs. Most hotels and major museums are wheelchair accessible (except in some older buildings) and most of the transport system is equipped with amenities. Guide dogs are also allowed on public transport.

Österreichische Bundesbahnen (ÖBB – Austrian Federal Railways) has mobility aids at around 100 train stations and offer discounted tickets and travel assistance. For further information on accessible travel, contact the **Austrian National Tourist Office**. **Barrier Free Holidays** also offer accessible holiday packages.
Österreichische Bundesbahnen
W oebb.at
Austrian National Tourist Office
W austria.info
Barrier Free Holidays
W barrierefreierurlaub.at

Language

German is Austria's official language but even those with a good grasp may find the Austrian dialect hard to understand, especially in more rural regions. English is commonly spoken in major towns, cities and ski resorts, but learning a few niceties in German goes a long way, even if you then continue in English (p326).

Closures

Monday Some museums and tourist attractions are closed for the day.
Sunday Some shops and most businesses close for the entire day.
Public holidays Schools, post offices, banks and some shops are closed for the day.

PUBLIC HOLIDAYS	
1 Jan	New Year's Day
6 Jan	Epiphany
Apr/May	Easter Sunday
Apr/May	Easter Monday
Apr/May	Ascension Day
1 May	Labour Day
May/Jun	Pentecost
May/Jun	Whit Monday
May/Jun	Corpus Christi
15 Aug	Assumption
26 Oct	Austrian National Day
1 Nov	All Saints' Day
8 Dec	Feast of the Immaculate Conception
25 Dec	Christmas Day
26 Dec	St Stephen's Day

GETTING AROUND

Whether you are visiting for a short city break, a ski weekend or a rural retreat, discover how best to reach your destination and travel like a pro.

PUBLIC TRANSPORT COSTS

VIENNA

€2.40

One way
train, metro, tram, bus

SALZBURG

€2.90

One way
bus, tram

INNSBRUCK

€2.50

One way
bus, tram

TOP TIP
Some cities offer a discounted day pass or multiple-trip day passes.

SPEED LIMIT

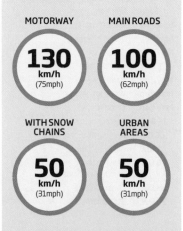

MOTORWAY

130 km/h (75mph)

MAIN ROADS

100 km/h (62mph)

WITH SNOW CHAINS

50 km/h (31mph)

URBAN AREAS

50 km/h (31mph)

Arriving by Air

Major airports in Austria include Vienna Schwechat International Airport, Innsbruck Airport and Salzburg Airport W A Mozart. Each offer flights to and from numerous European cities with the national carrier, **Austrian Airlines**, as well as other airlines including Air France, British Airways, Lufthansa, KLM, SAS and SWISS. Smaller airports, including Graz, Klagenfurt a nd Linz, also serve destinations within Europe. Flights to Austria are also available with the following budget airlines – eurowings, flybe, easyJet and Ryanair.

For information on getting to and from Austria's airports, see the table opposite.
Austrian Airlines
w aua.com

Arriving by Boat

DDSG Blue Danube shipping company operates a fast City Liner catamaran service between Vienna and Bratislava daily from mid-April to September, with a reduced service for the rest of the year. A number of companies also offer cruises through Austria along the Danube between Germany and the Black sea, including **Scenic** and **Viking**, which stop at Vienna, Linz, Melk and other destinations along the way.
DDSG Blue Danube
w ddsg-blue-danube.at
Scenic
w scenic.co.uk
Viking
w viking.co.uk

Train Travel

International Train Travel
Situated at the heart of Europe, Austria has great international rail links. Regular high-speed trains connect the country with major cities in neigh-bouring countries. Most of Austria's rail services are operated by Österreichische Bundesbahnen *(p311)*. The fastest train, the Railjet, can travel at speeds of up to 230 km/h (143 mph) and links major Austrian cities, including Vienna, Graz

Airport	Distance to city	Taxi fare	Public Transport	Journey time
Graz Airport (GRZ)	9 km (5.5 miles)	€20	bus	30 mins
Innsbruck Airport (INN)	5 km (3 miles)	€15	bus	20 mins
Klagenfurt Airport (KLU)	5 km (3 miles)	€15	bus	20 mins
Linz Blue Danube Airport (LNZ)	13 km (8 miles)	€30	bus	22 mins
Salzburg Airport W A Mozart (SZG)	4 km (2.5 miles)	€25	bus	15 mins
Vienna Schwechat Airport (VIE)	19 km (12 miles)	€35	bus	20–40 mins

RAIL JOURNEY PLANNER

This map is a handy reference for intercity rail travel between Austria's main towns and cities.

Vienna to Graz	2 hrs
Vienna to Innsbruck	4.5 hrs
Vienna to Linz	2 hrs
Vienna to Salzburg	3 hrs
Graz to Innsbruck	4.5 hrs
Graz to Linz	2.5 hrs
Graz to Salzburg	3 hrs
Innsbruck to Linz	3.5 hrs
Innsbruck to Salzburg	2 hrs

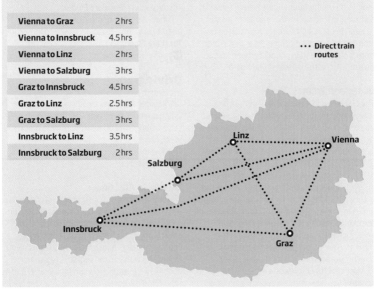

••• Direct train routes

and Linz, with cities across Germany, Italy, Hungary, the Czech Republic and Switzerland. Early booking is recommended, especially on overnight sleeper trains. **Eurail** and **Interrail** also sell tickets for multiple international journeys.

Eurail
W eurail.com

Interrail
W interrail.eu

Regional Trains

Travelling between towns on the reliable regional rail network is one of the best ways to see the country. There are a dozen small mountain and regional rail companies, but to reach the more off-the-beaten-track locations in the Alps you will need to change to local bus services. The railway timetable is well coordinated with buses and other forms of public transport.

Public Transport

Austria's larger cities operate multiple public transport services, comprising bus *(Autobus)*, tram *(Strassenbahn)* and local urban rail networks (S-Bahn). Vienna also has an underground rail network (U-Bahn). These transport systems work largely on an honesty system – there are no ticket barriers at stations, allowing passengers to hop on and off. However, formal checks by transport authority staff do take place – occasionally you'll be asked for your *Fahrschein* (ticket) by a uniformed guard. Travellers caught without a valid ticket will receive a hefty on-the-spot fine.

Tickets

You can purchase tickets from newsagents, station counters and ticket machines, or at automatic ticket machines at most bus and tram stops, and these are usually valid on all modes of transport. In most towns, the public transport network is divided into zones; the more zones you traverse the more expensive the ticket. They can also be valid for a limited period, from one hour to a full day or longer. Multi-trip tickets tend to be cheaper than single tickets, so worth considering if you plan to use public transport several times. All tickets must be validated by stamping them at a machine either at the bus or tram stop, on the train or underground station platform, or on the vehicle as you board.

Buses and Trams

The quickest and easiest way of getting around towns and cities is by bus or tram. Vienna, Graz, Innsbruck and Salzburg also operate a good night-bus service.

Vienna's transport system is more extensive and therefore more complicated than that of other Austrian cities, but, even so is relatively straight-forward and clearly signed. Vienna city is zone 100 of the Austrian regional fare system, which means a standard ticket covers all areas of the city and allows you to change trains and lines and switch from the underground to a tram or a bus, as long as you take the most direct route and don't break t your journey.

Vienna's **EASY CityPass** is a good value option if you intend to use public transport a number of times during your city break; it offers unlimited travel within the city for 24, 48 or 72 hours or a week.

EASY CityPass
W easycitypass.com/en/city/wien-en

Long-Distance Bus Travel

Although train is the most popular way of travelling between cities in Austria, ÖBB postbuses offer reasonably priced bus travel throughout the country, and are especially useful for reaching mountainous regions and ski resorts. **FlixBus** also provides a popular low-cost intercity coach network with easy online booking and direct services between Vienna, Salzburg, Linz, Graz and Klagenfurt, as well as international destinations. **Eurolines** offers a variety of international coach routes; fares are reasonable, with discounts available for students, children and seniors.

Eurolines
W eurolines.eu
Flixbus
W flixbus.com

Taxis

Taxis throughout Austria are generally very safe and of a high standard. However, as bus and tram services are comprehensive and inexpensive, taxis are generally not used for daily transportation around town but more often for trips to the airport or train stations (typically with fixed fares). They can easily be booked in advance or engaged at a taxi rank and they are metred by distance; charges are higher at night and at weekends. To estimate a fare in advance, check **Taxi Fare Finder**.

Uber, and other app-based taxi services, operate in Vienna, Salzburg, Graz and Innsbruck.

Taxi Fare Finder
W taxifarefinder.com/at

Driving

Driving licences issued by any of the European Union member states are valid throughout the EU. If visiting from outside the EU, you may need to apply for an International Driving Permit. Check with your local automobile association before you travel.

Driving to Austria

With the exception of Switzerland, all of Austria's neighbours are EU members, meaning there are no border checks. Austria is easy to reach from other European countries by car. If you bring your own foreign-registered car into Austria you must carry with you the vehicle's registration documents, insurance documents, your ID and a valid driver's licence.

Driving in Austria

A well-maintained network of motorways and major roads link Austria's major towns and cities, and provide some highly scenic rural routes to more remote towns and villages in Alpine regions. Extra caution is advised on narrow, winding Alpine roads, especially in winter months, when winter tyres are strongly advised.

Fuel prices in Austria are generally lower than in neighbouring countries. Petrol stations are usually open from 8am to 8pm. In large cities and on motorways, some are open 24 hours a day. There are no automatic petrol pumps. Every car driving on the motorway must display a Mautvignette toll sticker – valid for 10 days (€9.20); 2 months (€26.80); or 1 year (€89.20) – available at the border or from all Austrian petrol stations.

Car Rental

To hire a car in Austria, drivers need to produce their passport, driver's licence and a credit card with capacity to cover the excess. Most rental agencies require drivers to be over the age of 19 (the age may vary according to car category), to have held a valid driver's licence for at least one year, and to have an international licence. Drivers under 25 may incur a young driver surcharge. Major international car-hire companies, with offices in the main cities and airports, include **Hertz** and **Sixt Rent-a-Car**.

Hertz
w hertz.com
Sixt Rent-a-Car
w sixt.com

Rules of the Road

Austrians drive on the right, as in the rest of mainland Europe. The legal car driving age is 18 (19–25 in a hire car, depending on the rental company), and seatbelts are compulsory.

It is illegal to use mobile phones while driving, or to drive under the influence of alcohol. The limit for alcohol is between 0.5 mg per ml of blood (about 330 ml or half a pint of beer or 1–2 glasses of wine) and is strictly enforced. Spot checks are common and anyone over the limit is likely to face a hefty fine and loss of licence.

Children under 14 must use special seatbelts adapted to their size or special child restraints. All vehicles must carry a warning triangle, a first aid kit and a reflective jacket in case of breakdown, and full headlights should be on at all times. Headlamps must have beam deflectors and dashboard cameras are prohibited. In winter, drivers are required by law to use snow tyres and/or chains on mountain roads when indicated by special warning signs. Any infringement of traffic regulations is likely to incur a hefty on-the-spot fine.

Parking

Apart from on Sundays, when shops are closed, finding a parking spot in city centres can be time-consuming and expensive. If you are lucky to find a space, there is usually a maximum stay of two hours allowed. Check time limits on roadside signs, or look out for pay and display schemes which usually allow longer stays. City car parks can be expensive: in Vienna expect to pay around €8 for one hour, up to €40 per day.

Hitchhiking

Austria is a popular country for hitchhiking, although it is illegal on motorways. However, you should always consider your own safety before picking someone up or before entering an unknown vehicle.

Cycling

Austria is a popular country for cycling, and a fantastic way to see both city and countryside.

Bicycle Hire

Most towns and cities have clearly marked cycle paths and there are a number of bike rental schemes, most usually free for the first hour. Bikes may also be hired from some stations (at a discount if you have a train ticket) or, in Salzburg and Vienna, from a **Citybike** station. In Vienna, **Radlkarte** has online maps of the city bike paths.

Long-distance cycle routes crisscross the entire country, including the 2,897-km (1,800-mile) Danube River cycle path – 390 km (245 miles) of which straddles Austria. Less ambitious, but equally delightful, are the 7-km (4-mile) cycle path round Vienna's celebrated Ringstrasse, and the 20-km (12.5-mile) circular ride through the lake district south of Salzburg.

Citybike
w citybikewien.at
w citybikesalzburg.at
Radlkarte
w radlkarte.at

Bicycle Safety

Always ride on the right and stick to the cycle paths wherever possible. If you're unsure, dismount. Do not walk with your bike in a bike lane. Do not cycle on pavements, on the side of the road, in pedestrian zones or in the dark without lights. Locals may not bother and it isn't compulsory, but wearing a helmet is highly recommended. Beware of tram tracks – cross them at an angle to avoid getting your tyres stuck.

Fiakers

Traditional horse-drawn open carriages, or *Fiakers*, are a relaxing way to get around the city centres of Graz, Innsbruck, Linz, Salzburg and Vienna. Expect to pay around €55 for four people for a 20-minute ride around the Hofburg in Vienna, or €110 for an hour. In Salzburg, it costs €200 for four to five people for a 50-minute tour of the centre. The following companies are reputable and adhere to animal welfare requirements:

Wiener Fiaker
w fiaker.at
Fiaker Winter
w fiaker-salzburg.at

PRACTICAL
INFORMATION

A little local know-how goes a long way in Austria. Here you will find all the essential advice and information you will need during your stay.

EMERGENCY NUMBERS

EMERGENCY	POLICE
112	**133**

AMBULANCE	FIRE SERVICE
144	**122**

TIME ZONE
CET/CEST: Central European Summer Time runs from the last Sunday in March to the last Sunday in October.

TAP WATER
Unless otherwise stated, tap water in Austria is safe to drink.

TIPPING

Waiter	Round up to the nearest €5 or €10
Hotel Porter	€5
Housekeeping	€2 day
Concierge	€2-5
Taxi Driver	Round up to the nearest €5 or €10

Personal Security

Austria is generally a safe place for visitors, but it is always wise to be vigilant, especially when walking in unlit streets late at night, withdrawing cash at an ATM, travelling on public transport or wandering in crowded public places and busy tourist areas. If you are a victim of theft, report it immediately to the police. Obtaining a police report will enable you to make an insurance claim. Contact your embassy if you have your passport stolen, or in the event of a serious crime or accident.

Health

Austria has a reciprocal agreement with all EU countries, so if you have an EHIC card (p311), present this as soon as possible. You may have to pay before treatment and reclaim the money later. Private health insurance is also strongly recommended, especially if you are planning a skiing, mountaineering or hiking holiday.

For visitors coming from outside the EU, payment of hospital and other medical expenses is the patient's responsibility, so it is important to arrange comprehensive medical insurance before travelling.

For minor ailments, seek medical supplies and advice from a pharmacy (Apotheke). Most are open during the week, and for a few hours on Saturday mornings. In large towns and cities, pharmacies also operate a night and Sunday rota system. Closed pharmacies will display the address of the nearest one open. Alternatively you can find one on the **Österreichische Apothekerkammer** website, or you can call the 24-hour **Pharmacy Hotline**.
Österreichische Apothekerkammer
W apotheker.or.at
Pharmacy Hotline
1455

Smoking, Alcohol and Drugs

Austria is one of the last European countries to ban smoking in all enclosed public spaces. It is illegal to drive under the influence of alcohol.

The BAC (blood alcohol content) limit is 0.05 per cent or 0.01 per cent for drivers with less than two years' driving experience. There are heavy penalties, jail sentences and fines for drug possession depending on the type of narcotic.

ID

There is no requirement for visitors to carry identification, but in the event of a routine check you may be asked to show your passport. If you don't have it with you, the police may escort you to wherever your passport is being kept so that you can show it to them.

Local Customs

Be respectful of the religious beliefs and political opinions of the local people and try to adhere to their local customs. Peace and quiet are highly valued by those who live outside the cities. Austrians also take sustainability seriously and expect tourists to do the same.

LGBT+ Safety

LGBT+ rights in Austria are less progressive than many European countries, although same-sex marriage has been legal since 2019. The LGBT+ scene is best in Vienna, which celebrates two weeks of EuroPride Vienna festivities annually.

Visiting Churches

Dress respectfully in places of worship: cover your torso and upper arms, and ensure shorts and skirts cover your knees.

Mobile Phones and Wi-Fi

Wi-Fi is widely available throughout Austria, and cafés and restaurants will usually give customers their Wi-Fi password. Visitors with EU tariffs are able to use their devices abroad without being affected by roaming charges. Check with your service provider for details.

Post

Austrian post offices are clearly identifiable by their bold yellow signs. They provide postage stamps (*Briefmarken*), can send registered letters and arrange the delivery of packages. Foreign currency is handled by the larger post offices.

The Austrian postal system is straightforward and efficient. Postage is charged by weight, and customers can choose between two postal tariffs: priority and economy. Post offices are generally open between 7am and 7pm Monday to Friday. In smaller resorts, they may only be open in the mornings. Stamps are also sold at newsagents.

Taxes and Refunds

VAT is 20 per cent in Austria. Non-EU residents are entitled to a tax refund for purchases over €75, subject to certain conditions. In order to do this, you must request a tax receipt and export papers (*Ausfuhrbescheinigung*) when you purchase your goods. When leaving the country, present these papers, your receipt and your ID at Customs to receive your refund.

Discount Cards

Many holiday regions offer summer cards or guest cards entitling visitors to enjoy attractions free of charge or at reduced prices. Some cities offer their own visitor's pass or discount card. For instance, the **Salzburg Card** and **Vienna City Card** (valid for 1, 2 or 3 days) offer free admission for museums, galleries, events and transport options too.
Salzburg Card
🅦 salzburg.info/en/hotels-offers/salzburg-card
Vienna City Card
🅦 viennacitycard.at

INDEX

Page numbers in **bold** refer to main entries.

Index

PHRASE BOOK

IN EMERGENCY

Help!	Hilfe!	hilf-er
Stop!	Halt!	hult
Call	Holen Sie	hole'n zee
...a doctor	...einen Arzt	...ine'n artst
...an ambulance	...einen Krankenwagen	...ine'n krank'n varg'n
...the police	...die Polizei	...dee pol-its-eye
...the fire brigade	...die Feuerwehr	...dee foy-er-vair
Where is a telephone?	Wo finde ich ein Telefon?	voh fin-der ish ine tel-e-fone?
Where is the hospital?	Wo ist das Krankenhaus?	voh ist duss krunk'n-hows?

COMMUNICATION ESSENTIALS

Yes	Ja	yah
No	Nein	nine
Please	Bitte	bitt-er
Thank you	Danke vielmals	dunk-er feel-malse
Excuse me	Gestatten	g'shtatt'n
Hello	Grüss Gott	groos got
Goodbye	Auf Wiedersehen	owf veed-er-zay-ern
morning	Vormittag	for-mit-targ
afternoon	Nachmittag	nakh-mit-targ
evening	Abend	ah b'nt
yesterday	gestern	gest'n
today	heute	hoyt-er
tomorrow	morgen	morg'n
here	hier	hear
there	dort	dort
What?	Was?	vuss?
When?	Wann?	vunn?
Where?	Wo/Wohin?	voh/vo-hin?

USEFUL PHRASES AND WORDS

Where is...?	Wo befindet sich...?	voe b'find't zish...?
Where are...?	Wo befinden sich...?	voe b'find'n zish...?
How far is it to...?	Wie weit ist...?	vee vite ist...?
Do you speak English?	Sprechen Sie englisch?	shpresh'n zee eng-glish?
I don't understand	Ich verstehe nicht	ish fair-shtay-er nisht
I'm sorry	Es tut mir leid	es toot meer lyte
big	gross	grohss
small	klein	kline
open	auf/offen	owf/off'n
closed	zu/geschlossen	tsoo/g'shloss'n
left	links	links
right	rechts	reshts
near	in der Nähe	in dair nay-er
far	weit	vyte
up	auf, oben	owf, obe'n
down	ab, unten	up, oont'n
early	früh	froo
late	spät	shpate
entrance	Eingang/Einfahrt	ine-gung/ine-fart
exit	Ausgang/Ausfahrt	ows-gung/ows-fart
toilet	WC/Toilette	vay-say/toy-lett-er

MAKING A TELEPHONE CALL

I'd like to place a long-distance call	Ich möchte ein Ferngespräch machen	ish mer-shter ine fairn-g'shpresh mukh'n
I'd like to call collect	Ich möchte ein Rückgespräch machen	ish mer-shter ine rook-g'shpresh mukh'n
local call	Ortsgespräch	orts-g'shpresh
Can I leave a message?	Kann ich etwas ausrichten?	kunn ish ett-vuss ows-rikht'n

STAYING IN A HOTEL

Do you have a vacant room?	Haben Sie ein Zimmer frei?	harb'n zee ine tsimm-er fry?
double room	ein Doppelzimmer	ine dopp'l-tsimm-er
twin room	ein Doppelzimmer	ine dopp'l-tsimm-er
single room	ein Einzelzimmer	ine ine-ts'l-tsimm-er
with a bath/shower	mit Bad/Dusche	mitt bart/doosh-er
key	Schlüssel	shlooss'l
I have a reservation	Ich habe ein Zimmer reserviert	ish harb-er ine tsimm-er rezz-er-veert

SIGHTSEEING

bus	der Bus	dair booss
tram	die Strassenbahn	dee stra-sen-barn
train	der Zug	dair tsoog
art gallery	Galerie	gall-er-ee
bus station	Busbahnhof	booss-barn-hofe
bus (tram) stop	die Haltestelle	dee hal-te-shtel-er
castle	Schloss, Burg	shloss, boorg
palace	Schloss, Palais	shloss, pall-ay
post office	das Postamt	dee pohs-taamt
cathedral	Dom	dome
church	Kirche	keersh-er
garden	Garten, Park	gart'n, park
museum	Museum	moo-zay-oom
information (office)	Information	in-for-mut-see-on

SHOPPING

How much does this cost?	Wieviel kostet das?	vee-feel kost't duss?
I would like...	Ich hätte gern...	ish hett-er gairn...
Do you have...?	Haben Sie...?	harb'n zee...?
expensive	teuer	toy-er
cheap	billig	bill-igg
bank	Bank	bunk
book shop	Buchladen	bookh-lard'n
chemist/pharmacy	Apotheke	App-o-tay-ker
hairdresser	Friseur/Frisör	freezz-er/freezz-er
market	Markt	markt
newsagent	Tabak Trafik	tab-ack tra-feek
travel agent	Reisebüro	rye-zer-boo-roe

EATING OUT

Have you got a table for... people?	Haben Sie einen Tisch für... Personen?	harb'n zee ine'n tish foor... pair-sohn'n?
The bill please	Zahlen, bitte	tsarl'n bitt-er
I am a vegetarian	Ich bin Vegetarier	ish bin vegg-er-tah-ree-er
Waitress/waiter	Fräulein/Herr Ober	froy-line/hair oh-bare
menu	die Speisekarte	dee shpize-er-kart-er
wine list	Weinkarte	vine-kart-er
breakfast	Frühstück	froo-shtook
lunch	Mittagessen	mit-targ-ess'n
dinner	Abendessen	arb'nt-ess'n

MENU DECODER

Ei	eye	egg
Eis	ice	ice cream
Fisch	fish	fish
Fleisch	flysh	meat
Garnelen	gar-nayl'n	prawns
gebacken	g'buck'n	baked/fried
gebraten	g'brart'n	roast
gekocht	g'kokht	boiled
Gemüse	g'mooz-er	vegetables
vom Grill	fom grill	grilled
Hendl/Hahn/Huhn	hend'l/harn/hoon	chicken
Kaffee	kaf-fay	coffee
Kartoffel/Erdäpfel	kar-toff'l/air-dupf'l	potatoes
Käse	kayz-er	cheese
Knödel	k'nerd'l	dumpling
Lamm	lumm	lamb
Meeresfrüchte	mair-erz-froosh-ter	seafood
Milch	milhk	milk
Mineralwasser	minn-er-arl-vuss-er	mineral water
Obst	ohbst	fresh fruit
Pfeffer	pfeff-er	pepper
Pommes frites	pomm-fritt	chips
Reis	rice	rice
Rind	rint	beef
Rostbraten	rohst-brart'n	steak
Rotwein	roht-vine	red wine
Salz	zults	salt
Schinken/Speck	shink'n/shpeck	ham
Schlag	shlahgg	cream
Schokolade	shock-o-lard-er	chocolate
Schwein	shvine	pork
Tee	tay	tea
Wasser	vuss-er	water
Weisswein	vyce-vine	white wine
Wurst	voorst	sausage (fresh)
Zucker	tsook-er	sugar

ACKNOWLEDGMENTS

The publisher would like to thank the following for their kind permission to reproduce their photographs:

Key: a-above; b-below/bottom; c-centre; f-far; l-left; r-right; t-top

123RF.com: Anton Ivanov 36-7t; Nikolay Korzhov 252t; Richard Semik 163br; tupungato 80tl; vvoennyy 16, 58-9.

4Corners: Olimpio Fantuz 249cra; Gianluca Santoni 87t; Reinhard Schmid 19t, 200t, 258-9; Giovanni Simeone 173t.

akg-images: 53tl, 53tr, 56tl, 56bc; Album / Oronoz 54tr; IMAGNO / Votava 57bc; Erich Lessing 52cb, 53br, 161cra; Ullstein Bild 56cla.

Alamy Stock Photo: aerial-photos.com 305tl; AGE Fotostock / Richard Semik 169bl; Agencja Fotograficzna Caro / Preuss 31clb; AGF Srl / Alberto Nardi 281tr; allOver images / Collection 120 29cl, / Viennaphoto 49t, 147bl; Jonathan Andel 70br; Frédéric Araujo 95br, 112br; Arco Images GmbH / K. Kreder 274b; Miroslava Arnaudova 238t; ART Collection 173cla; Austrian National Library / Interfoto 53cla; Bart Pro 35cl, 257ca; Pat Behnke 33cl; Bildarchiv Monheim GmbH / Florian Monheim 244br, / Barbara Opitz 146cra; Jon Bilous 128t; blickwinkel / McPHOTOx / Alfred Schauhuber 136bl, / Erwin Wodicka 154-5b; Boelter 80b; imageBROKER / Helmut Meyer zur Capellen 105cla; Cavan / Aurora Photos / Steve Outram 127tr; Chronicle 56crb; Classic Image 53cb; Sorin Colac 64, 118-9; CoverSpot Photography 137cra; Ian Dagnall 129bl; Ian G Dagnall 54clb, 145t; Danita Delimont / Walter Bibikow 186cra, 186clb; Werner Dieterich 285br; dpa picture alliance archive 137tl; eFesenko 93b, 241b; Etabeta 299br; F1online digitale Bildagentur GmbH / Pritz 201b; Andrew Fare 52t; Jess Gibbs 8cla; GL Archive 55clb, 82clb; Glenstar 50clb; Manfred Glueck 10-1b; Manfred Gottschalk 69br; Tim Graham 266tr; Hackenberg-Photo-Cologne 112la, 112tl; Gavin Hellier 282tr; hemis.fr / Maurizio Borgese 300cl, / Bertrand Gardel 85tl, 105tr, / Hervé Hughes 243br, / Ludovic Maisant 101cra, / Pierre Witt 34-5t, / Pawel Wysocki 167cra; Heritage Image Partnership Ltd / © Fine Art Images 139bl; Roger Hollingsworth 265cra; Image Professionals GmbH / Hauke Dressler 71b, / TravelCollection 8cl; imageBROKER / Norbert Eisele-Hein 39tl, 276bl, 308-9, / Thomas Hoflacher 273tl, / Günter Lenz 82c, / Petr Svarc 199tr, / Alfred Schauhuber 167t, 295cr, / Daniel Schoenen 283b, / Martin Siepmann 45br, 50cl, 197bl, 203br, 228tl, 272cl, 303t, / Franz Waldhäusl 167cr, / Moritz Wolf 193tr, / Gerhard Zwerger-Schoner 244clb; INSADCO Photography / Willfried Gredler 226bl; INTERFOTO / History 186fcrb; Karl Jena 122cl; Jon Arnold Images Ltd / Doug Pearson 231br; John Kellerman 57tr, 78-9t, 105cr, 106-7b, 114tr; Keystone Press 194bc; KH-Pictures 13t; Karl Kost 160t; Lothar Kurtze 47tr, 48br; Yadid Levy 40bl; LianeM 170b; Look / Hauke Dressler 42tr, / Georg Knoll 223tr; / Tom Lamm 198bl, 230-1t, / Konrad Wothe 277t; Marshall Ikonography 45t; mauritius images GmbH / Walter Bibikow 30br, / Rainer Mirau 195t, 208, 222b, / Rudolf Pigneter 286bl, / Matthias Pinn 287tl, / Wolfgang Weinhäupl 248-9b, 249tr; Paul Mayall Austria 13br; McPhoto / Bilderbox 77ca, / Waldhaeusl 297clb; Hercules Milas 10clb, 77cla, 94tr, 114tl; June Morrissey 243cra; Manfred Muenzl 257br; National Geographic Image Collection / Robbie Shone 12-3b, 255tr; NB Photos 8clb; Newscom / BJ Warnick 51tl; North Wind Picture Archives 55br, 101cla; Werner Otto 221clb; Painters 100tl; Ian Patrick 46bl; Mo Peerbacus 132cl; Franz Perc 165tr; Pictures Colour Library 170cb; Pictures Now 37cla; Benny Pieritz 280-1b; The Print Collector / Heritage Images 55tr, / Keystone Archives / Heritage Images 57clb; Prisma Archivo 52bc; Prisma by Dukas Presseagentur GmbH / Raga Jose Fuste 279tr; / Sonderegger Christof 11t, / Van der Meer Rene 300-1b; Alexander Rochau 268-9t, 285tl; RooM the Agency / coberschneider 10ca, 43tr; Royal Armouries Museum 186crb; Marcin S. Sadurski 86bc, 131br; Peter Schickert 242bl; Frank Schneider 302br; Burghard Schreyer 270t; Sedmipivo 158cra; Kamlesh Sethy 175tl; Robbie Shone 77br; Shotshop GmbH / Classic Collection 304bl; Alan Smithers 29crb; Marina Spironetti 88-9t; Myron Standret 232-3b; Stockimo / andyamc 43clb; Sueddeutsche Zeitung Photo / Jose Giribas 33t; Petr Svarc 185tr; Jochen Tack 204tl, 227t; Georgios Tsichlis 84-5b; Universal Images Group North America LLC / Education Images 12t; Lucas Vallecillos 68br, 186cr, 186cb, 187; 271br, 292b; Viennaslide 11tr, 176, 216cb; volkerpreusser 18tl, 20cr, 22crb, 24-5ca, 45clb, 51cr, 91bl, 106tr, 111bl, 137tr, 143tr, 144tr, 156t, 161cla, 166bl, 168t, 172bl, 189br, 207tl, 210-1, 220-1t, 221bc, 253br; Westend61 GmbH / EJW 220br, / Christina Falkenberg 4, / Martin Moxter 218-9t, / Martin Siepmann 28-9t / Uwe Umstätter 13cr, / Wilfried Wirth 27tr; Scott Wilson 164b, 182-3t, 244bl, 256-7t; World History Archive 55tl; Ernst Wrba 41bl, 123tr; Xinhua 50crb; Zoonar GmbH / Silvia Eder 22cr, / travelphoto 254b.

AWL Images: Jon Arnold 90-1t; Moreno Geremetta 273cla; Christian Handl 148-9; Hemis 65, 134l; imageBROKER / Manfred Schmidt 8-9b; Katja Kreder 18cb, 234-5; Stefano Politi Markovina 246bl.

Belvedere, Vienna: 124bc.

Brauhaus Mariazell: 25tr.

Depositphotos Inc: Pressdigital 146t.

Dreamstime.com: Anton Aleksenko 82cl; Alexirina27000 20t, 250-1b; Beataaldridge 38-9t; Bhofack2 33br; Maciej Bledowski 108-9b; Eva Bocek 272-3b; Andrei Bortnikau 192-3b; Boris Breytman 190clb; Daliu80 158t; Ekinyalgin 196-7t; Emicristea 11cr, 141; Eugenesergeev 126-7b; Frank Gärtner 184-5b; Hakoar 297bl; Hansenn 22t; Fritz Hiersche 40-1t; Irakite 20bl; Jjfarq 48br, 49clb, 188cl, 227cl, 240tr; Jorisvo 161tc; Josefkubes 193c; Gergo Kazsimer 28-9b; Vichaya Kiatyingangsulee 138-9t; Tetyana Kochneva 56-7t; Nikolai Korzhov 2-3; Gábor Kovács 130bl; Aliaksei Kruhlenia 51clb; Pawel Lipskiy 44br; Peter Lovás 44tl; Luftklick 228-9b; Karl Allen Lugmayer 221bl; Zdeněk Matyáš 6-7, 51tr; Ewa Mazur 202-3t; Mdworschak 162t; Minnystock 117br; Montypeter 31br; Ncristian 139clb; Sergey Novikov 298t; Palinchak 50cra; Photoflorenzo 43br, 206bl; Roman Plesky 24-5t, 92tr, 113br, 171tl; Olimpiu Alexa-pop 306; Radub85 66t; Rbiedermann 294bl; Rosshelen 125ca; Stefan Rotter 17t, 150-1; Saiko3p 26tl, 38-9b, 214b, 216-7b, 265t; Brian Scantlebury 109tr; Siempreverde22 22bl; SlavkoSereda 36b; Sonyakamoz 32tl; Nikolai Sorokin 34bl, 249ca; Calin Andrei Stan 51crb; TasFoto 66bl; Trazvan 39cla; Lev Tsimbler 107cr; Vladimir Vinogradov 49br; Vvoevale 48tl, 114-5b, 139crb; Xantana 224-5t; Xbrchx 142-3b; Yup265 62, 72-3; Zoryanchik 12clb.

Electronic Mountain Festival: Rudi Wyhlidal 42-3b.

Getty Images: AFP / Barbara Gindl 51cl, 243t; / Georg Hochmuth 131t, / Robert Jaeger 50cla, / Thierry Roge 57crb; ASAblanca / Josef Polleross 110t; Atlantide Phototravel / Corbis / VCG 83; Corbis Documentary / Franz-Marc Frei 17bl, 178-9t; De Agostini / DEA 139br, / A. Dagli Orti 202cla, / G. Nimatallah 54tl; Alexander Hassenstein 66crb; Hulton Archive / Heritage Images 224bc, / Imagno 57cr, 139bc, 140bl, 167clb, 205b, 225br; The LIFE Picture Collection / Nat Farbman 101tr; Lonely Planet Images / Amos Chapple 133br, / Andy Christiani 68-9t; LOOK-foto / Andreas Strauss 221tr; Moment Unreleased / Giovanni Chiaia 301tr; Photolibrary / Gonzalo Azumendi 63, 96-7; Manfred Schmid 50cr, 70-1t; David Silverman 32-3b; Martin Steinthaler 296-7t; Laszlo Szirtesi 267br; ullstein bild 55cra.

Grafenegg Festival: Klaus Vyhnalek 31t.

iStockphoto.com: AleksandarNakic 66cl; E+ / DaveLongMedia 30tl, / Saro17 24tl, / Umkehrer 251tl; FooTToo 35b; Robert Ford 167br; steve-goacher 26cra; lucentius 278b; Uwe Moser 26-7t; nevereverro 20crb; Olezzo 262t; RelaxFoto.de 19bl, 288-9; RomanBabakin 41crb; TPopova 27cla.

Kaffemik: 69cl.

KHM-Museumsverband: 104-5b, 107tl, 107tr, 107clb.

Leopold Museum, Vienna: 103crb.

MAK-Osterreichisches Museum fur ange wandte Kunst: Georg Mayer 87cra.

Mozartkino /Altstadthotel Kasererbraeu Mozartkino GmbH & Co KG: 46-7t.

MUMOK: 43bl.

Österreichisches Freilichtmuseum Stübing: Reinhart Nunner 190-1b; Wolfram Strohschein 190cra, 191tr.

Reuters: Dominic Ebenbichler 82cra.

Robert Harding Picture Library: Jan Greune 297br.

Shutterstock: by Paul 273tc.

SuperStock: AGF / Masci Giuseppe 125tc; hemis.fr / Bertrand Gardel 102-3b; / Ludovic Maisant 125tr; Iberfoto 54br; Mauritius 144bl.

Swarovski Kristallwelten: un attimo Photographie 275cra; Werner Elmer 275t.

VIENNALE: Roland Ferrigato 47br.

ZOOM Children's Museum: J.J.Kucek 103tr.

Front Flap
Alamy Stock Photo: allOver images / Viennaphoto bl; imageBROKER / Moritz Wolf cra; RooM the Agency / coberschneider br; volkerpreusser cla; **Dreamstime.com:** Mdworschak c; **Getty Images:** Martin Steinthaler t.

Cover
Front and spine: **iStockphoto.com:** serts.
Back: **Alamy Stock Photo:** blickwinkel tr; Westend61 GmbH / Martin Siepmann c; **Dreamstime.com:** Emicristea cl; **iStockphoto.com:** serts b.

Mapping
Original cartography from BEV, Magdalena Polak, Olaf Rodowald, Dariusz Romanowksi.

For further information see: www.dkimages.com

Penguin Random House

Main Contributors Donna Wheeler, Craig Turp, Teresa Fisher, Janina Kumianiecka, Ewa Dan, Marianna Dudek, Konrad Gruda, Małgorzata Omilanowska, Marek Pernal, Jakub Sito, Barbara Sudnik-Wójcikowska, Roman Taborski, Zuzanna Umer

Senior Editor Alison McGill

Senior Designer Tania Da Silva Gomes

Project Editor Zoë Rutland

Project Art Editor Dan Bailey

Designers Stuti Tiwari Bhatia, Bharti Karakoti, Simran Lakhiani, Bhagyashree Nayak, Priyanka Thakur

Factchecker Melanie Nicholson-Hartzell

Editor Matthew Grundy Haigh

Proofreader Stephanie Smith

Indexer Helen Peters

Senior Picture Researcher Ellen Root

Picture Research Jen Veall, Sumita Khatwani, Rituraj Singh, Vagisha Pushp

Illustrators Michał Burkiewicz, Paweł Marczak, Bohdan Wróblewski

Senior Cartographic Editor Casper Morris

Cartography Rajesh Chhibber, Simonetta Giori, Mohammad Hassan

Jacket Designers Dan Bailey, Maxine Pedliham

Jacket Picture Research Susie Watters

Senior DTP Designer Jason Little

DTP Rohit Rojal, Tanveer Zaidi

Producer Rebecca Parton

Managing Editor Rachel Fox

Art Director Maxine Pedliham

Publishing Director Georgina Dee

First edition 2003

Published in Great Britain by Dorling Kindersley Limited, 80 Strand, London, WC2R 0RL

Published in the United States by DK Publishing, 1450 Broadway, Suite 801, New York, NY 10018

Copyright © 2003, 2020 Dorling Kindersley Limited
A Penguin Random House Company
19 20 21 22 10 9 8 7 6 5 4 3 2 1

A CIP catalog record for this book is available from the British Library.

A catalog record for this book is available from the Library of Congress.

ISSN: 1542 1554
ISBN: 978 0 2414 0933 6

Printed and bound in China.

www.dk.com